HUMAN NATURE, CONTEMPLATION & THE POLITICAL ORDER

HUMAN NATURE, CONTEMPLATION & THE POLITICAL ORDER

Essays Inspired by Jacques Maritain's *Scholasticism and Politics*

EDITED BY PETER KARL KORITANSKY

AMERICAN MARITAIN ASSOCIATION

Distributed by

THE CATHOLIC UNIVERSITY
OF AMERICA PRESS
Washington, D.C.

Manufactured in the United States of America

Distributed by the Catholic Univesity of America Press
620 Michigan Avenue, N.E., 240 Leahy Hall
Washington, D.C. 20064

Cataloging-in-Publication Data available from the Library of Congress
ISBN 978-0-9827119-5-8

For my mother, Jeanne Carolyn Koritansky

Contents

Acknowledgements

I wish to express my gratitude to all those who helped me put together this volume of essays. Most especially, I wish to thank Michael Torre of The University of San Francisco and Giuseppe Butera of Providence College, both of whom have served at different times of this book's production as general editor of the American Maritain Association book series of which this volume is a part. I also wish to acknowledge the generous hospitality of John O'Callahan and Alice Osberger of the Jacques Maritain Center at the University of Notre Dame, where I spent much of the 2012–13 academic year working on this project as a visiting fellow. Most of all, I wish to thank my wife, Pam, and my children, Matthew, Eva, and Joseph, all of whom uprooted their lives to make the long journey from our home in Prince Edward Island to South Bend, Indiana (and back again) in order to support their husband's/father's work.

PETER KARL KORITANSKY

Introduction

Recovering Maritain's Personalism Amidst the Challenge of Modernity

I. Maritainian Reflections on the "Crisis of Modern Times"

In Jacques Maritain's 1951 *Man and the State,* one of the most forthright statements of his political philosophy, he makes the following well-known claim: The 1948 *Universal Declaration of Human Rights* illustrates that, whatever the various and often incompatible theoretical justifications of our shared commitment to human rights, widespread agreement as to what those rights are is surprisingly possible. Consensus is therefore achievable in practice where it could never have been achieved in theory, an impossibility owing to the divergent "ideological allegiances," "religious traditions," "cultural backgrounds," and "historical experiences" of the persons involved. Far from revealing a skepticism as to human reason's ability to discern the true basis of human rights, Maritain's observation is that true conclusions, and therefore right practical initiatives, can even be derived from false theoretical principles, the falsity of which may still be known through the subtle application of philosophical analysis. Maritain puts it this way:

> I am fully convinced that my way of justifying the belief in the rights of man and the ideal of freedom, equality, and fraternity is the only one which is solidly based on truth. That does not prevent me from agreeing on these practical tenets with those who are convinced that their way of justifying them, entirely different from

mine or even opposed to mine in its theoretical dynamism, is likewise the only one based on truth.[1]

These words may strike some readers as exhibiting a certain naiveté, albeit an understandable one in the immediate wake of the Nazis' defeat and the successful signing of the 1948 *Declaration*. As we read on, however, Maritain himself cautions us against hoping for too much practical consensus where philosophical consensus is completely lacking. This is probably because Maritain was well aware that, although the post-war achievements came largely with a renewal of natural law thinking in Western Europe and the United States, the version of natural law in play was predominantly that of the Enlightenment derived from the philosophy of Kant and his intellectual forebears (Rousseau and Hobbes). Whereas agreement between this tradition and the older one to which Maritain adheres (in *Man and the State*, he traces it all the way back to Sophocles[2]) may be reached to forge an acceptable list of human rights, we must not overestimate how deep or how far that agreement will go. The "theoretical dynamisms" of these two natural law theories are so divergent that we have reason to be wary of whatever common practical results they may yield. Whereas Maritain's natural law is rooted in an understanding of divine providence and the human dignity that derives from the *Imago Dei*, the other "philosophy of rights ended up, after Rousseau and Kant, by treating the individual as a god and making all the rights ascribed to him the absolute and unlimited rights of a god."[3] In doing so, the Enlightenment account of natural law and natural rights leaves open the door to the same terrible consequences those who invoke it want to rebuke. It is a doctrine of rights without purpose, without hope, and without a compelling account of human nature. Whatever the temporary agreement Maritain may have had with its adherents, there is no fooling the great Thomist as to its serious problems:

> This philosophy built no solid foundations for the rights of the human person, because nothing can be founded on a illusion: it compromised and squandered these rights, because it led men to conceive them as rights in themselves divine, hence infinite, escaping every objective measure, denying every limitation imposed upon the claims of the ego, and ultimately expressing the absolute independence of the human subject and a so-called absolute right—which supposedly pertains to ev-

1. Jacques Maritain, *Man and the State* (Chicago: University of Chicago Press, 1951), 78.
2. See Maritain's reference to *Antigone* in ibid., 85 n. 8.
3. Ibid., 83.

erything in the human subject by the mere fact that it is in him—to unfold one's cherished possibilities at the expense of all other beings.[4]

If we examine the current culture wars taking place in the same Western democracies, and especially in the United States, that defeated fascism seventy years ago, Maritain's words seem prophetic. What better example of an appeal to human rights that advances the "absolute independence of the human subject" (often described as "autonomy") and allows us to unfold our "cherished possibilities at the expense of all other beings" than the contemporary argument for legalized and government-sponsored abortion? That this argument proceeds by an appeal to natural rights is clear by looking no further than the current legal opinion to which all American laws on abortion must conform. "At the heart of liberty," the US Supreme Court infamously tells us, "is the right to define one's own concept of existence, of meaning, of the universe, and of the mystery of human life."[5] Thus understood, the Court insists that for the state to adopt any one understanding of personhood or human nature would be a violation of liberty at its very core. If he had lived to read these fateful words, Maritain would have seen immediately the philosophical problems they raise (not even to mention the legal ones) and the practical disaster they would create.

For his part, Maritain derived an understanding of human rights from a theory of natural law and ultimately from a philosophical anthropology that was unapologetically Thomistic: "there is no right unless a certain order—which can be violated in fact—is inviolably required by what things are in their intelligible type or their essence, or by what the nature of man is, and is cut out for: an order by virtue of which certain things like life, work, freedom are due to the human person, an existent who is endowed with a spiritual soul and free will."[6] In short, whereas Maritain recognizes that human rights may only be consistently sustained by a certain understanding of human nature, the US Supreme Court has opted to hinge human rights upon a certain *agnosticism* about human nature, a human nature that is inherently "mysterious," and about which we must not expect to find any answers, as a society, that could provide the basis for law.

To be sure, the Court does not take a position of moral relativism. The

4. Ibid., 84.

5. Supreme Court Justice Sandra Day O'Connor's majority opinion in *Planned Parenthood of Southeastern Pennsylvania v. Casey*, 505 US 833 (1992).

6. Maritain, *Man and the State*, 96–97.

claims it makes about the moral requirements of liberty are intended as universal moral claims. What Maritain would have found so troubling about the *Casey* majority decision is that the moral claims contained therein are based upon a certain kind of *anthropological* relativism.[7] The implication appears to be that, since we are without any clear answers as to the nature of the human person, his destiny, the source of his dignity, or the moment at which he comes into existence, the maximization of his "liberty" should be the obvious practical initiative. Applied to abortion, it is not difficult to see the relevance of Maritain's warning that such a "basis" of liberty ends up exalting the individual and his "cherished possibilities at the expense of all other beings." What *Casey* shows us is that the defenders of abortion believe in human rights just as much as do opponents of abortion. Like the signatories of the 1948 *Declaration*, each participant in the abortion debate, moreover, could likely agree on a list of human rights. But the theoretical differences in how those rights are conceived clearly, in this case, has led to radically divergent positions on one of the most controversial issues of the day. Whatever Maritain's thoughts would have been about this and other contemporary moral issues, one thing is clear: he would insist that meaningful progress will never be made in resolving difficult moral questions, especially where human rights are invoked, without a proper understanding of human nature. Contrary to Kantian morality, philosophical anthropology must precede moral philosophy. If it does not, moral claims will be arbitrary and will easily crumble under scrutiny.

For these reasons, Maritain's philosophical anthropology is at least as (perhaps more) relevant today as his moral and political philosophy, and this is the reason for turning to *Scholasticism and Politics*, published eleven years before *Man and the State*. As Maritain states in the forward, "however varied the topics dealt with [in this book] may be, the general purpose, which makes the organic unity of the volume, is easily perceptible. It is entirely permeated with the idea of the human person, considered in his spiritual dignity and the concrete conditions of his existence."[8] As the first chapter of *Scholasticism and Politics* shows, the study of the human person to follow is far from a dispassionate exercise motivated solely by intellectual curiosity. The title of the chapter, "Integral Humanism and the Crisis

7. I am grateful to Russell Hittinger for sharpening my understanding of this distinction.

8. Jacques Maritain, *Scholasticism and Politics,* translated and edited by Mortimer J. Adler (New York: Macmillan, 1940), vii.

of Modern Times," conveys the practical significance, even the urgency, of the chapters to come. The modern world is truly embroiled in a crisis, Maritain thinks, precisely because it has misunderstood human nature in a fundamental way. This misunderstanding is, again, the result of the prevailing Enlightenment account of human nature and morality that follows from it, which has driven a wedge between that which is distinctive about the human person, namely, human reason, and the rest of human nature. More specifically, Enlightenment thought, most evidently in Kant but certainly finding its roots in Descartes, defines human nature as nothing other than reason itself. As Maritain explains, this apparent attempt to elevate the human being only succeeds in distorting him. It prevents him from defining himself in relation to anything beyond reason to the point of denying anything transcendent or supernatural. "Instead of an *open* human nature and an *open* reason ... people pretend that there exists a nature and a reason isolated by themselves and *shut up* in themselves, excluding everything which is not themselves."[9] In the realm of morality, the moral law can only be a self-imposed law, obedience to the "idea of law itself," as Kant put it. It turns out to be a calculated morality that ignores all human desire, both crude and profound, because desire is one of those things from which reason supposedly needs to be purified. Because everything pertaining to desire is "put in parentheses and religiously forgotten,"[10] Enlightenment morality is a morality that fails to give the whole person a compelling reason to be moral.

The doctrine of human rights and human dignity that is developed in the absence of an adequate philosophical anthropology is, thus, vulnerable to the devastating criticisms that have been leveled against it. Against those, such as Kant, who speak of a human dignity derived solely from human reason, has come a spirited, and not unjustified, criticism of rationality in defense of the sub-rational. But here, too, the great thinkers of modernity only get if half right: "I am thinking of Nietzsche, of Kierkegaard, of Karl Barth, of Chestov. But even here, no matter with what intelligence they develop the theme that intelligence comes from the serpent, and no matter with what generosity they try to salvage human values, this position unmistakably gives way to what one may call a *counter-humanism*." As Maritain continues, "my point is precisely that if we set out to defend man not against a certain use of reason, but against reason itself, the result—

9. Ibid., 3; emphasis in original.
10. Ibid.

inevitably and in spite of everything—will be a counter-humanism."[11] If Kant and the Enlightenment thinkers failed to distinguish clearly enough between man and God, Nietzsche and his fellow "unmaskers" have failed sufficiently to distinguish between man and beast. After eviscerating the unpersuasive moral, even moralistic, claims of the Enlightenment based on autonomy and other such dubious concepts, they have concluded that morality itself is a sham. Maritain understands well that, all the while, Nietzsche longs to erect something noble in its place. It is only, perhaps, the benefit of hindsight that allows Maritain to understand that Nietzsche's project cannot work:

> Poor Nietzsche! The truly terrifying voice, the fatal voice is not the voice of Nietzsche; it is the voice of that mediocre and base multitude whose mediocrity and baseness, and disgrace, themselves appear as apocalyptic signs, a voice which scatters to the four winds of humanity the gospel of the hatred of reason, in the form of the cult of the fecundity of war or in that of the cult of race and blood.... Nietzsche could not bear the sight of the lame and halt of Christianity; more even than Goethe, he rebelled against the Cross; he dreamed of a Dionysian superman, who was a fiction. Dionysius! The newspapers and radio give us news of him every morning and tell us how he leads his dance through the concentration camps and the new ghettos, the cities of China and Spain eviscerated by bombs, Europe maddened in the armament race and feverishly preparing for suicide. Nietzsche could not see that man must choose between two ways: the way of Calvary and the way of slaughter.[12]

In a way, the contemporary situation presents us with a great irony. If one may summarize modern philosophy so broadly, one might say its fundamental motivation was to reconsider man *as he is*.[13] Whether we examine the thought of Hobbes, Rousseau, Kant, or even "poor Nietzsche," we observe a thinker pleading with us to be honest with ourselves and about ourselves like we have never been before. What Maritain suggests, however, is that this plan, so central to modern thought, has belied its promise. Whether we conceive of man as a rational substance to the exclusion or diminishment of the sub-rational, or we conceive of man as primarily a beast

11. Ibid., 4–5; emphasis in original.

12. Ibid., 6.

13. See, for example, Spinoza's complaint that philosophers of the past had unrealistically conceived of men, "not as they are, but as they themselves [the philosophers] would like them to be," with the result that "no men are esteemed less fit to direct public affairs than theorists or philosophers." Benedict de Spinoza, *Political Treatise*, translated by A. H. Gosset (London: Bell and Son, 1883), chap. 1, sec. 1; available online at http://www.constitution.org/bs/poltr-00.htm

to the exclusion or diminishment of his intellect and will, we fail precisely to be sufficiently realistic. We fail to grasp that realism which acknowledges what is both high and low in us and which appreciates the rich complexity that emerges when we discover how interwoven the high and the low actually are. It is a true testimony to the legacy of Descartes and Kant that modern society has failed to see the humanity of the human organism whose rational faculties are not yet developed, as in the human embryo, or in whom reason is truncated or lies dormant as in the severely mentally handicapped or the patient in a vegetative state. How ironic that the dualism imbedded in Cartesian and Kantian morality, that same morality upon which so many human rights claims have been made, is also used to justify the free and lethal exercise of violence against the weakest and most vulnerable. In the unfolding of history where the consequences of ideas are played out, what separates the Cartesian and Kantian celebration of pure reason and the Hobbesian or Nietzschean will to power may actually be very little. Again, the antidote for this crisis of culture must be, even more fundamentally than a new conception of morality, a new philosophical anthropology; or, in Maritain's case, the rediscovery of a philosophical anthropology long forgotten.

And so we return to the "general purpose" that establishes the "organic unity" of *Scholasticism and Politics,* namely, "the idea of the human person." To be sure, the nine essays comprising the work do not simply constitute an enquiry into the principles of human nature. Maritain's point of view, in his own words, is "that of the philosophy of culture, and not that of metaphysics."[14] As the essays in this volume will demonstrate, however, Maritain's concept of the human person has far reaching implications for the understanding of human knowledge, the meaning of human freedom, the distinction between good and evil in human affairs, the political common good, and even the ultimate aim of human life itself. It is, therefore, with a view to developing Maritain's thought upon these broad but fundamental issues (and certainly not uncritically) that the authors of the present volume have set to task. As I have already suggested, Maritain's philosophical insights have a new meaning for the twenty-first century, but which is grounded in a perennial philosophy that never ceases to be relevant.

14. Maritain, *Scholasticism and Politics,* 1.

II. The Present Volume

The essays of this volume are divided into three categories. The first, entitled "Human Nature and the Challenge of Modernity," examines from numerous perspectives Maritain's personalism developed in *Scholasticism and Politics* and elsewhere. The first of these essays, "Jacques Maritain and Yves R. Simon on Freedom of Choice" by Michael Torre, provides an account and defense of the Thomistic notion of freedom in light of the modern dismissal of human freedom that frequently accompanies more recent philosophical anthropologies. Using Maritain and Simon as the primary spokesmen for St. Thomas, Torre carefully explains that while the notions of freedom and necessity are commonly understood to be mutually exclusive, there is in fact no defensible account of freedom without necessity. As Torre expounds upon Maritain's thought, "the will's *freedom* of choice is rooted in and deduced from its *nature* and *necessity*." To say that the will naturally longs for happiness, and even to identify human happiness in a single activity as St. Thomas and Aristotle do, is not to eliminate freedom of choice but to provide a context in which the human person may undertake intelligible free actions in pursuit of that happiness. This intelligibility, Torre shows, emerges only after the kind of painstaking consideration of the human will's relation to the human intellect one finds in Maritain, Simon, and St. Thomas Aquinas himself.

Among those responsible for undermining human freedom and the philosophical anthropology found in Maritain's thought, probably no figure looms larger than Sigmund Freud. And yet Maritain's own posture towards Freud reveals that he is just as capable of learning from and appreciating the great founder of psychoanalysis as he is in pointing out Freudianism's limitations. As John Conley shows in his essay, "Freud as Political *Adversarius*," Maritain acknowledges that Freud may even be credited with rediscovering elements of the Thomistic doctrine of the human mind's powerful connection with the sub-rational. As Conley explains, "unlike rationalist epistemologies, which tend to reduce the mind to the conscious possession of a series of concepts, Thomistic epistemology, like Freud's theory of the unconscious, recognizes what is hidden and obscure in the workings of the mind which elude conscious grasp but which powerfully shapes emotive and moral temperament." Still, because Freud's anthropology is rooted in an uncompromising, almost pre-reflective, materialism, his teaching will always be dogged by an inferior and indefensible philosophy of human nature. Conley explains well that, for Maritain, whatever clarity one may gain from Freud's understanding of the connection between the rational and sub-rational is quickly undermined by his theory that the rational is entirely *reducible to* the sub-rational. In Conley's view, in fact, Maritain may not have understood the extent to which this faulty anthropology vitiates even the practical efficacy of Freud's psychoanalytic method.

Maritain's analysis of Freud is taken up again in Stephen Chamberlain's "Aquinas, Psychoanalysis, and the Internal Sense Faculties." Chamberlain explores in greater detail what Conley put forth regarding the relation between the higher and lower forms of human cognition. In particular, he shows, contrary to Freudian reductionism, how the lower faculties are in human beings ordered to the higher faculties as to their proper end. As he explains, "although sensible and intellectual powers are distinct, in any specific operation that unfolds as a process, there exists a dynamic unity in which the higher powers flow through to the lower powers such that the lower ones are subordinated to the higher powers and also are raised up to a greater degree of perfection or functionality." Chamberlain then proceeds to develop Maritain's provocative claim that scholastic anthropology "implied the existence" of the Freudian unconscious by locating the unconscious in the internal sense faculties, and in particular what St. Thomas Aquinas calls the "estimative power." By relying upon Maritain's Thomistic analysis of the human soul, Chamberlain argues, one is able to appreciate the insights of modern psychoanalysis without being hindered by the materialism that often accompanies it.

Bernadette O'Connor develops even further the theme of the previous two essays in her analysis of Maritain's relation to Freud entitled, "The Freudian and Maritainian Theories of Sublimation and Their Ontological Bases." It is, in particular, Freud's and Maritain's respective understandings of sublimation in which one sees the clearest example of Maritain's simultaneous correction of Freud and acknowledgment of Freud's genuine contribution. Freud's identification of sublimation, the process by which lower instincts may be redirected towards something "finer and higher," is, O'Connor concurs with Maritain, ultimately unexplainable solely on the basis of Freud's materialism and empiricism. Turning to key passages, both in *Scholasticism and Politics* and *Creative Intuition in Art and Poetry*, O'Connor presents Maritain's Thomistic hylomorphism as a basis upon which to explain what Freud could not, namely, the harnessing of sub-rational impulses in the service of the sublime human activities that come to define whole civilizations, such as artistic expression, and that are specific to the rational creature. According to O'Connor, Maritain borrows Freud's understanding of the powerful connection between the high and the low in human beings in order to derive a "spiritual unconscious" that serves as a kind of wellspring for what can become humanity's greatest achievements. Instead of reducing sublimation to a rerouting of neurological phenomena, we may understand it better as, to use O'Connor's words, a "final integration of spirit and flesh."

It is precisely in avoiding Freud's materialistic reductionism, therefore, that Maritain is able to account for a broader range of human phenomena and experience. Another way one might put the matter is that Maritain develops a superior philosophical anthropology only because, contrary to Freud, he offers an understanding of the human *person*. Even more specifically, Maritain's teaching is instructive to a world overly influenced by materialism in light of his all-important distinction (developed in *Scholasticism and Politics*) between the person and the individual. Raymond Hain's essay, "Individuality and Personality in Maritain and Classic Hindu Philosophy," calls attention to precisely this distinction and its philosophical importance. As Hain explains, a materialist anthropology only understands human beings as "individuals," that is to say, as beings who consume food, breathe air, and take up material resources that cannot be shared. As individuals, moreover, our being is entirely shaped by the material and historical forces at work from outside and from within our bodies, reducing all that was formerly attributed to the immaterial soul to blind laws of nature. To be sure, Hain insists, humans are profoundly influenced by such material causes, but the world nonetheless has much to learn from Maritain's teaching that some dimensions of human existence require the notion of the person: "For the individual to possess food is for that food to be transformed into the individual himself. But for the personality to possess knowledge, or to possess another person through love, is to possess without consuming. In this sense ... the goods of the person [contrary to those of the individual] ... are sharable goods." As Hain convincingly shows, Maritain's doctrine is not only a retrieval of Thomistic philosophy, but of a much-needed ancient wisdom found in Eastern thought as well. As Hain's essay proves, elements of the very same Maritainian distinction between individuality and personality are also discernible in the classical texts of Hindu philosophy.

In fact, according to one author, Maritain's resistance to the materialism of his age even leads him to overstate the spiritual dimension of human nature, leading to a doctrine that could even be categorized as dualist when compared with a genuinely Thomistic anthropology. According to Federico Tedesco's "From Maritain to Aquinas: Beyond the Polarity between Individual and Person," this is precisely the mistake made by Maritain in his efforts to correct the reductionism that surrounded him. As Tedesco argues, only by returning to Aquinas's hylomorphism itself, in which the rational human soul's close ontological connection to the body is fully appreciated, does one truly find the antidote to the anthropological confusion of modern thought. Moreover, by returning to Aquinas, one also finds the centrality of divine providence for the notion of human personhood. As Tedesco puts it, "there are persons only if there is God."

The essays that constitute *Scholasticism and Politics* are, in Maritain's words, parts of a broader "philosophy of culture" as opposed to a thematic metaphysical study of human nature. For this reason, the moral and political dimensions of Maritain's 1940 publication deserve attention as much as those dealing with philosophical anthropology. Hence, the second section of the present volume is entitled "Freedom, Morality, and Civil Society" and explores another spectrum of profound implications of Maritain's teaching for modern thought and society. The first of these essays, written by Terry Hall, is entitled "Dirty Hands in Politics? Maritain's Answer to Machiavelli." Though not directly concerned with *Scholasticism and Politics*, this essay explores what is one of the most important questions raised by that book, namely, Maritain's relationship to modern thought, and in this case, modern political thought. As in his treatment of Freud, Maritain considers Machiavelli a formidable opponent. As Hall demonstrates, though, this does not deter Maritain from meeting Machiavelli's argument on its own terms. Otherwise stated, Maritain's critique of the great Florentine is not merely a moral critique that simply exposes Machiavelli as a "teacher of evil." It is also a political critique in which Maritain argues, in Hall's words, that Machiavelli's evil not only corrupts the ruler, [but] [also] corrupts the polity itself."

According to Peter Pagan Aguiar, the author of the next essay entitled "The End of Democracy: Authority or Freedom from Truth?" the evidence from contemporary American society shows that the corruption of the polity has been precisely the result of the modern project of which Machiavelli was the founder. In particular, Pagan challenges the modern view that freedom and democracy can be maintained in a culture that denies the possibility of knowing the truth about life's deepest and most profound questions, questions of course that Maritain devoted his life to answering. What results, Pagan asks, if we become convinced that human life has no inherent meaning or direction? As he answers, "if one holds that the last end of human action in society is purely arbitrary, the unbridled will to power resurfaces as the ultimate norm of human conduct, which leads to the idea of anarchic democracy discussed by Maritain." Such a change creates an environment especially inhospitable to Christianity, Pagan argues, and paves the way for replacing the gospel of Jesus Christ with the cold and bleak civil religion advocated in Jean-Jacques Rousseau's *On the Social Contract*.

To reiterate a central point in the first section of this introduction, Maritain's prescription for the social disease identified by Pagan is a new integral humanism, a humanism that, according to Denis Scrandis, was independently championed by Josef Ratzinger (both as Pope Benedict XVI and as Josef Cardinal Ratzinger). In his essay, "Maritain and Ratzinger on the Crisis of Modern Times," Scrandis reports that both men blame the Enlightenment for the crisis. While Maritain condemns philosophical causes, Ratzinger assails the resulting moral relativism. Yet, "both men agree that the recovery of our culture from its secular crisis lies in heroic Christian witness." Furthermore, whereas Maritain went so far as to label the contemporary intellectual climate as "anti-Christ" (as opposed merely to anti-Christian), Ratzinger says vibrant Christian witness is our "greatest need." While Progressives herald government as the way of salvation, they bitterly reject the gospel and salvation of Christ as dead roots of a dead culture.

In a larger sense the revulsion against Christianity in Western culture observed by Pope Benedict is against, not only Christianity, but revealed religion as such, a phenomenon that creates a particularly urgent need for Christians to cultivate their relationship with the youngest and fastest growing monotheistic religion of the West, namely, Islam. In her essay, "Perceptions of Islam: Pope Benedict XVI and Jacques Maritain," Cornelia Tsakiridou reveals the various ways in which Benedict's and Maritain's thought opens the door for Christians and Muslims to understand one another and the unique challenges facing both religions in the twenty-first century. Her essay discusses ambiguities in Maritain's approach to Islam that stem from his view of its mysticism as implicating Christ and thus a tacit conversion to Christianity, and relates his fascination with Islam to the work of Louis Massignon, Louis Gardet, Georges Anawati, and Charles de Foucauld. With particular emphasis upon Benedict's "Regensberg Lecture," Tsakiridou explains the former Pontiff's insistence that Christianity is based upon a "sacramental, incarnational rationality," which must be firmly in place before a Christian mysticism can be meaningfully developed, and which prevents any such mysticism from devolving into an empty spiritualism. In their various and respective overtures to Islam, Benedict and Maritain agree that both religions must draw upon the same understanding of faith's coherence with reason in order to resist modernity's attempt to render both traditions culturally irrelevant. In fact, one learns from Tsakiridou's profound analysis that both religions are in a position, not only to reintroduce the modern world to the mystery of God, but also to the capabilities of human reason itself, with which modernity appears to be no less disillusioned than with religious faith.

If Benedict's and Maritain's analysis that modernity suffers from a crisis of reason no less than from a crisis of faith is correct, what may seem to give their followers hope is the relatively recent "virtue ethics" movement, which is often hailed as a recovery of Aristotelian and Thomistic moral philosophy, a recovery emanating from the thought of Maritain, G. E. M. Anscombe, and Alasdair McIntyre (among others). According to Jonathan J. Sanford's essay, "Maritain, Anscombe, and Contemporary Virtue Ethics," however, the new virtue ethics from which so much enthusiasm is derived actually has very little to do with that of the tradition championed by Maritain. As Sanford points out, the recent virtue ethics movement was intended by many as an alternative to the utilitarian and deontological bases for ethics dominant in the twentieth century. Unfortunately, however, contemporary virtue ethicists, such as Rosiland Hursthouse and Michael Slote, provide only a moral theory that is either woefully inadequate in answering the fundamental questions of moral philosophy, or one that is ultimately reducible to the very same utilitarian and Kantian systems to which it was originally supposed to provide an alternative. In the end, Sanford warns the followers of Aristotle, Aquinas, and Maritain that contemporary virtue ethicists are not the fellow travelers they seem to be, and like most other modern philosophers, they "have low regard for your teleology, your natural law, your ethical absolutism, and your faith."

A similar phenomenon that exemplifies the misappropriation of Maritain's thought is, perhaps, the contemporary celebration of "natural rights." For followers of Maritain, however, it is essential to understand that, unlike their contemporary counterparts, any compelling doctrine of natural rights must be rooted in a doctrine of natural law. Making this very point, Anne Wiles, in her essay "Habit, Natural Law, and Natural Rights," argues that, for Maritain, "there are no human rights unless a certain order 'is inviolably required by what things are in their intelligible type or their essence, or by what the nature of man is, and is cut out for, an order by virtue of which certain things like life, work, freedom are due to the human person, an existent who is endowed with a spiritual soul and free will.'" Wiles's essay, like Sanford's, is therefore a sobering reminder of the gulf that lies between Maritainian Thomism and contemporary thought, and that a return to that Thomism is essential if human rights are to receive the philosophical underpinnings that render them ultimately defensible.

As Eric Manchester argues, once this Maritainian perspective is adopted a much fuller and richer interpretation of Western democracy's, and especially American democracy's, founding principles are able to emerge. In his essay, "Beatitude as the Foundation of Freedom: Re-Reading the First Amendment in Light of Maritain," Manchester recalls Maritain's critical distinction between the individual and the person to point out that the political freedom Americans hold so dear only possesses an inherent value on the understanding that they are persons, that is to say, naturally social beings with a spiritual dimension that transcends the fulfillment of immediate bodily desires. This is why, according to Manchester, for the state to promote political freedom adequately it must remember the crucial role of institutions, like the Church, specifically concerned with man's supernatural destiny, only by reference to which political freedom is rightly understood. Drawing upon Maritain's *Scholasticism and Politics*, Manchester writes, "given that a democracy which authentically champions truly *personal* freedom must recognize humanity's eternal end that transcends the state, proper democratic government humbly recognizes that ecclesial institutions are equipped to facilitate the pursuit of humanity's greatest end in a way that the state cannot."

Of course, a careful reading of Maritain's work, and especially the argument developed in *Scholasticism and Politics*, reveals that a full account of human personhood requires coming to terms with the Aristotelian and Thomistic dictum that true human happiness, the ultimate end of human life, consists in contemplation. As difficult as this doctrine is for a modern audience to accept (much less understand), there is no doubt that Maritain considers it essential for properly addressing the "crisis of modern times" identified at the outset of his 1940 publication. With a view to exploring this dimension of Maritain's work, the final four essays of the present volume constitute a third section entitled "Contemplation and Human Perfection." In the first of these, "The Mountain and the Valley: Medieval Orderings of Contemplation and Action," Heather Erb helps us understand the rich medieval tradition upon which Maritain develops his understanding of contemplation's place in human affairs. Unlike the oversimplifying criticism of modern figures like Martha Nussbaum and Pierre Hadot, Erb shows that the medieval elevation of the contemplative life (not without its own critics, such as Henry of Ghent) is far from constituting a hatred of this world or of all things corporeal. In fact, much of the medieval worldview is taken from Augustine, for whom, according to Erb, "the motive of charity is central, demanding a balance of both dimensions [active and contemplative], creating a unity of hearts and a common life." Even in Aquinas, she notes, for whom the contemplative life unquestionably possesses an inherent superiority over the active life, we find an extraordinarily nuanced view, which includes a special place for the "mixed apostolate of prayer, study, teaching and preaching favored by Dominicans," and which, Erb explains, "mirrors the life of Christ to the extent that service to others flows from a superabundance of contemplation."

It is precisely the nuance of the medieval treatment of contemplation that allows Maritain to find such fertile ground for addressing what he called the crisis of modern times. In "Contemplation in America? Maritainian Reflections on Life in the New World," Michael Krom develops this point by showing how Maritain sought to rediscover the truth of the ancient claim that human happiness is essentially contemplative while simultaneously upholding Christian virtues, such as charity, that require action and constitute a perfection of our social nature. "As a being whose fulfillment is found through contemplation as an act of self-transcendence," Krom explains, "man can never be sacrificed to politics; and yet, as a being situated in a political community, his transcendence must somehow serve the common good." After comparing Maritain's thoughts on the contemplative life with his philosophy of education, Krom finds that Maritain provides an extremely valuable ideal for American society that, despite the pronounced pragmatism of its founding, is far from alien to the American regime.

Developing many of the central claims in Krom's essay, James Hanink's "Contemplation, Martyrdom, and the Principle of Gratuitousness" sets out to show just how much the good of the contemplative life extends far beyond the intellectual or spiritual perfection of the contemplative himself. "Contemplation itself," says Hanink, "remains in the one who contemplates; it is an intransitive or immanent activity. But if one who contemplates shares in God's life, contemplation overflows in the free gift of self." Nowhere does this free gift overflow for the good of others more than in martyrdom. Whereas the modern world views the explicit choice for death for the sake of holiness as fanatical and perverse, Hanink reminds us that history tells a much different story. It is, in fact, the witness of contemplative Christian martyrs that has both resisted and confounded the most fanatical and perverse regimes in modern times. Such martyrs, Hanink shows, are far more than mere innocent victims of tyranny. Their openness to (not desire for) death flows directly from their love of the God who is truth itself and is therefore efficacious for resisting injustice as nothing else can be.

The more one concentrates upon the contemplative life of the saints, as opposed to that of the philosophers, the more compelling is Maritain's claim that *all* people are capable of sharing, not just in the good effects of the contemplative life, but in a participation of that life itself. This notion lies at the heart of Anne Frances Ai Le's essay, "*Contemplata aliis tradere*: The Universal Call to Contemplation and Its Implications," in which she argues that Maritain's teaching that all are called, in some form, to the contemplative life anticipates the Second Vatican Council's declaration of the universal call to holiness. "Both Maritain and the Council Fathers," Ai Le says, "based their teachings on the universality of Christ's command to perfection (Be ye perfect as thy heavenly Father is perfect) and the role of the gifts of the Holy Spirit as the cause of such perfection which is then displayed in the various forms of holiness or contemplation." Unlike its ancient Greek counterpart, Maritain's Christian understanding of contemplation involves a reciprocity between contemplation and action. Action may be the fruit of contemplation and vice versa. Maritain's teaching also opens the doors of contemplation to the ordinary, simple soul, not as a watered-down version of what the few wise philosophers are able to accomplish, but, due to the active presence of the Holy Spirit, in a form even higher than the pre-Christian philosophical ideal.

If Maritain is right to say that the modern world is in a state of crisis, and that a new integral humanism is the only way of addressing that crisis, then we have much to learn from *Scholasticism and Politics*, the contemporary relevance of which the authors of this volume have only begun to explore. To understand correctly the "philosophy of culture" contained therein is to see that Maritain sets out, not to condemn, but to engage modernity on the most urgent philosophical questions facing the human person, questions that require our attention now as much as it required Maritain's in 1940.

I

HUMAN NATURE AND THE CHALLENGE OF MODERNITY

MICHAEL D. TORRE

Jacques Maritain and Yves R. Simon on Freedom of Choice

I. Introduction

Surely there were few people more knowledgeable about the debated idea of free choice than Mortimer J. Adler. His dialectical study of freedom—a collaborative work of many colleagues, which took eight years, and reached to two volumes and over one thousand four hundred pages[1]—remains required reading for anyone writing on the subject who does not wish to re-invent the wheel. Of all the philosophers referred to in the index to the first volume, only Aquinas, Dewey, Hegel, Kant, and Locke receive more space than Jacques Maritain, and Yves R. Simon is also amply mentioned (some sixty times); both also continue to figure prominently in the second volume. Evidently, Adler regarded them as the preeminent modern

1. Mortimer J. Adler, *The Idea of Freedom*, 2 vols. (Garden City, New York: Doubleday, 1958 and 1961). As his two prefaces and his signature on the title pages make clear ("*for* The Institute for Philosophical Research"; emphasis added), Adler wrote up a collective work of many, overseeing a staff of some 18 "Research Workers," who collectively put in some 33 years of service over five years for volume 1, along with one "Associate Director" (William J. Gorman) and two "Assistants to the Director" (Herman C. Bernick and Peter C. Wolff) for that volume, with the last named remaining as Adler's closest "associate" (vol. 2, p. x) for the second volume, along with Robert G. Hazo, earlier named as a "Research Worker" for volume 1. In addition, five "Consultants" are named for volume 1: Jacques Maritain (then at Princeton University) being first named, along with Paul Weiss of Yale University, Richard P. McKeon of The University of Chicago, V. J. McGill, formerly of Hunter College and Associate Editor of the *Journal of Philosophy and Phenomenological Research*, and Otto Bird of The University of Notre Dame. A current member of the American Maritain Association and former colleague, Desmond FitzGerald, is named as one of the "Research Fellows" who worked for one year on the first volume. (He also worked for three years on volume 2 and helped prepare the text of Simon's *Freedom of Choice* [New York: Fordham, 1969]. Peter Woolf acknowledges him as his "co-editor" in his "Editor's Preface," xvi.)

interpreters of Aquinas, regularly identifying their thought with his while schematizing different theories of freedom. Save Locke and Montesquieu, he held that they alone distinguish with Aquinas four differing senses of freedom: that of natural self-determination, acquired self-perfection, circumstantial self-realization, and political liberty (a significant instance of the third).[2]

My concern here is with the natural freedom of self-determination or freedom of choice: the subject of "The Thomist Idea of Freedom," in Maritain's *Scholasticism and Politics*,[3] and of Yves R. Simon's dense yet clear account in his *Freedom of Choice*.[4] In his "Editor's Preface" to that latter work, Peter Wolff informs us that the Institute for Philosophical Research "relied greatly on Professor Simon's exposition" when "dealing with free choice" in *The Idea of Freedom*.[5] For his part, Adler asserts in his foreword to Simon's work that it "is the perfect antidote for the errors, misunderstandings—or worse, the ignorances—that beset the modern discussion of free choice."[6]

2. Ibid., 1: 594.

3. Jacques Maritain, "The Thomist Idea of Freedom," in *Scholasticism and Politics*, translated and edited by Mortimer J. Adler (New York: Macmillan, 1940; Freeport, New York: Books for Libraries Press, 1972), 94–113. According to the Foreword to *Scholasticism and Politics* (p. vii), its chapters represent a series of lectures Maritain gave in the United States in the Fall of 1938. However, the substance of these lectures had already appeared in a book in Spanish: *Para Una Filosofia de la Persona Humana* (Buenos Aires: Cursus de Cultura Catolica, 1937), in which the essay was titled simply "La Libertad." That essay then appeared in French as "L'Idée Thomiste de la Liberté" (*Revue Thomiste* 45 [1939]: 440–59), before appearing in *Scholasticism and Politics*. It seems likely that this French text was translated into the English one, seemingly by Maritain first, with someone aiding him, and then with Adler finally editing their work.

4. Yves R. Simon, *Freedom of Choice*, with a foreword by Mortimer J. Adler, edited by Peter Wolff (New York: Fordham University Press, 1969). This works translates most of Simon's *Traité du libre arbitre* (Liége: Georges Thone, 1951), to which it then supplies one addition (namely, its last pages: 152–58), taken from his unfinished project of a philosophical encyclopedia. (Wolff mentions this addition in his preface, xvi.) The last chapter of the French work was not included in the English one and was later published as "Law and Liberty" in *The Review of Politics* 52:1 (1990): 105–18, again as translated by Peter Wolff. Simon's "Réflexions sur la connaissance practique," *Revue de Philosophie* 3 (1932): 449–73 and 551–55 marks his first attempt to deal with matters touching on free choice (e.g. the final practical judgment) and was written some 20 years after Maritain's own first effort. (It later formed part of his *Critique de la connaissance morale* [Paris: Desclée de Brouwer, 1934]; in English: *A Critique of Moral Knowledge*, translated with an introduction by Ralph McInerny [New York: Fordham, 2002].) In fact, however, he never really addresses freedom itself until his "Liberty and Authority," *Proceedings of the American Catholic Philosophical Association* 16 (1940): 86–114; his first book dealing with it was *Par delà de l'expérience du désespoir* (Montreal: Lucien Parizeau, 1945); in English: *The Community of the Free*, translated by Willard R. Trask (New York: Henry Holt, 1947; Lanham, Maryland: University Press of America, 1984), 17–21.

5. Simon, *Freedom of Choice*, xiv and xv.

6. Ibid., xi.

It is thought-provoking that two of those most knowledgeable about the idea of free choice, and who ever associated Maritain and Simon in their account of it, should single out Simon's book in particular for such praise. It makes one wonder whether, in that work, Simon has somehow articulated ideas or made distinctions that are absent in Maritain's own treatment of the matter.

If one puts the question in just those terms—"Is there any new *idea* or *distinction* present in Simon that was not in Maritain?"—then my straightforward and simple answer to it here may perhaps disappoint: no, there is nothing importantly new in Simon. Nevertheless, the "devil is in the details," as anyone who has ever taken up this matter knows. And, as I will try to show in this essay's second half, Simon *does* bring a distinctive feature of free choice into sharper focus. First, however, I will summarize the "general outline" of their common position, one first given by Maritain. Only then will I turn to Simon, to underline one or two of what I take to be the most crucial and most difficult distinctions to grasp clearly in their mutual defense of free choice.

II. Maritain: The Common Account

Maritain's first exposition of free choice was given in a series of lectures at the Institut Catholique the year before World War I. He had just begun his academic career, and he published these lectures the following year, in the second chapter of his first book, on Bergson.[7] He adds little to his exposition of free choice in his next treatment of the matter, twenty years later, in "Une philosophie de la liberté,"[8] the immediate antecedent to his treatment in *Scholasticism and Politics*, which, in turn, continues to follow

7. Jacques Maritain, *La Philosophie Bergsonienne: Études Critiques* (Paris: Marcel Rivière et Cie, 1914). The work can be found in Jacques and Raïssa Maritain, *Oeuvres Complètes,* vol. 1 (Fribourg: Éditions Universitaire Fribourg Suisse; Paris: Éditions St. Paul, 1986), 97–492; in English: *Bergsonian Philosophy and Thomism,* translated by Mabelle L. Andison, in collaboration with J. Gordon Andison (New York: Philosophical Library, 1955; New York: Greenwood Press, 1968). The material on freedom is pp. 415–58 for the French and pp. 252–77 for the English.

8. Jacques Maritain, "Une philosophie de la liberté," in *Du Régime Temporal et de la Liberté* (Paris: Descleé, 1933); in English: "A Philosophy of Freedom," in *Freedom in the Modern World* (London: Sheed and Ward, 1936), 3–73. (The essay in *Para una Filosofia de la Persona Humana* [see n. 3] was given the year after the English version of "Une philosophie de la liberté" and only three years after it was first published. In truth, his later two essays are nothing more than different *versions* of the account he gave of it in his first book.)

the teaching of his earlier works. Thus, it is to his first treatment that we should turn to discover his view and its bases.[9]

As to the latter, he is relying heavily on the theologian with whom he would become more intimately associated a decade later in his project of the *Cercles Thomistes*: Reginald Garrigou-Lagrange, O.P.[10] This Dominican had just begun his own academic career, and one of his first articles (indeed, arguably his first important article) was an account, and defense, of the Thomistic idea of freedom, especially as it had been articulated by his classic Dominican predecessors.[11] From first to last, Maritain understood Thomism to have been substantively—even if not "unexceptionally"—passed on by these commentators, and we already see his preference for them here, in referencing both his favorite among them—John of St. Thomas—and the contemporary Dominicans who continued this tradition: not only Garrigou-Lagrange, but the older Norberto Del Prado, at the University of Fribourg.[12] Maritain indeed is not attempting to be "original" in his own treatment of freedom, but only to give a "review" of the "essential points" of this classic position.[13]

9. Before beginning what he takes to be the right analysis of *how* choice is free, Maritain had asserted there is no doubt *that* choice is free: "the existence of free will is the most certain *fact* there is. As evidenced by the judgments of practical reason in each one of us and the principles of social life and the universal consent of mankind, freedom is an immediate datum of consciousness; it is perceived by an intuition as infallible as the intuition of the active self by the consciousness, or of the external world by the senses, or of being by intelligence; not that we immediately apprehend, through consciousness, the essence of the will or its power; but because we immediately apprehend in its action,—by reason of the immanence of spiritual things to themselves,—the dominating indetermination of our will, because we perceive as an existing fact in the operation of the will that it is we who give to the determining motive its determining value, and to the sufficient reason of our act its complete sufficiency or its efficacity; which means that our will is not determined by any of the particular goods presented to it; whence it follows that we could, in the same circumstances, have acted differently or not at all." Maritain, *Bergsonian Philosophy*, 252–53. (The commas before and at the end of the dashed section are in the text.) As he summarily says in "The Thomist Idea of Freedom" (p. 95), "the average man … troubles himself very little [about free will], knowing he possesses it."

10. Jacques Maritain, *Bergsonian Philosophy*, 253 n. 1 (at the beginning of his account of freedom, where the article is fully cited), and then 266 n. 2 (where Maritain acknowledges his indebtedness).

11. Reginald Garrigou-Lagrange, "Intellectualisme et Liberté chez saint Thomas," *Revue des Sciences philosophiques et théologiques* (1907): 649–73, and (1908): 5–32. Garrigou-Lagrange's first article (on Thomas' Fourth Way) had only been published three years previously: see B. Zorcolo, "Bibliographia del P. Garrigou-Lagrange," *Angelicum* 42 (1965): 200–50. (His work on freedom preceded his going to the Angelicum in 1909, where he then taught for fifty years, before removing to Santa Sabina in 1960; he died in Rome, in 1964.)

12. Jacques Maritain, *Bergsonian Philosophy*, 272 n. 4, references both Del Prado and John of St. Thomas.

13. Ibid., 266.

As a good example of his adherence to that tradition, one can cite a lengthy footnote, in which he defends the "Dominican position" on the relation between our final practical judgment and free choice.[14] Given the former—a decision that this good here and now is to be preferred to others, or this action to non-action—our choice infallibly follows. While choice is *by nature* posterior to that judgment, or supposes it, it occurs at the same time or same instant, and we cannot but *in fact* choose what we deem choiceworthy.[15] In *this* sense, both Garrigou-Lagrange and Maritain concede that Leibniz was right to think that our final motive and judgment is determinative (whereas Suarez and others had argued that we are able in fact not to choose according to our final practical judgment). It is in this sense that the Dominican tradition that Maritain defends might be described as "intellectualist."

Yet this tradition also argued that our final practical judgment itself remains within the power of our will, and that the will's freedom extends to whether we make or do not make our final judgment: an ability for opposites that antecedes our final judgment both naturally and temporally.[16] As Simon notes, starting with Cajetan, the Dominicans had worked out the reciprocal relation of the acts of intellect and will of which Thomas speaks in his "Treatise on Human Acts" (in the *Prima Secundae*, qq. 11–17), a relation especially close in choice, as is already clear in Aristotle's definition of it as "desiderative reason" or "ratiocinative desire."[17] Thus Maritain, again following Garrigou-Lagrange, cites the adage "*causae ad invicem sunt causae*": in choice, intellect and will cause each other, but in diverse ways.[18] The in-

14. Ibid., 273 n. 1.

15. Maritain writes: "At the instant that the final practical judgment is made, the will cannot choose otherwise *in sensu composito* (the ACT of choosing otherwise is incompossible with the positing of the final practical judgment)." Ibid. Nevertheless, as he states just prior to this, "the judgment which determines my choice does not suppress the *power* that I have of willing or not willing [i.e. my ability to choose otherwise "in sensu diviso"], since it is precisely in exercising this power that I bring this judgment to bear." Emphasis in original.

16. "If it is a question of prerequisite conditions of a priority *in time* [as is true throughout the *time* of deliberation that antecedes one's final judgment] it can act or not act *etiam in sensu composito*." Ibid.

17. Yves R. Simon, "Law and Liberty," 112 n. 3. See Cajetan, *In I-II*, q. 16, a. 4. (For the *loci classici* in Aristotle, see the *Nicomachean Ethics* 1113a11 and 1139a33.) In fact, Dominicans after Cajetan, in particular Antonin Reginald (1606–1676)—e.g. in his *Doctrinae Divi Thomas Tria Principia* (Paris: Lethielleux, 1878), Principle I, n. 766–77—had developed the account of the interrelation of intellect and will as this was then being given by contemporary Thomists: see Matthieu-Maxime Gorce, O.P., "Reginald, Antonin," in the *Dictionnaire de Théologie Catholique*, 13b (Paris: Lethielleux, 1937), 2105–14.

tellect supplies the formal cause or determining motive to the will, as the "material cause" or subject of choice; but the will itself applies the intellect to its very act of judgment, which is under its control.[19] This application is prior by nature to final judgment (being its efficient cause) and makes a given good or motive become finally determinative. Thus, our choice is free precisely because our final judgment is caused by the will, as agent.[20]

This conclusion is based on a classical analysis of the will's nature, one that Maritain follows. To will is to desire. Its object is the desirable, or the good. Yet the will is a certain kind of desire, a rational one: it is an intellectual appetite. Thus, its object is the known good, or a good apprehended as such by the intellect. Desire is not blind, nor is will: we always want what we apprehend or judge to be good, and should we find nothing good about an object or act, then we will not be attracted to it or want it.[21] Because the will is an intellectual desire or appetite, it follows that its natural range of attraction is as wide as the intellect's: and, since the latter is open to all reality or being—and thus to the full amplitude of the true and the good—the will's natural thirst or desire is for the universal good.

It is thus that the will's freedom of choice is rooted in and deduced from its nature and necessity. Since, "*in very virtue of what it is*,"[22] it necessarily seeks, inclines towards, is attracted to, or desires "good in all its fullness,

18. Jacques Maritain, *Bergsonian Philosophy*, 271; see Garrigou-Lagrange, "Intellectualisme et Liberté chez saint Thomas," 18.

19. See Thomas Aquinas, *Summa Theologiae* (ST) I-II, q. 9, a. 1, ad 3: "The will *moves* the intellect as to the exercise of its act"; a. 1: "the will *moves* the other powers of the soul to their acts, for we *make use* of the other powers when we will"; q. 16, a. 1: "it is the will which *moves* the soul's powers to their acts, and this is to *apply* them to operation"; and q. 16, a. 4: "since the will, in way, *moves* the reason also, and *uses* it, we may take the use of the means as consisting in *the consideration of reason*, according as it refers the means to the end. In this sense use *precedes* choice." Emphasis added. Our will applies our reason, or moves it, using our reason to consider aspects of a good. The English quotations of these texts and others from the *Summa* are from *Summa Theologica*, translated by the English Dominican Province, 5 vols. (Westminster, Maryland: Christian Classics, 1948).

20. In *Bergsonian Philosophy*, 273 n. 2, Maritain quotes John of St. Thomas on this point: "The indifference of freedom consists in the will's dominating power (*potestate dominative voluntatis*), not only over its own act to which it moves, but also over the judgment (*super judicium*) by which it is moved; and this is necessary so that the will may have full dominion (*plenum dominium*) over its own act (*de Anima*, q. xii, a. 2)."

21. Even to act without motive or good, "for no good reason," or simply "for no reason," can still be judged good; and only were it so judged could we want it. (Sensitive desire is no more blind than the intellectual one; the former always supposes the given of sensation, an "apprehensive" power.)

22. Jacques Maritain, *Bergsonian Philosophy*, 267; emphasis in original.

universal good,"[23] it is not necessitated to desire or choose any "particular or partial good."[24] Quoting Garrigou-Lagrange, he thus proclaims that "any particular or partial good remains inadequate to ... [the will's] infinite capacity for loving"[25]; in regards to a particular good, it remains "*undetermined*" and "*indifferent*."[26] Or, as Simon will later felicitously put the same point, while we all naturally and necessarily want to be happy (as our end), we are free to place our happiness in any particular good that solicits our desire (as a means to it), at any given time.[27]

Maritain is careful to underline that, in speaking of our will's infinite capacity for loving, and thus to its indetermination to a particular good, he is not referring to the will as passive or potential, as being able to be acted on by any particular good. Rather, he is referring to the will as being active and thus as possessing an "active and dominating indifference" to the partial good before it.[28] In a footnote, he insists that this active and dominating indifference is the essence of freedom, and that it is precisely because some thinkers confuse it with a passive indetermination that they misunderstand Thomas's doctrine.[29] Later, in his *Preface to Metaphysics* (written at the same time as "Une philosophie de la liberté"), he makes this point by speaking of the will's "*superabundant* determination," as opposed to an "*in*determination."[30]

Our final practical judgment occurs at the end of a process involving previous acts of intellect and will. We first apprehend a possible good and are attracted to it or love it simply, just as good. By our simple apprehension and volition, our faculties of intellect and will are in act. Because we

23. Ibid., 268.

24. Ibid.

25. Ibid., n. †. The quote is from an offset printing of Garrigou-Lagrange, "Intellectualisme et Liberté chez saint Thomas," 15 n. 10.

26. Ibid.; emphasis in original.

27. Yves R. Simon, *Freedom of Choice*, 148.

28. Jacques Maritain, *Bergsonian Philosophy*, 268.

29. Ibid., 272 n. 3.

30. Jacques Maritain, *A Preface to Metaphysics* (New York: Sheed and Ward, 1939), 103. *Sept leçons sur l'être et les premiers principes de la raison speculative* was originally published by Pierre Tequi, in Paris, in 1934. It was Maritain's next book, after publishing *Du Régime Temporel*, with its essay on freedom. In *A Preface*, he writes: "[the will] pours out upon ("surabonder") the particular good, of itself wholly incapable of determining it, the *superabundant* ("*trop plein*") *determination* it receives from its necessary object, good as such. It gratuitously makes that good purely and simply good for itself—the subject—in virtue, to put it so, of the *fullness* ("plenitude") of intelligible determination with which it overflows ("regorge")." Emphasis added. (Simon references this passage in his *Freedom of Choice*, 150–51 n. 19.)

see and love a good insofar as good, we then move ourselves, or use our intellectual power, to consider it more deeply: to determine if we should choose it under our present circumstances or "all things considered," including our dispositions towards it. In this process of deliberation, we can discern and judge many aspects of the object before us, in relation to our most cherished principles and our best inclinations. Yet any object save the Absolute Good (a good that corresponds to the will's infinite reach, its desire for all that is good)—any particular good, then, save God seen in Himself—can be good for us considering a certain aspect and not-good considering another. Any good, then, can be seen as desirable or not desirable, depending on what we consider in it, and we judge as we do because we apply our intellect to consider just these aspects of the object and to judge according to them. Our final practical judgment, then, derives from our will's inclination and direction. Simon later makes the same point: "The object of the practical judgment is one that cannot be grasped by looking at it. It is delivered by love to the docile intellect. As John of St. Thomas says in words of Augustinian beauty, *Amor transit in conditionem objecti*, 'Love takes over the role of object.'"[31]

In sum: a free choice is not uncaused. Rather, it is caused by a final practical judgment: we choose what we decide here and now is best for us. Further: since we always choose for a reason or motive, neither is our freedom founded in irrationality. Yet it is from the will itself that a judgment becomes our final one.[32] Faced with two differing goods, or simply to act or not to act,[33] we are free to focus our attention on differing aspects of the object, and to make them be decisive for our final decision. Thus is our choice freely made. Being moved to will, and with our volition then in act

31. Yves R. Simon, *Practical Knowledge*, edited by Robert J. Mulvaney (New York: Fordham University Press, 1991), 17–18. (John of St. Thomas was his favorite commentator, as well as Maritain's.) The first chapter of this work was first published as "Introduction to the Study of Practical Wisdom," *New Scholasticism* 34 (1961): 1–40, one of his last two articles published, in the year of his death.

32. Again referencing Garrigou-Lagrange ("Intellectualisme et Liberté chez saint Thomas," 43), Maritain says "*the will is thus the cause* [of the final judgment and thus] *of the very attraction it undergoes* [in choosing the judged good]." Ibid., 272; emphasis in original.

33. See ibid., 275, where Maritain gives the classic distinction between the freedoms of specification and exercise. There are in fact some goods that, when considered, are necessarily judged good, namely those that fulfill our natural desires: e.g. life, health, sensation, knowledge. Yet the act of willing itself, or the act of using our intellect to consider, are not such goods, and thus we are always free to exercise the act of willing or to continue considering these specifying goods; indirectly, then, we are not necessitated to choose even those acts.

towards our natural end, we move ourselves to judge a particular good here and now the means to our end, and thus we move ourselves to choose it. And thus is free choice rightly understood as *self*-determination.

This, then, is Maritain's version of the classic Thomistic defense of free choice. Let us turn, now, to what Simon underlines in an account that he entirely makes his own.

III. Simon: The Account Exemplified

From the beginning to the end of his life as a philosopher, Simon sought to understand the order of practical reason and especially prudence, or practical wisdom, and its defining act: the final practical judgment that is determinative of choice.[34] And, from first to last, he was above all intent on purifying our concept of free choice from false coin, from ideas that entice us into thinking it is something other than it is.

One of the most obvious mistakes we can make about freedom is to think that it resides in *indetermination*. Simon signals for us the way we make this mistake: it is

> due to the similarity in name of two notions which are sharply opposed to one another, although they are connected by a thin analogy. There is an indifference which results from a lack of determination, from an ontological poverty, from a state of potency, an indifference of potentiality. A subject which lacks determination, which is unachieved and thereby *open* to several possibilities, is indifferent to the special nature of each of them. On the other hand there is an indifference which is based upon the achievement of a being, the fullness of its determination, an indifference to several possibilities which results from the higher actuality of a cause, its plenitude, its superabundance.[35]

34. Simon's following works (in English translation, but also with their original date of publication) bear on practical wisdom, the final practical judgment, and freedom of choice: *A Critique of Moral Knowledge* (1932 [as an article], 1934 [as a book], 2002); "Liberty and Authority" (1940); *Foresight and Knowledge* (1944, 1996, as edited posthumously by Ralph Nelson and Anthony O. Simon [New York: Fordham University Press]); *The Community of the Free* (1945, 1947); "On the Foreseeability of Free Acts" (1948: see n. 37 below); *Freedom of Choice* (1951, with English additions, 1969); "Introduction to the Study of Practical Wisdom" (1961 and [in a book, edited posthumously, *Practical Knowledge*] 1991), *The Tradition of Natural Law*, edited posthumously by Vukan Kuic (New York: Fordham University Press, 1965); and *The Definition of Moral Virtue*, edited posthumously by Vukan Kuic (New York: Fordham University Press, 1986).

35. Yves R. Simon, "Liberty and Authority," 90–91; emphasis in original. Simon cites Thomas in his *Summa Contra Gentiles* (I, chap. 82) for an account of these two indeterminations, as

Ever alert to finding a concrete example that makes a distinction clear, he later strikes on a difference in wealth, as a happy means of explication: "One indifference results from abundance and another from deficiency. There is the indifference of the *rich* man, who feels sure that he will not lack anything and that of the *poor* fellow, for whom all is good, because he has nothing.... One indifference consists in the power to *produce* a multiplicity of effects and the other indifference consists in an ability to *receive* a multiplicity of influences."[36]

Another mistake in the analysis of freedom is to identify it with an irrational spontaneity. This again occurs because free choice *does* come from the personal depths of our own will and being and *is* uncoerced; but this does not make it irrational. No one can ever forget the brilliant way Simon also exposes this mistake, by giving two examples of a driver swerving to miss an object that suddenly is on the road, even at risk to his life. The first driver acts like Epicurus's famous "causeless swerve." Driving carelessly, and almost asleep, he instinctively reacts to a dog barely glimpsed, thus going down an embankment and seriously injuring himself. When queried by relatives as to why he chose to risk his life for a dog, he rightly protests that he did not choose at all, but reacted instinctively. Simon contrasts this with a driver in full control of his faculties who makes the split second decision to swerve, to avoid killing a child suddenly before him on the road, even at risk to his own life. This example brings home forcefully the point he is ever intent on making: freedom consists in self-mastery, and in deliberately acting *for* a reason. By contrast, to be driven by sub-rational forces to act "spontaneously" is not to choose at all, much less freely.

Correlate to the idea of irrational spontaneity is the false association of unpredictability with freedom. As he points out, it would indeed be odd were we to think that the more virtuous we became, and therefore the more we could be relied upon to do the right thing, the less free we became! This is surely wrong. Indeed, the degree to which we master ourselves and become virtuous is the degree to which we become free from self-conflict, perplexity, and irresolution; and thus the degree to which we attain the self-mastery proper to freedom is the degree to which we can be counted on and become relatively predictable. Yet, even where only one

---

well as John of St. Thomas's *Cursus Philosophicus, Phil. Nat.* IV, 12, 2 (Marietti ed., vol. 3, p. 387 b 12). I know of no place where Maritain had cited these sources first.

36. Yves R. Simon, *Freedom of Choice,* 118–19; emphasis added.

choice is available to the virtuous person, his choice remains free; for he chooses it knowing it is a particular good, one that remains at "an infinite qualitative distance... [from] the all-embracing essence of the good. In this extreme but not so infrequent case, it is still the gratuitous initiative of the will which gives to the particular good the character of absolute desirability"; and thus he concludes that "here as elsewhere freedom is *mastery over means*: in this definition lies the *whole of its essence*."[37] He goes so far as to posit a person whose will is totally virtuous (a case surely true only in heaven, or through an exceptional or heavenly grace) and who is confronted both with the need to choose and with only one good means available. In such a case, Simon argues, his free act would be both predictable and even foreseeable (since it would be determined in its virtuous cause);[38] and yet the act would still be free, and for the same reason as just given.

We come, then, to one of the two points Simon makes in regards to freedom that are especially valuable. First, just as irrationality and irresolution lessen our self-mastery and thus lessen our freedom, so do morally disordered or evil acts.[39] The reason is this: we are free insofar as we possess an active and dominating indifference over means that can lead to our end; but morally evil means do not lead *to* our end, but *away* from it.[40]

37. Yves R. Simon, "On the Foreseeability of Free Acts," *The New Scholasticism* 22, no. 4 (1948): 357–70, 362–63; emphasis added. Note that, so long as a particular good is recognized to be less than the comprehensive good, it can be freely chosen. Normally, this is recognized in deliberation, one that can terminate in diverse judgments. Yet this is not essential: it might be seen immediately and before all deliberation. Simon makes this point as well in *Freedom of Choice*, 116–17.

38. Ibid., 366. If God commands an angel to do a particular act, it will infallibly, yet freely, choose to do it. Again, any first act in the state of charity or first acts caused by the infusion of sanctifying grace are infallibly good ones (see ST I-II, q. 113, a. 8 and III, q. 85, aa. 5 and 6, esp. a. 6, ad 1), even though they are free acts. However, when God is not seen face to face and or one's will is not rendered infallibly good by the infusion of sanctifying grace, it is able to deflect from its true good. Lucifer was virtuous at his creation (see ST I, q. 63, a. 5, esp. ad 4) and—Thomas at least thinks—even in a state of grace (ST I, q. 62, a. 3) or, at a minimum, called to this by an actual grace (ST I, q. 62, a. 2, ad 3). He was without moral blemish, yet could sin. For men in this life, there is the additional "tinder of sin": temperamental inclinations away from virtue, the remnants of Original Sin. Simon may be thinking of the free acts caused by the infusion of sanctifying grace or by one confirmed in grace. Or, possibly, he may have been motivated here simply by his desire to distinguish as sharply as possible between the essence of freedom and the accidental fact of its usual unpredictability. (His argument is original here, going beyond what Maritain held, a position he initially had defended without qualification: see *Foresight and Knowledge*, 61–64 n. 54.)

39. Simon already makes this point in his first treatment of freedom, "Liberty and Authority," 95–98 (1940), and then in his first book treating of freedom (1945), in *The Community of the Free*, 19.

40. The point is as old as Plato's argument in *Gorgias* 466b-e that the power to choose what

Freedom is rooted in our active love of the comprehensive good, of a good fulfilling to our nature; but this love that gives rise to freedom is undercut by the choice of a means not in accord with our nature, but disordered, as is every morally evil means. Simon asks us to imagine whether our choice to travel from America to Europe—say, in a luxury liner, or in a cargo ship, or taking an airplane instead—is somehow rendered more free by being able to consider or choose going on a cheap vessel that is to be scuttled on the way by its corrupt and clever owner, to supply himself with a needed insurance payout.[41] This means does not lead to our end, and having scope to consider it only distracts us from the free choice we *do* have: of diverse means that *can* lead us to our end, each being possibly best for legitimate reasons (for a much-needed enjoyment of leisure, for thrift, or for speed).

As an aside, this point allows us to see that God—in moving our will or placing it in act—does not empower our will to choose moral evil. For to empower us freely to choose means is to empower us to choose *true* means, ones that lead towards our end or that will fulfill us, as any honest good will do (even the imperfect good not chosen according to charity, or freedom's perfect mode). In creating our will, and moving it in accord with its nature, God is moving us to the true or honest good. Thus, our will being moved or activated towards *that* good, it is empowered to use the intellect to consider the moral rule that should govern any choice. True, we are fallible and we can turn aside from our end, for God also moves us in accord with the fallible mode natural to our free will. While we are empowered to use our freedom well, then, we can misuse it; but such misuse is *our* doing, not God's. We may fail to use our intellect to consider the moral rule, even though we in fact could have, but this failure and non-use of our power undermines freedom; it does not perfect it.[42]

We come, then, to the last and most important point that Simon's exposition of freedom brings into the clearest possible focus. This consists in his treatment of the principle of causality and its relation to the will's active indifference or its "superdetermination," a neologism he gets from his teacher, but that he underlines more forcefully: "*the indifference of the*

---

is evil is not a true power, but rather undermines it, since such means are so only in appearance and do not lead to what one wants.

41. Ibid., 359–60.

42. Note that, by contrast, the *use* of our reason to consider the rule of reason (amongst other aspects of a given good) is caused by the will, supposing it is in act (or moved by God): see Thomas's texts cited in n. 19 above.

practical judgment does not originate in any indetermination of intellect and will, it originates in the natural superdetermination of the rational appetite."[43] Or, again: "few thinkers awoke to the theory that *freedom is superdetermination* rather than indetermination, and that … freedom proceeds … from a particular *excellence* in power, from a *plenitude* of being and an *abundance* of determination."[44] He regards this idea as a "conceptual treasure,"[45] one by which we can respond to our inevitable tendency to think that freedom violates the principle of causality.

Our free choice is one that comes into being and thus, as with any change, it requires a cause. First, this cause must be other than the caused, and this has been seen: the will's act is caused by the intellect's; for, however much will and intellect are intertwined in the process of free choice, to judge is different than to desire, and to judge finally is different than to choose freely. Second, the cause must resemble the effect, and this it most certainly does, since the intellect's judgment is the very form of the will's choice. Finally, and most crucially, the cause must possess full actuality, for something acts or causes only in virtue of being in act. And this is just what the intellect receives from the active and dominating indifference proper to the will in act towards its natural object, the comprehensive good.

Thus, suppose that we are trying to decide between two gifts for a friend: say, a book (A) and an engraving (B).[46] Let us suppose that, focusing on the pleasure the book gave us and one we are confident our friend will share, we judge it preferable and choose it. The theory posits that our final decision, as free, derives from the active indifference of our will. Let us label this active indifference (C). This, then, is the cause of our judgment and choice of (A), just as being free. Yet the theory also posits that it lay within that active power of our will to focus on some other good and make a different judgment and choice. Prior to determining ourselves in our first direction, we could in fact have focused on the beauty of the engraving

43. Yves R. Simon, *Freedom of Choice,* 106. Simon's emphasis in the first phrase, mine in the last three words.

44. Ibid., 152–53. This is at the start of those pages Peter Woolf chose to excerpt from Simon's unpublished encyclopedia of philosophy; see n. 4, with which he concludes the book.

45. The importance Simon attributes to the correct idea of "indetermination" can be seen from the fact that he devotes an entire chapter to this idea in "De l'idée d'indétermination," chapter 9 in his *Traité du Libre Arbitre,* 117–22, material largely incorporated later into *Freedom of Choice,* 106ff.

46. See Yves R. Simon, "On the Foreseeability of Free Acts," 363, for an analysis similar to what is given here.

and its particular subject matter (dear, let us suppose, to our friend), and could have judged this preferable and chosen (B), instead. In that case, our very same active indifference (C) would be the cause of our judgment and choice of (B), just as being free. The *super*-determination of our will that is the cornerstone of the theory insists that the will's *energy* ("or activity") is such that it causes (A) while possessing the *actual* ability to terminate in (B) or that it causes (B) while possessing the *actual* ability to terminate in (A).[47] The determination that renders its judgment and choice to be what it finally is *comes from itself*, as already *in act*. Our will, desire, or love being in act, in either case the answer to "why" we finally judged (A) or (B) preferable remains the same: simply because it pleased us to make that judgment.[48]

47. When Thomas speaks of an active power, in distinction from a passive one (see ST I, q. 77, a. 3, the *Commentary on De Anima* II, lect. 6, and his *Disputed Questions on De Anima*, a. 13), he asserts that an active cause can terminate in different objects. It does not require more activity to do so. Thus, a flame (with its heat staying the same) can cause this or that object to burn; and a medicine's active ingredient need not become more active for its ingestion to cure this or that person (or for a poison to harm this or that person). The application of the cause does not make it more active. Furthermore, even if applied, a determinate effect need not follow, since some other cause can impede it, even though its power is sufficient to cause the effect. In the case at hand, the will has been applied and is in act; but the nature of its act or energy is such that it does not require the intervention of some other cause to terminate diversely: this lies within its own active power. That is why the will is free in its choice, and not "determined to one," whereas the above causes *are* (heat to burn, medicine to its cure, poison to its harm). What the specific form is in such cases, the final practical judgment is in that of the will. Prior to this finally determining act, however, the will remains free to give itself to opposite goods. (On this last point, see the illuminating aside of Francisco Marín-Sola, O.P., in "Respuesta a algunas objeciones acerca del sistema tomista sobre la moción divine," *La Ciencia Tomista* 97 [1926]: 57 n. 1.)

48. Inevitably, someone will ask: "Why does *this* good please at one time and *another* good at another?" If this is asking about the *motive* of what pleases, the answer is: "Because at one time *this* motive pleased me (e.g. the pleasure of a shared good read) and at the other time *that* motive pleased me (the subject beautifully engraved)"; in other words, the theory is always able to point to some good initially seen as good and motivating. Yet the objector is likely asking, "What *moved* you to be pleased about one and not the other?" (that is, "What is the *efficient* cause that accounts for you being diversely pleased?"). Simon well knew that the question would return this way, and gave this reply: "Obstinately, the initial question returns. We know that the will possesses all the actuality necessary in order to make this or that determinately desirable. One wants to assign a reason to this preference, one demands *why* the choice is made one way rather than another.... What does this *why* signify? (a) One could mean that it relates to a cause sufficiently characterized by altereity, actuality and resemblance to the effect: the free cause is not excluded, if it presents all these characteristics. If the question is thus understood, it receives the answer: 'the will insofar as it adheres to the universal essence of the good and to the practical judgment of its choice is a cause presenting these characteristics and it is free.'" Simon, *Freedom of Choice*, 151–52. He had just argued that altereity results from judgment being different than choice, and yet its very form (thus fulfilling the condition of resemblance). The condition of actuality derives from the will's adherence "to the universal essence of good" (or, as he often terms

Let us join this analysis to the earlier aside I made, in relation to God empowering us only for the true, honest, or moral good. He does so just in placing our will in act (or moving it). Now we also see that, just in placing our will in act towards its natural object of the comprehensive good, He has empowered it for different good choices. Let us then suppose we choose (A). As free, this act is caused by our active indifference (C), and this in turn is caused by God (who first places us in act). Let us now suppose we choose (B), instead of (A). This act, as free, is also caused by this same active indifference (C) caused by God. In each case, our will is the cause of our free choice, as is God: we as secondary causes, acting with a God-given energy already supplied, and God as the one who supplied it, by first placing our will in act. That will is by nature not determined to one choice, and God, in activating or moving our will according to its nature, empowers us to choose the morally good acts within our power. This, it seems to me, is the fruitful way of thinking about God's movement of our will to its free choice that Simon proposes for our consideration.[49]

---

this, the "comprehensive good"), which adherence antecedes judgment (and communicates its actuality to it). Again, then, the crucial concept that needs to be understood to its depths is that of a cause already in act that can terminate in diverse effects. With necessary causes (e.g. heat) that diversity is based on different objects being applied, or on the interference of a cause, impeding its effect (even though the cause has already been being applied); see Thomas's account in the texts quoted in n. 47 above. In the case of free will, the diversity of termination lies in the free will itself and the plenitude of its activity, which permits it to terminate in diverse ways: "*This* pleased me then, although *that* could have then (as, indeed, it did at some other time); I judged *this* preferable then, although I could have judged *that* so (as I did at some other time). It pleased me to judge *this* preferable, although *I could have judged otherwise* (as I did later): that is just why I assert that my judgments are *free*."

49. Note that God is here asserted to move our will itself, which is the same as moving it "physically" (and not just "morally," by proposing an attractive good for choice). Note, further, that God's activation of our will (towards the comprehensive good) precedes its free decision (and thus could be termed a "pre"-motion relative to that act). Note, even, that one can speak of the will being "pre-determined" to its particular free choice by the naturally prior judgment of the intellect. Note, finally, that the will here acts as a sub-ordinate (not co-ordinate) cause, with all of its activity and goodness being caused by God (and it only "non-acts" as an insubordinate and independent first cause when it fails to act and does not use the intellect to consider the moral rule, as it could do during deliberation and as it should do in making a final judgment). Yet Simon's account fully respects both the transcendence of God (since the final judgment is not "pre-determined," or willed by God "before" it occurs) and the basis of the will's freedom is grounded in God's moving it to the "universal good" (as Thomas himself says and upon which many have insisted), with it not being "determined to one" particular good or choice. If it be challenged that somehow the will "alone" is using the intellect to consider what it does and directing it to make this decision, not another, it should be said in reply that this very use and direction is, in its turn, caused by the will's prior God-given activity and thus also is being caused by God; see also n. 42 above.

Simon makes all of the specific points just noted in a number of different places in his works. But all of his trenchant observations, as well as his strong insistence on the importance of the will's "superdetermination," are brought together in his work on *Freedom of Choice*. All of its ideas are ones Maritain himself had first defended, of which Simon, his greatest pupil, has availed himself. Yet one will find these ideas always supported by the concrete examples and analytic precision for which Simon is justly famous. I therefore conclude that, while his book cannot be said to advance new ideas or distinctions absent in Maritain, Adler's judgment in its foreword remains sound: his remains the single best work on the subject of freedom that has issued from the pen of any contemporary Thomist.

JOHN J. CONLEY, S.J.

Freud as Political *Adversarius*

I. Introduction

In one of the odder chapters of *Scholasticism and Politics*, Jacques Maritain criticizes Freud and Freudianism.[1] The parallel operated between Freud and Luther, one of the old antagonists from *Antimoderne*,[2] indicates Freud's status as a modern adversary to be overcome. But the critique developed by Maritain is a mitigated one. As a therapeutic technique, Freudian analysis can heal certain neuroses. Its account of the unconscious can illuminate the arational psychic background of the human mind, which more rationalist theories of the psyche obscure. Nonetheless, Freudianism proposes an erroneous anthropology inasmuch as its theory of the libido and the sexual instinct rests on a materialist account of the mind and of human action. It cannot adequately account for the emergence of religion, morality, art, and science in human cultures. Such phenomena owe more to the work of the intellect and will than to the obscure play of non-rational instincts. Freudianism is a political opponent to the extent that it can neither account for nor cultivate the human faculties which fabricate the religious, moral, aesthetic, and technological orders of society, particularly in complex societies at their speculative and practical apex of development.

1. See Jacques Maritain, *Scholasticism and Politics*, translated and edited by Mortimer Adler (New York: Macmillan, 1940).

2. See Jacques Maritain, *Antimoderne* (Paris: Editions de la *Revue de la Jeunesse*, 1922).

II. Figures of Freud

A preliminary problem in Maritain's critique of Freud is discerning which Freud one is reading. Maritain cites several works of Freud himself: *Interpretation of Dreams*, *Psychopathology of Everyday Life*, and *Essays in Psychoanalysis*. But he clearly relies more directly on the synthesis of Freudian theory written by his friend Roland Dalbiez.[3] He also relies on another synthesis by his colleague at the University of Chicago, Mortimer Adler,[4] who was central in the development of and collection of the essays which came to be called *Scholasticism and Politics*. As Maritain himself notes, he is also referring to the diffuse Freudianism which had influenced so much of the French literary world since the 1920s. His friend and correspondent Jean Cocteau represents one of the major artistic figures to produce film, drama, and prose shaped by a neo-Freudian exploration of the unconscious.[5]

Not only does Maritain analyze a Freud refracted through a particular therapeutic, philosophical, and artistic lens; his sympathetic interpretation of Freud assimilates Freud's theories and practices to the canons of Maritain's own personalist and Thomistic philosophy. This assimilation clearly occurs in the treatment of Freud's practice of psychoanalysis and of Freud's account of the unconscious.

In Maritain's perspective, the psychotherapeutic relationship is unusual inasmuch as it involves an intimate relationship between two persons. It is in fact a conflict between the analyst and the patient. "This very special relationship which places the psychoanalytical act, not in the realm of the (practical) science which is medicine, but in the realm of a conflict between two persons,—where the individual event and accidental aspect are much more absorbing,—would perhaps also explain why psychoanalysts more than others usually find it difficult to observe the canon of objectivity in scientific method."[6] In this interpersonal conflict of analysis, such phenomena as transference from patient to doctor in terms of conflict and

3. See Roland Dalbiez, *La méthod psychanalytique et la doctrine freudienne* (Paris: Desclée de Brouwer, 1936). Dalbiez's sharp distinction between Freudian psychoanalytic method (which he approves) and Freudian doctrine (which he criticizes) clearly influences Maritain's own judgment of Freud.

4. See Mortimer Adler, *What Man Has Made of Man: A Study of the Consequences of Platonism and Positivism in Psychology* (London: Longmans, Green and Company, 1937).

5. See Jacques Maritain and Jean Cocteau, *Art and Faith: Letters between Jacques Maritain and Jean Cocteau*, translated by John Coleman (New York: Philosophical Library, 1948).

6. Maritain, *Scholasticism and Politics*, 157–58.

belief are common. Maritain describes the psychoanalytic relationship as "the intromission of one soul into another."[7]

In limning the personalist dimension of the psychoanalytic relationship, Maritain insists on the difference between psychotherapy and sacramental confession. In the setting of the confessional, the priest must remain as anonymous as possible. He presents the forgiveness of Christ to the penitent; in his judicial and medicinal role, he must remain as restrained as is possible. In the same way, the penitent must avoid rummaging around in the images and feelings of the subconscious. The penitent uses intellect, memory, and will to construct the narrative of sin to be confessed with contrition, either perfect or imperfect.

The psychoanalytic relationship operates in a different manner. The very purpose of the analyst-patient relationship is to probe the unconscious, the reservoir of the forces covertly causing the neuroses or psychoses troubling the patient. The emotional force of the relationship lies in accessing this hidden mind through techniques such as free association. So powerful and dangerous is the brooking of the unconscious that the psychoanalyst must undergo extensive psychoanalysis himself or herself before attempting to help others through this means. According to Maritain, this charged psychoanalytical relationship can lead to authentic but limited success in resolving neuroses and psychoses by revealing to the patient the hidden causes—the repressions—which have led to the emotional trauma.

In treating Freud's theory of the unconscious, Maritain assimilates it to the Thomistic theory of the powers of the intellect and the will. Like Freud, Thomas recognizes that many of the operations of these powers take place unknown to the conscious mind. "For St. Thomas Aquinas, not only is the human soul obscure to itself—knowing its own concrete existence only by reflection upon its acts—not only after its basic tendencies, called powers or faculties, among the realities whose intimate nature escapes introspection, but, in addition, the instincts, the inclinations, the acquired tendencies, the habitus or internal improvements of the faculties, the virtues and the vices, the deep mechanisms of the life of the spirit—all these constitute a world or reality whose effects alone reach consciousness."[8] Unlike rationalist epistemologies, which tend to reduce the mind to the conscious possession of a series of concepts, Thomistic epistemology, like Freud's theory

7. Ibid., 157.
8. Maritain, *Scholasticism and Politics*, 146.

of the unconscious, recognizes what is hidden and obscure in the workings of the mind which elude conscious grasp but which powerfully shape emotive and moral temperament.

Maritain recognizes that the effort to assimilate Freudian theory to the categories of Thomistic and personalist philosophy has clear limitations. Maritain, argues, for example, that the effort of some Christian philosophers to interpret the Freudian libido as a contemporary variant of concupiscence is deceptive, since the irrational impulses described by Freud are decoupled from earlier Christian considerations of sin and responsibility. Nonetheless, in his positive appreciation of the successful new therapeutic techniques developed by the Freudian school and of the enriched map of the unconscious mind provided by Freud, Maritain considers Freudianism a healthy antidote to the thin positivist anthropology of the late nineteenth century. In Freudianism's pity for the patient enslaved by emotional repression, Maritain even finds an analogue to Christian charity.

III. Freud as Opponent

Despite his sympathy for certain contributions of Freud, Maritain considers Freudianism fundamentally mistaken in its basic account of human nature. Like many contemporary Catholic philosophers, Maritain criticizes the hypersexuality of Freud's theory of childhood and of the hidden motives for human action. But his major concern is the materialism of Freud's anthropology. In his reduction of human behavior to arational instincts, reason itself disappears and free will, the foundation of human moral responsibility, crumbles. The Freudian theory of the unconscious ultimately dismantles thought and will in a sea of unconscious but determinative impulses.

According to Maritain, Freud simply denies the properly rational and conscious nature of part of the human mind. In doing so, he destroys the freedom and dignity of the human person. "[Freud ignores] the life proper and the energy proper of the whole region of the psychic to which consciousness is necessarily linked, that is, the rational part of the soul. The judgments of the mind, the free choices of the will—these are necessarily and in themselves conscious, and they are essential to our behavior. In contrast, there is, for Freud, no free choice; even the highest functions of the mind can be accomplished in the unconscious like the rest. If there is any efficacy in the conscious, it consists only in the fact of being known."[9] In the denial of reason as truly different from animal instinct, Freud proposes "the violent negation of spirituality and liberty."[10] The sublimation celebrated by Freud, as a means to overcome psychic conflict through high cultural expression such as art or religion, is a false sublimation, since it does not recognize the role of the higher powers of intellect and will (and the virtues perfecting these faculties) as the architects of such an expressive overcoming of internal psychic conflict.

For Maritain, Freud is a political opponent inasmuch as he cannot explain the origin and nature of the most enduring achievements of human society, such as religious practice, the moral code, and artistic creation. "Let us be content to record here the failure of the effort, made by Freud and his school, to explain by psychoanalysis and by an empiricism or radical sensualism of a sexualist tendency, the superior activities of the human being: art, morality, religion."[11] Moreover, the hypersexualism of Freud and his disciples conceives the principal purpose of political society to be the encouragement of human happiness through primary attention to the sexual conflicts of individuals and the abolition of constraining sexual codes denounced as repressive. The recognition and the cultivation of the rational soul, with its transcendental aspiration toward God and toward the good, the beautiful, and the true is simply ignored in a distorted anthropology which has reduced human nature to certain basic material instincts and which has reduced politics to the fulfillment of these instincts and the resolution of the conflicts encumbering them.

In criticizing Freud's naturalistic account of sublimation, Maritain attempts to rehabilitate the concept of sublimation along more religious lines. A properly spiritual account of sublimation needs to be resurrected. "The rapture of the lyrical or religious soul is in itself specifically spiritual, and, therefore, specifically distinct from the animal instinct. Does this mean that this rapture is separated from instinct? It is absurd to absorb the superior in the inferior, but it is inhuman to disjoin them."[12] As in the earlier *Degrees of Knowledge*,[13] it is mystical experience which reveals what

9. Maritain, *Scholasticism and Politics*, 147.

10. Ibid., 165.

11. Ibid., 167.

12. Ibid., 163–64.

13. See Jacques Maritain, *Distinguish to Unite or The Degrees of Knowledge*, translated by Gerald Phelan (New York: Charles Scribner's Sons, 1959).

human beings are capable of in the most exalted use of their higher powers. Emotions and animal instincts may accompany such ecstatic expressions of the rational soul, but such expressions cannot be reduced to these accoutrements. Only a society which acknowledges and encourages such sublimations can construct a political order and a pedagogy which respects the human soul in its fullness and with its highest aspirations.

IV. Critical Evaluation

At the distance of sixty years, Maritain's treatment of Freud merits critical evaluation. Maritain's irenic effort to assimilate Freud to the concerns of Thomism and associated Catholic philosophies is not always convincing and he may have underestimated one way in which Freud's theories are a salutary antidote to our political illusions.

First, Maritain's distinction between Freudian method and Freudian doctrine is not as convincing as he claims. The classical Freudian practice of psychoanalysis does indeed aim at unlocking the unconscious by piercing the defenses articulated by the ego and superego's laws and reasons. But this unconscious is still the reservoir of the instincts and conflicts which have been shaped by biological and social determinants hidden from the rational and volitional purview of the subject. As opposed to other methods of counseling, such as the rational-emotive or the existential, the classic psychoanalytic method tends to discount the import of formal reason and of the free, conscious, deliberate decisions made by the moral agent. The interpersonal method of psychoanalysis is still very much shaped by the determinist theory of human nature which undergirds it. Psychoanalytic practice, broadly praised by Maritain, would appear closer to the determinist, materialist theory of the human person which Maritain condemns.

Similarly, Maritain's effort to assimilate the Freudian concept of the unconscious to the non-reflective working of the operations of the human mind according to Aquinas seems willfully irenic. While both give weight to the emotions which erupt in the human mind, the Thomistic pays far greater attention to the intellectual and volitional faculties, minimized by Freud. The Thomist discussion of the virtues, specifically cited by Maritain, finds no parallel in the Freudian discussion of instinct, conflict, and repression. The effort to cultivate the habits of justice, fortitude, temperance, and prudence so that the intellect might reach the goal of the true and the good is passed over in silence. The difference between the rational soul of Thomism and the libidinous network of mortal desires in Freud receives little excavation.

If Maritain might appear too sympathetic to Freud in certain dimensions of the latter's thought, he appears to underestimate the political contribution of Freud in another area. Freud's account of the conflicted and suffering nature of the human person is a caution against the utopian impulse to construct an ideal order out of the dictates of reason and an enlightened will. The Freudian account does not accept the Rousseauesque argument that human unhappiness is solely caused by social factors external to the human person; the roots of anxiety and despair cannot be eliminated through the proper dose of social engineering, based on objective scientific analysis. Behind our concepts and decisions stands a series of potent impulses and conflicts usually veiled from view. Even in the best therapeutic circumstances, this reservoir of arational forces never comes to full consciousness and its broiling tensions never achieve complete resolution. As Maritain argues, this grasp of human illusion and veiled motivation should not be quickly assimilated to the theological concept of concupiscence, but it does underscore the limitations of human thought and decision. As such, it cautions against the illusion of human perfectibility and the political schemes founded upon such an illusion.

It is in his reconstruction of sublimation that Maritain provides the clearest critique and rehabilitation of Freudianism in the political sector. It is the false, materialist account of sublimation that precisely makes Freud a political adversary. The attempt to construct civilization on the basis of a sublimation of conflict which is only biological and emotional is to negate the properly intellectual and volitional sublimation that is the hidden source of humanity's enduring achievements in the religious, artistic, scientific, and legal orders. The rights of the human person and the nature of the human soul as a rational soul must be properly appreciated for the nature of the political order to be conceived properly and for the great symbolic achievements of humanity in this social order to be nurtured. As in his transformation of Bergson's intuition, Maritain's transformation of the Freudian sublime manifests Saint Thomas's intellectualism and Maritain's own.

STEPHEN CHAMBERLAIN

Aquinas, Psychoanalysis, and the Internal Sense Faculties

In his essay "Freudianism and Psychoanalysis" Jacques Maritain acknowledges the wealth of insight offered by Freudian psychology, particularly in regard to Freud's discovery of the psychoanalytic method by which the hidden workings of the unconscious may be disclosed. At the same time, Maritain is quick to point out the philosophical shortcomings of Freudianism that typically go unrecognized by Freud's followers and which reveal an inadequate "pseudo-metaphysics." While considering Maritain's analysis of Freud's theory, this essay will attempt to sketch the outlines of a philosophical psychology or anthropology that situates some of the basic and most fruitful aspects of the Freudian unconscious and psychoanalysis within a contemporary Thomistic account of the human person.

I will begin by specifying the distinct, internal sense faculties according to a Thomistic psychology. I will then identify the fundamental principles for the dynamic interrelations between these faculties according to their normative and unified operations. Thirdly, I will consider the possibility of psychic disorders that can persist latently within the unconscious. In conclusion, I will offer a suggestion of how imagination, reason, and language play essential roles in the psychoanalytic process of retrieving, recollecting, and in turn restructuring such disorders.

I. Aquinas's Account of the Internal Sense Faculties

As is well known, Aquinas identifies four internal sense powers, namely, *sensus communis, imaginatio, memoria,* and the *vis aestimativa or vis cog-*

itativa.[1] Common sense or sense consciousness is the power by which one is able to recognize and in turn discriminate between the proper and common sensibles that are received by the five external senses. Traditionally, *sensus communis* has also been viewed as the power through which the sense data is synthesized insofar as the data are referred to a singular material entity. Hence, one can distinguish between tartness and greenness while referring these qualities to the same object, namely, the apple. More recently, this view has been challenged and the cogitative power has been assigned that role.[2] Although I am not entirely convinced by these recent arguments, for the purposes of this essay I will bracket consideration of this question as my main concern will be the relation and distinction between imagination and memory.

Aquinas defines imagination as a *thesaurus* or "a treasure-store of forms received through the senses."[3] What is noteworthy is that the power of imagination is given a function that we typically assign to memory, namely, the act of conserving or retaining an image or sign of something that initially was received in the past. This aspect is important in that for Aquinas memory is delimited and so takes on a narrower function. The intentional forms that are initially received by *sensus communis,* then, are expressed and conserved within the power of imagination. Imagination is in turn capable of arranging or rearranging these species in order to construct or create a more complex and comprehensive image of the object (actual or possible).[4] And so, on the one hand, imagination is subordinated to common sense insofar as it depends upon the initial reception of those intentional forms of the impressed species.[5] On the other hand, imagination elevates

1. See Thomas Aquinas, *Man (Ia. 75–83),* vol. 11 of *Summa Theologiae* (ST), translated and edited by Timothy Suttor (Cambridge: Cambridge University Press, 2006), q. 78, aa. 3–4, pp. 129–43. All English quotations of the *Summa* are from this translation.

2. See, for example, Stephen J. Laumakis, "The *Sensus Communis* Reconsidered," *American Catholic Philosophical Quarterly* 82, no. 3 (2008): 429–43 and Anthony J. Lisska, "A Look at Inner Sense in Aquinas: A Long-Neglected Faculty Psychology," *Proceedings of the American Catholic Philosophical Association* 80 (2006): 1–19.

3. "(F)antasy or imagination is, as it were, a treasure-store of forms received through the senses"; "(E)st enim phantasia sive imaginatio quasi thesaurus quidam formarum per sensum acceptarum." ST I, q. 78, a. 4. All Latin text citations of the *Summa* are from the Leonine edition and are included in the Suttor translation; see n. 1 above.

4. Aquinas says, "As when from the image of gold and the image of mountain we compose the single form of a golden mountain which we have never seen." "(U)t patet cum ex forma imaginata auri et forma imaginata montis componimus unam formam montis aurei quem nunquam vidimus." ST I, q. 78, a. 4.

5. Hence, the limitation of a finite imagination that cannot itself create images *ex nihilo,* such

those initially received forms insofar as it builds, creates, or expresses more complex and comprehensive objects (actual or possible).

Although Aquinas refers to imagination as a *thesaurus* or storehouse of sense forms, he also refers to memory as a *thesaurus* or "treasure-store." The difference between these two faculties is determined by the intentional forms that are received and in turn stored within the distinct faculties. Whereas imagination retains the impressions initially received by sense consciousness, memory retains those objects grasped by the *estimative* or *cogitative* faculty, which in animals is akin to instinct. As Aquinas says, "Instinct grasps intentions which are not objects of simple sensation. And the power of memory conserves these; it is a treasure-store of intentions of this kind."[6] And so, as we shall see further below, the estimative or cogitative power perceives the sensible object in an *evaluative* manner, which is to say, as pleasurable or painful, or as beneficial or harmful; in turn, this evaluated intentional object is then stored in memory.

Now in understanding Aquinas's account of the internal sense powers, one must appreciate two essential features of his analysis. First, the internal sense faculties that human beings possess are shared by other sensate beings, namely, animals or at least the higher animals. Initially, then, these faculties are considered generically as common to all higher animals. Secondly, though, the faculties that belong more precisely to the human animal will be modified according to its specific difference, namely, its rationality. So, at first, the estimative power is distinguished from imagination and memory generically in terms of animal being. Animals act on the pleasures or pains of the senses and so require two distinct acts within its unified operation, namely, sense cognition and appetite. The external senses in conjunction with appetite are sufficient to explain how any number of sense objects are apprehended as pleasurable or painful and so are immediately sought or avoided. Other sense objects, however, are grasped not as immediately pleasing or displeasing but rather as useful or harmful to the overall well being of the animal knower. Aquinas states, "Thus a lamb, when it sees a wolf approach, flees, not because it does not like the color or

---

that even the most deranged of imaginations nonetheless preserves a sense of realism in the dependence of its sense content upon the extramental real.

6. "Ad apprehenendum autem intentiones per sensum non accipiuntur ordinatur vis aestimativa,. Ad conservandum autem eas, vis memorativa, quae est thesaurus quidem hujusmodi intentionum." ST I, q. 78, a. 4.

shape, but because it is its natural enemy. And likewise a bird collects straw, not because it pleases its senses, but because it needs it for building a nest. So, the animal has to perceive things which no external sense perceives."[7] These objects are often referred to as "difficult goods." It is the estimative faculty, then, that perceives the practical value of a sense object according to its overall utility. These objects are not purely sensible but are to some extent interpreted insofar as they are evaluated according to their practical utility or harmfulness.[8] The form expressed, therefore, communicates the utility of the object, though, not without the help of the soul's power since the object is now interpreted in relation to the knower as being beneficial or harmful.[9]

Memory is distinguished from imagination, then, as that specific internal sense power that conserves or retains those intentional objects judged to be "harmful or serviceable" to the animal knower within its environ-

7. "Sicut ovis videns lupum venientem fugit, non propter indecentiam coloris vel figurae, sed quasi inimicum naturae. Et similiter avis colligit paleam, non quia delectat sensum, sed quia est utilis ad nidificandum. Necessarium est ergo animali quod percipiat hujusmodi intentiones quas non percipit sensus exterior." ST I, q. 78, a. 4.

8. Aquinas states, "Each particular sense judges its proper object, discerning it from other things that come under the same sense, for instance discerning white from black or green. But neither sight nor taste can discern the difference between white and sweet, because to discern a difference between two things you have to know both. Hence it must belong to a common sense to discriminate; all sense perceptions are referred to it as to a common terminus. It also perceives sense-perceptions, as when someone is aware that he is seeing. This could not take place through any particular sense, which knows only the sensible form by which it is affected. Sight arises from the physical impression and this leads to another impression in the common sense, which perceives the act of sight." "Ad secundum dicendum quod sensus proprius judicat de sensibili proprio, discernendo ipsum ab aliiis quae cadunt sub eodem sensu, sicut discernendo album a nigro vel a viridi. Sed discernere album a dulci non potest neque visus neque gustus, quia oportet quod qui inter aliqua discernit, utrumque cognoscat. Unde oportet ad sensum communem pertinere discretionis judicium ad quem referantur sicut ad communem terminum omnes apprehensions sensuum. A quo etiam percipiantur intentiones sensuum, sicut cum aliquis videt se videre. Hoc enim non potest fieri per sensum proprium, qui non cognoscit nisi formam sensibilis a quo immatatur; in qua immutatione perficitur visio, et ex qua immutatione sequitur alia immutatio in sensu communi, qui visionem percipit." ST I, q. 78, a. 4.

9. Moreover, Maritain, in following St. Thomas and John of St. Thomas, states, "A dog does not merely know various visual, audible, etc., variables linked together in some way; he knows his master, without the knowledge or power of saying it to himself. On a purely sensitive level, and thanks to numberless comparative associations, he has an analogate of the knowledge we have—of that transobjective subject we call his master... And if the sheep flees from the wolf, it is not, as St. Thomas points out, because the colored object he has seen at that moment has wounded the retina of his eye; it is because the sheep sees in the wolf 'his natural enemy.'" Jacques Maritain, *Distinguish to Unite or The Degrees of Knowledge*, translated by Gerald B. Phelan (Notre Dame, Indiana: University of Notre Dame Press, 1995), 101.

ment.[10] Furthermore, Aquinas identifies the sense image retained in memory to be referred specifically to its temporal aspect, i.e., in the "fact of its pastness."[11] Here Aquinas notes that the phantasm or image is not only known materially in terms of its content but also formally in terms of its function as a sign referring to some past event. Klubertanz in his work *The Discursive Power* states the difference between memory and imagination in the following manner:

> It must be likewise noted that the mere retention of sensory experience as such is not memory. Nor is the act of again presenting to internal sensation some sensible form the same as remembering. Rather, that is the proper function of imagination. To the actual presence of what is in fact an image there must be added the knowledge that it is in fact an image. This is another way of saying that in memory the phantasm is known as referring to a past experience.[12]

This distinction is critical because the estimative power, which in Aquinas is identified as the highest power proper to animals, is an interpretative power which judges the various sense objects, images, or signs within the contextual totality of its environment.[13] For non-rational animals, this contextual totality is signified as a purely bio-semiotic nexus, that is, a complex and interwoven *Umwelt* or environment that is determined primarily by the instinct for survival and the pleasure principle.[14]

10. "Instinct grasps intentions which are not objects of simple sensation. And the power of memory conserves these; it is a treasure-store of intentions of this kind. A sign of this is that the reason for remembering in animals is an intention of this kind, the fact that something is harmful or serviceable, and the fact of pastness, which is what memory bears on, falls into this category." "Ad conservandum autem eas, vis memorativa, quae est thesaurus quidem hujusmodi intentionem. Cujus signum est, quod principium memorandi fit in animalibus ex aliqua hujusmodi intentione, puta quod est nocivum vel conveniens, et ipsa ratio praeteriti, quam attendit memoria, inter hujus-modi intentiones computatur." ST I, q. 78, a. 4.

11. ST I, q. 78, a. 4.

12. George P. Klubertanz, *The Discursive Power: Sources and Doctrine of the* Vis Cogitativa *According to St. Thomas Aquinas* (St. Louis: The Modern Schoolman, 1952), 260. Likewise, Timothy Suttor, in providing a gloss on Aquinas's distinction between imagination and memory, describes the difference in the following way: "Imagination differs from sense-memory by its power to decontextualize images. Memory holds to the whole *gestalt*. When it seems that memory has lost the context of an image, what has really happened is that imagination has taken over." Timothy Suttor, translator and editor of Thomas Aquinas, *Treatise on Man*, vol. 11 of *Summa Theologiae* (Cambridge: Cambridge University Press, 2006), 141 note c.

13. As Klubertanz also puts it, "Because the estimative is the highest power of the animal, it follows that all purely sense cognition will *ultimately* be practical. In other words, the final limit, the highest type of purely animal knowledge is the apprehension of the individual in so far as the latter is the term of material action or passion." Klubertanz, *The Discursive Power*, 274–75.

14. This biosemiotic nexus or *Umwelt* I take to be similar to what Heidegger has in mind by

Now although Aquinas identifies the estimative power as generically proper to all higher animals, he specifies more precisely its function within animals endowed with reason. Whereas non-rational animals may make the estimative judgment by natural instinct,[15] humans do so by a comparative or discursive process. This process unfolds via particular reason (*ratio particularis*), which is also called the cogitative power (*vis cogitativa*).[16] This discursive process differs from animal estimation in that the involvement of reason in the practical judgment means that individual sensible objects are cognized as standing under a common nature. Although both irrational and rational animals estimate the value of a given sense object by a process of comparison, in rational animals this process is more complex in that it involves rational deliberation that includes considering the specific object according to its common nature. And so, in pragmatic terms, the singular, concrete object is interpreted not merely as useful or harmful to oneself in the particularity of this situation but also as useful or harmful (i.e., desirable or undesirable) in general. The sheep sees the particular wolf before it and by comparing it to past sense images stored in memory judges this object to be harmful and so flees; I see the particular wolf and reflect

---

his notion of *Zuhandenheit*, which is the apprehension of beings according to their instrumental value within a contextual totality and that is prior to the theoretical or objective apprehension of *Vorhandenheit* or the present-at-hand. For Heidegger's analysis of *Zuhandenheit* see *Being and Time*, translated by John Macquarrie and Edward Robinson (New York: Harper and Row, 1962), Part I, Division I, Section III, pp. 91–149. Also, for a Thomistic reading of Jacob von Uexkull's notion of *Umwelt*, see Josef Pieper, "The Philosophical Act," in *Leisure, The Basis of Culture*, translated by Alexander Dru (San Francisco: Ignatius Press, 2009), 95–97.

15. This is the case whether the instinctual judgment is hardwired into the animal's genetic complex or acquired habitually through past experiences of survival.

16. "Consider now that so far as sense forms are concerned there is no difference between men and other animals; they are affected in the same way by external sense objects. But when it comes to the intentions just discussed there is a difference, for other animals perceive such intentions solely by natural instinct, whereas man perceives them by a process of comparison. And so what we call natural instinct in other animals in man we call cogitation, which comes upon intentions of this kind in question through a process of comparison. Which is why it is also called the particular reason, to which medical scientists assign a fixed part of the body, the middle of the head; for it compares individual intentions the way reasoning intellect compares universal intentions." "Considerandum est autem quod quantum ad formas sensibiles non est differentia inter hominess et alia animalia; similiter enim immutantur a sensibilibus exterioribus. Sed quantum ad intentiones praedictas differentia est, nam alia animalia percipunt hujusmodi intentiones solum naturali quodam instinctu, homo autem etiam per quandum collationem. Et ideo quae in aliis animalibus dicitur aestimativa naturalis in homine dicitur cogitative, quae per collationem quondam hujusmodi intentiones adinvenit. Unde etiam dicitur ratio particularis, cui medici assignant determinatum organum, scilicet mediam partem capitis; est enim collative intentionum individualium, sicut ratio intellective intentionum unversalium." ST I, q. 78, a. 4.

that such objects are generally by their nature dangerous to human beings, and so I also keep my distance.

II. Significance of These Distinctions in the Dynamic Interrelation of the Unified Operations

Before considering the Freudian Unconscious within this schema, four more principles need to be clarified in regard to a Thomistic psychological analysis of the human person. First, although Aquinas is careful to distinguish faculties according to their determinate activities and proper objects, he is also careful to maintain the unity of specific operations. He does so by positing a hierarchal order among the faculties such that the lower ones are ordered to the higher ones as to their proper end. Although sensible and intellectual powers are distinct, in any specific operation that unfolds as a process, there exists a dynamic unity in which the higher powers flow through to the lower powers such that the lower ones are subordinated to the higher powers and also are raised up to a greater degree of perfection or functionality.[17] Here, then, within this unified, emanative process the lower powers are considered instrumental in relation to the principal source of the higher power, which is both the origin and end of the specific operation. The active or agent intellect, for example, is the principal of all rational cognition since that which is only potentially intelligible, namely, the sense object, must be actualized by something already in act. Likewise, the estimative or cogitative faculty in a human being, when functioning properly, is ordered to a rational deliberative assessment of a given sense object according to a proper understanding of the common nature of that object.[18]

Secondly, for Aquinas, the intentional relations that are essential to the functioning of all faculties, be they sensitive, appetitive, or rational, are perfected through habit. Hence, although the cogitative faculty in human

17. So, for instance, in the relation between sense and intellect, although humans and non-rational animals generically share similar sense faculties, these sense faculties, when functioning properly in human beings are raised to a higher order. (For example, the sense gratification of eating that is typical of all higher animals is raised to a higher order through the cultivation of an aesthetically refined cuisine.)

18. Here I might note, the given "sense object" or "image" can of course be extended to an interrelated sequence of objects, signs, or intentions that refer to a unified and more complex experience, situation, or state of affairs.

beings is properly directed toward reason in that a proper judgment of a particular sense object is made through a comparison of past sense singulars stored in memory along with the knowledge of the common nature, a long, deliberative process is not necessary each time one is exposed to the object; rather, through habit one is properly (or improperly) and rationally (or irrationally) disposed or oriented toward that given object. Every time I see a dog, for example, I need not deliberate about its utility or harmfulness by comparing it to past experience and considering the common nature of dogs; rather I am properly disposed to not fearing a dog unless some concrete evidence suggests otherwise (e.g., its snarling or foaming mouth, etc.).

Thirdly, a distinction can be made between the initial apprehension of a common nature in a confused and general "concept" and the more determinate, scientific or speculative understanding of the universal nature grasped in and through a formal concept. As Leo White puts it:

> We acquire these tentative, confused concepts by comparing individuals and discovering various commonalities among them. According to Aquinas, the cogitative power's perception of what is common to many individuals serves as the basis of our initial, pre-scientific grasp of the nature of things. This grasp of the 'one in the many," which he calls 'experience' (*experiencia* or *experimentum*), typically takes place within the context of practical reasoning.[19]

In a practical comportment, then, the object is considered under the aspect of the *good* and so oriented toward an action; hence, the object is judged to be desirable or undesirable, useful or harmful. In a theoretical comportment the object is considered under the aspect of the *true* and so judged according to its universal nature. In the full intentional and linguistic life of the human being, these knowledges of course overlap. Hence, by theoretically understanding the universal nature of a given object, one has a better understanding of its potential utility or harmfulness. In order to achieve this universal understanding, however, one's practical orientation toward the given sense object or image must be suspended. For, although the knowledge sought may, at some future time, be employed practically or instrumentally, in the intentional relation of theoretical thought the object to be known is sought as an end-in-itself. Now, as we saw earlier, for Aqui-

19. Leo White, "Perception, Experience, and Practical Reason in Aquinas," in *Being and Thought in Aquinas*, edited by Jeremiah Hackett, William E. Murnion, and Carl N. Still (Binghamton, New York: Global Academic Publishing, 2004), 202.

nas those sense images considered under the practical aspect of the good are conserved in memory, whereas those sense images considered under the theoretical aspect of the true are conserved or at least employed in and through the imagination. In this sense, the imagination is more "objective" insofar as it considers the object or image devoid of its subjective and practical value and in turn its relation to the knower's personal and temporal experience or situation. In other words, a proper understanding of the universal nature of an object in one's theoretical orientation toward that object means that those sense images to which the intellect refers should be accessed through the imagination and not memory. As Aquinas states in his *Commentary on Aristotle's "On Memory and Recollection"*:

> So then it is clear that when the soul turns itself toward an image as it is a form preserved in the sensitive part of the soul, in this way there is an act of the imagination or phantasia, or even of the intellect considering the universal involved in this image. If, however, the soul should be turned toward the image inasmuch as it is a likeness of what we have previously seen or understood, this belongs to an act of remembering. In addition, since to be a likeness marks an interest with respect to this form, Avicenna fittingly observes that *the memory focuses on the interest, whereas the imagination focuses on the form apprehended through the sense.*[20]

The significance of the distinction, then, is that even if one wishes to shift the Thomistic vocabulary into a more contemporary terminology such that any sense image that is conserved belongs in a broader sense to the power of memory, one must keep intact the conceptual significance of Aquinas's distinction. For within the intentional theoretical orientation the sense image is modified so that its formal, intelligible content is considered devoid of its temporal and practical aspects. In this way, there is a kind of conversion or *trans-form-ation* of the sense object or form such that it is considered universally or objectively as a common nature, rather than practically or subjectively through particular reason or the cogitative power. This conversion is necessary since the object is usually perceived vaguely or distortedly in a practical context. In fact, the very capacity to dispose or comport oneself toward objects in the world in a theoretical rather than practical manner is the very *habitus* of the scientific mode of being. That is, it is a mode of being that is oriented toward objects in order to attain

20. Thomas Aquinas, *Commentaries on Aristotle's "On Sense and What is Sensed" and "On Memory and Recollection,"* translated by Kevin White and Edward M. Macierowski (Washington, D.C.: The Catholic University of America Press, 2005), 203.

knowledge for its own sake, rather than as instrumental means directed towards a practical action. Although the distinction between theoretical reason and practical reason is often acknowledged, the specific role of the inner sense power of imagination, as opposed to memory, is less frequently recognized.

Fourthly, though, the discursive, abstractive process that unfolds in theoretical reasoning happens in language. Here I would distinguish between thought and understanding in that although there is thought without language, there can be no understanding without language (be this understanding theoretical, practical, or experiential). We saw earlier that the internal sense faculties are what form or express sense images that are retained or conserved by the knower. At the same time, however, for Aquinas the intellect of the rational animal is always active (as agent intellect) and so is perpetually casting its light upon sense images so as to draw out intelligible aspects (*species intelligibles*) inherent within them. These aspects (or "inspects" as they are sometimes called) are impressed upon the mind, though often at the preconscious or unconscious level. Maritain refers to these intelligible impressed species as impressed patterns or intelligible germs, which are capable of being brought into the daylight of conscious, conceptual, and articulated thought. Likewise Yves Simon identifies these intelligible impressed patterns as existing halfway between potency and act.[21]

For instance, as I glance around the room, all sorts of intelligible aspects may be impressing themselves upon my mind, but only when these aspects or inspects are taken up thematically and so consciously considered in language are they developed and so solidified into actual objects of understanding. This is significant in that all sorts of intelligible and interpretative meanings are drawn from the world and the things in it, but only in a very vague, inchoate, and dispersed way. Not until these meanings are raised up and brought into the daylight of conscious, articulated thought can they be understood according to their proper, common or universal nature.

21. Yves R. Simon, *An Introduction to the Metaphysics of Knowledge*, translated by Vukan Kuic and Richard J. Thompson (New York: Fordham University Press, 1990), 133.

III. The Unconscious and the Possibility of Psychic Disorder within a Bio-Semiotic Complex

Against the background of this normative structure we may now consider the unconscious and in turn the practice of psychoanalysis. Jacques Maritain credits Freudian psychology for its exposition of psychic dynamism and for "having obliged philosophers to acknowledge the existence of unconscious thought."[22] Moreover, although Aquinas and the schoolmen in general did not work out any theory of the unconscious, "their doctrines implied its existence."[23] I would suggest, then, that for human beings, as rational animals, this unconscious thought exists in the "realm" in which the sensible, biosemiotic nexus first touches reason and yet remains prior to a clearly articulated experiential or theoretical understanding. Hence, the "space" where the unconscious "fits" into a Thomistic psychology and ontology of knowledge is precisely where sense and reason first meet, though in a latent state, which is to say, at the estimative or cogitative power.[24]

Now in cases of traumatic experiences that are undergone at a prelinguistic and so pre-conceptual stage of development, complex sense objects are interpreted through the cogitative power, which at this point in the developmental stage is more akin to the estimative power in non-rational animals. Hence, the sense objects are vitally interpreted according to survival (and the pleasure principle) within a biosemiotic nexus. This means the sense object is "understood" according to the interpreted instrumental value within the totality of the knower's environment or *Umwelt*. In turn, these sense objects are stored in memory and their deep and lasting impression can serve as the standard or model by which subsequent, similar objects or experiences are compared and judged according to what is thought latently and at this point "pre-rationally" to be a "common" nature. Repeated exposure to similar objects or signs (i.e., experiences) may, in

22. Jacques Maritain, *Creative Intuition in Art and Poetry* (Cleveland, Ohio: Meridian Books, 1955), 70.

23. Ibid.

24. Maritain states, "Whether or not the will suffices to evoke them, it is under a psychic form, that the crowd of memories and images is preserved in us in a latent state; and many psychic operations, even operations of knowing, as those of the external sense, can be performed by us without our being explicitly conscious of them by a reflective act of intelligence, turning back on them and taking hold of them in order to express them to itself." Jacques Maritain, "Freudianism and Psychoanalysis," in *Scholasticism and Politics*, translated and edited by Mortimer J. Adler (New York: Image Books, 1960), 141.

Heidegger's language, "throw" or cast one into a mood or state in which one's whole world is permeated or colored (or discolored) by the evaluative affect aroused by the presence of this particular sensible object(s) as sign(s). Continuous exposure to these sensible objects or signs can evoke a repetitive, anxious reaction that over the course of time becomes affectively-habitually ingrained.

For example, an infant or toddler, prior to the formation of linguistic and conceptual capacities, may experience some form of physical or psychological abuse over a prolonged period. Various associations connected to the abuse may attach to sensible objects such that the phantasms formed in sensible expressed species may have been evaluated by the estimative power in terms of survival and the avoidance of pain; in turn these evaluated sense images are stored in memory, though again at a very deep unconscious level. In adult life similar sense images that are associated with the abuse might provoke anxiety or fear. For instance, this could be the common physical features of the abuser (a particular look or a sound of the voice), or the surrounding characteristics of the setting if the abuse took place in the same room or house (such as a particular shade of color on the wall), or even a distinct feeling, such as hunger if the abuse took place during or around mealtimes.

In fact, in more extreme cases, the latent complex that developed may be determined precisely by the added anxiety of the "illogic" of the experience; hence, when interiorized (and not expressed), the anxiety results in neuroses, obsessions, dissociations, and phobias that are repressed within the unconscious and yet are repeated automatically. The present is then distorted by the past but without being recognized as such. Hence, the distinction between memory and habit or what Paul Ricoeur calls marked and unmarked modes.[25] Aquinas, as well, identifies the different ways in which one can be disposed toward an object of memory depending upon whether or not the object is truly a mnemonic object and whether or not it is recognized as such. In regard to the object being experienced, which means imagined, but without being recognized as an object of memory, Aquinas has this to say:

25. Paul Ricoeur, "Memory and Imagination," chapter 1 in *Memory, History, Forgetting*, translated by Kathleen Blamey and David Pellauer (Chicago: The University of Chicago Press, 2004), 5–55.

For sometimes, although there may be within us motions of the images that were made *by what we have sensed before,* motions that are left over from the first immutation of the sense by the sensible object, nevertheless *we do not know whether* these motions happen to be in us *because of* the fact that we have sensed something before, and consequently *we are in doubt* as to whether we are remembering or not.[26]

Aquinas also states,

[W]hen the movement of the thing to be remembered and of the past time occur in the soul together, then there is the act of memory.... sometimes one remembers and does not think that he does so, but it escapes his notice, because the thing occurred to him but not the time.[27]

Moreover, for Aquinas, whereas non-rational animals have memory, only rational animals can recollect; recollection involves the active, rational search for that which has been forgotten. Of course, what is both problematic and interesting in regard to psychoanalysis is that insofar as traumatic memories are repressed, they cannot be recalled or recollected voluntarily. As Maritain notes, what marks the unconscious is "not the fact of being absolutely inaccessible, but of being inaccessible to voluntary evocation."[28] Here is precisely where Maritain credits Freud's technique of free-association as a "stroke of genius" and as constituting "the essential factor of psychoanalysis."[29] For in this method of free-association the higher, rational faculties have to be suspended in order to allow the "logic" of what was initially experienced and interpreted by the estimative power at the level of animal instinct and which has resulted through repetition and habit in the informed pattern of the automatic unconscious. Maritain states,

The primary step in exploring the unconscious is the disrupting of the control and inhibitions normally exercised by the superior psychic functions over the inferior ones; ... to suspend this control for a while in order to obtain an emergence of inferior psychic states into the field of consciousness.[30]

But in order for the hidden experience to be brought into the daylight of conscious and—I would add—articulated, thought, which subsequent-

26. Aquinas, *Commentary on Aristotle's "On Memory and Recollection,"* 203; emphasis added.

27. Ibid., 228.

28. Jacques Maritain, "Freudianism and Psychoanalysis," 140.

29. For, "(t)he psychoanalytic cure essentially consists in dissolving morbid habits by reducing them to a memory of the events which gave birth to them." Ibid., 147.

30. Ibid., 142–43.

ly results in the dissolution of the morbid symptoms, what is required is the emergence or resurfacing of the sense images or phantasms that have been retained and repressed in memory and that must be recalled or conjured up as a concrete, rather than abstract, intuition. Again, though, these sense images or intentions, which sequentially amount to an experience or state of affairs, are not directly accessible since the force of the repression in extreme cases remains too strong. This is why Aristotle rightly recognizes that recollection, despite belonging only to rational animals, is nonetheless a bodily affection. He states,

> A sign that this affection, viz. recollection, is something bodily and an inquiry for an image within such a thing is the fact that some people get very upset whenever they cannot recollect. And, even though they strain intensely to hold back their thought from cogitating and are no longer trying to recollect, they are none the less distressed—especially those of melancholic temperament, since images move these persons most of all.[31]

Here, as in so many other areas, Aristotle and in turn Aquinas anticipate and exceed modern psychology by not falling into dualism or physicalism. For the complex of the melancholic or depressive temperament is precisely that it cannot adequately remember or forget. What is required, then, is a kind of hermeneutic detour in which the lower sense faculties are permitted to express their pre-rational, experiential, and symbolic interpretation of the sensible signs prior to an abstractive, conceptual or theoretical understanding of them. As we saw above, the mature, normative process is that the cogitative power under the guidance of practical reason judges a given sense singular through a comparative process and with reference to the object's common nature. This common nature, as we also saw, can be grasped in varying degrees of clarity, specificity, and universality. Again, as a normative process, theoretical reason serves practical reason by providing a higher degree of clarity and specificity concerning the universal nature of the object and in turn its potential utility or harmfulness. In this case, however, theoretical reason obstructs the therapeutic act of remembering since what needs to be recollected is the associative logic of the bio-semiotic complex that is retained in memory and remains operative in the automatic unconscious. Hence, as Maritain states, "psychoanalysis is not an impartial scientific research, but a therapeutic act; it does not seek

31. As cited and translated in Aquinas, *Commentary on Aristotle's "On Memory and Recollection,"* 229.

to prove something, but to modify something."[32] In order to achieve the modification as a curative effect that dissolves the morbid symptoms the traumatic memory must be reintegrated into the field of consciousness.[33] Here too Maritain criticizes Freud for privileging the unconscious as the "essential reality" and for not admitting in theory its teleological directedness toward rationality and consciousness, a principle which is proven by the efficacious effect of the psychoanalytic method in which neuroses are healed precisely by moving from the unconscious to conscious, articulated understanding.

One final Thomistic principle that I might mention in closing and that supports, explains, and in a certain sense corrects the therapeutic value and practice of psychoanalysis is the Thomistic notion that causes are known through their objects and acts. Repressed memories that act as causes for certain disordered conditions, then, are accessible only insofar as they manifest themselves through images and signs experienced in the present. The "method" or "technique" by which the associative logic of the impressed pattern of the unconscious, biosemiotic complex can be best accessed, then, is by a kind of phenomenological or pre-theoretical descriptive analysis or interpretation. For the experiential significance of the sensible signs are not universal or pre-determined, which is why Maritain criticizes the Freudians for falling into a symbolic dogmatism.[34] Rather, the significance and value of the signs are more analogous to an aesthetic logic that should be interpreted within the context of the narrative whole, which in this case would be the entire intentional life or "life-world" of the individual.

32. Maritain, "Freudianism and Psychoanalysis," 145.

33. Hence, the need for interpretation. As Maritain also states, "To the process of liberation must therefore be added the process of interpretation. It enlightens the repressing element and transfers it to the field of consciousness, where it loses its automatic character and is disintegrated." Ibid., 143.

34. For example, there is Freud's overemphasis upon sexuality within the Oedipus Complex. See Maritain, "Freudianism and Psychoanalysis."

BERNADETTE E. O'CONNOR

The Freudian and Maritainian Theories of Sublimation and Their Ontological Bases

I. Introduction

In this essay I will consider the theories of Sigmund Freud and Jacques Maritain on sublimation with special reference to the ontological factors in each theory that ground the process of sublimation. Freud, that master of suspicion,[1] as Paul Ricoeur refers to him, gives us the more elaborated theory of sublimation, and Maritain presents an outline of a theory of his own in the process of critizing the Freudian theory. So I will begin with Freud's theory of sublimation and then move to that of Maritain. My thesis is twofold. First, I concur with Ricoeur in holding that the Freudian theory of sublimation itself requires but does not provide a source higher than bodily instincts. And, second, Maritain is able to ground what he calls "'sublimation'" "in quite a different sense," "a psychic process of the greatest importance,"[2] in our human nature itself, composed as it is of material body and spiritual soul.

1. Paul Ricoeur, *Freud and Philosophy: An Essay on Interpretation,* translated by D. Savage (New Haven, Connecticut: Yale University Press, 1970), 35. In this rich and difficult work, Ricoeur shows conclusively that Freud's theory cannot account satisfactorily for our ability to sublimate, for our ability to create new, forward-looking and redemptive meanings in arts works and in cultural achievements generally; however, Ricoeur fails to ground the human capacity to sublimate in human nature itself and must appeal to something like the figures of Hegelian Absolute Spirit (ibid., 462–63) to account for our ability to sublimate.

2. Jacques Maritain, "Freudianism and Psychoanalysis," in *Scholasticism and Politics,* translated and edited by Mortimer J. Adler (Garden City, New York: Image Books 1960), 156.

Two other thinkers ought to be acknowledged as participating in this discussion. Roland Dalbiez (1893–1976), was a philosopher and a student of psychology who wrote a two-volume work on Freud, *Psychoanalytical Method and the Doctrine of Freud,*[3] and who was a guest of the Maritains at Meudon. Jacques encouraged Dalbiez to study Freud and praised his work in the article "Freudianism and Psychoanalysis" in *Scholasticism and Politics* and seems to have depended on it for part of his assessment of Freudianism.[4] Quite interestingly, Paul Ricoeur was a student of Dalbiez. Gustave Thibon (1903–2001) was a self-taught philosopher-peasant and a follower of Charles Maurras who, nonetheless, admired Maritain's work. When Maritain discusses that sense of sublimation different from Freud's he largely relies on Thibon.[5]

II. Freudian Sublimation

Let us now turn to Freud's theory of sublimation. Sublimation is of great importance for Freud, and yet, as Ricoeur points out, there is no complete work of his dealing explicitly with this topic.[6] The problematic character of sublimation prevented him from satisfactorily thematizing it within his metapsychology. Freud, himself, was well aware of the problematic nature of sublimation as he understood it. In the work in which Freud makes the first published use of the word "sublimate," "Three Essays on the Theory of Sexuality" of 1905, he approaches the topic with considerable reserve. While Freud is certain that the process exists,[7] he writes that "the

3. Roland Dalbiez, *Psychoanalytical Method and the Doctrine of Freud,* translated by T. F. Lindsay, 2 vols. (London: Longmans, Green and Company, 1948). The French version of this work was published in 1936. Biographical material on Dalbiez may be found in Jean-Luc Barré, *Jacques and Raïssa Maritain: Beggars for Heaven,* translated by Bernard E. Doering (Notre Dame, Indiana: University of Notre Dame Press, 2005), 159, and from *Gale Dictionary of Psychoanalysis,* "Roland Dalbiez," available at http://www.answers.com/topic/dalbiez-roland.

4. An earlier publication of Maritain's article "Freudisme et Psychanalyse," which became chapter four of *Scholasticism and Politics,* appeared in *Revue Thomiste* 44, no. 4 (1938): 712–34. Biographical material on Dalbiez may be found in Jean-Luc Barré, *Jacques and Raïssa Maritain: Beggars for Heaven,* 159, and from *Gale Dictionary of Psychoanalysis,* "Roland Dalbiez," available at http://www.answers.com/topic/dalbiez-roland.

5. The work of Gustave Thibon to which Maritain refers is "Mystique et Amour humain," *Études Carmélitaines* 21, no. 1 (1936): 61–90. Biographical material on Thibon is from an obituary, "Gustave Thibon," by Douglas Johnson in *The Independent,* January 25, 2001, available at http://license.icopyright.net/user/viewFreeUse.act?fuid= MTAzMjIOMjc%3D.

6. Ricoeur, *Freud and Philosophy,* 484.

7. Sigmund Freud, *Three Essays on the Theory of Sexuality,* in *A Case of Hysteria, Three Essays*

inner causes are quite unknown to us."[8] And as late as 1933 and the "New Introductory Lectures on Psychoanalysis" Freud will be admitting that he does "not understand ... very well" how "one instinctual satisfaction can be replaced by another."[9] We shall see more about the problematic character of Freudian sublimation below, but let us turn first to his description of sublimation.

In his 1915 paper on "Instincts and Their Vicissitudes" Freud states that sublimation is one of the vicissitudes to which an instinct is subject, the other vicissitudes listed being "reversal into its opposite, turning around upon the subject's own self, and repression."[10] Sublimation, then, is a possible form of change open to an instinct.

And what does Freud mean by an instinct (*Instink*) or a drive or force (*Trieb*)? In "An Outline of Psycho-Analysis," left unfinished and posthumously published, Freud writes:

> The forces which we assume to exist behind the tensions caused by the needs of the id are called *instincts*. They represent the somatic demands upon the mind. Though they are the ultimate cause of all activity, they are of a conservative nature; the state, whatever it may be, which an organism has reached, gives rise to a tendency to re-establish that stage so soon as it has been abandoned.[11]

In his "New Introductory Lectures" Freud distinguishes the instincts from stimuli by the fact that instincts have their source within the body.[12] Because instincts arise from within the subject they operate as constant forces which the subject cannot escape as he or she might an external stimulus.

Freud distinguishes a source, a pressure or motor force, an object, and

---

on Sexuality, and Other Works, vol. 7 of *The Standard Edition of the Complete Psychological Works of Sigmund Freud*, translated and edited by James Strachey (London: Hogarth Press and the Institute of Psycho-Analysis, 1953), 206.

8. Freud, *Three Essays on the Theory of Sexuality*, 7:239.

9. Sigmund Freud, *New Introductory Lectures on Psychoanalysis*, in *New Introductory Lectures on Psychoanalysis, and Other Works*, vol. 22 of *The Standard Edition of the Complete Psychological Works of Sigmund Freud*, translated and edited by James Strachey (London: Hogarth Press and the Institute of Psycho-Analysis, 1964), 97.

10. Sigmund Freud, "Instincts and Their Vicissitudes," in *On the History of the Psychoanalytic Movement, Papers on Metapsychology, and Other Works*, vol. 14 of *The Standard Edition of the Complete Psychological Works of Sigmund Freud*, translated and edited by James Strachey (London: Hogarth Press and the Institute of Psycho-Analysis, 1957), 126.

11. Sigmund Freud, *An Outline of Psycho-Analysis*, in *On the History of the Psychoanalytic Movement, Papers on Metapsychology, and Other Works*, vol. 23 of *The Standard Edition of the Complete Psychological Works of Sigmund Freud*, translated and edited by James Strachey (London: Hogarth Press and the Institute of Psycho-Analysis, 1964), 148.

12. Freud, *New Introductory Lectures on Psychoanalysis*, 22:96.

an aim of an instinct. The concept of an instinct's aim will be especially important in understanding the Freudian concept of sublimation. An instinct's "source [*Quelle*] is a state of excitation in the body, its aim [*Ziel*] is the removal of excitation; on its path from its source to its aim the instinct becomes operative psychically."[13] An instinct's pressure (*Drang*) is its "motor factor, the amount of force or the measure of the demand for work [or upon energy] which it represents."[14]

And what about the object of an instinct? The aim of an instinct, which "is in every instance satisfaction," is achieved in regard to or through the instinct's object:

> The object [*Objekt*] of an instinct is the thing in regard to which or through which the instinct is able to achieve its aim. It is what is most variable about an instinct and is not originally connected with it, but becomes assigned to it only in consequence of being peculiarly fitted to make satisfaction possible.[15]

This variability of an instinct's object will also be a factor in making sublimation possible.

We can make the various aspects of an instinct more concrete by considering an example. The hunger instinct has its source in the bodily excitation resulting from a nutritional deficiency. The aim of the hunger instinct is to remove the bodily excitation resulting from the lack of nutrition. The pressure or force of the hunger instinct varies according to the severity of the lack of nutrition; the more severe the lack the greater the force of the instinct or the demand upon the subject's energy. The object of the hunger instinct is ultimately the food, the consumption of which will allow the subject to return to the stasis enjoyed before the instinct arose, and frequently the hunger instinct can achieve its aim by means of a great variety of possible objects. With this general understanding of the source, pressure, aim and object of an instinct, we may return to the question of sublimation.

Sublimation is a vicissitude of an instinct in which the instinct undergoes a change in its aim.[16] The fact that an instinct can change in respect of its aim is simply stated by Freud. And he adds that the object of an instinct is more easily changed than its aim:

13. Ibid.
14. Freud, "Instincts and Their Vicissitudes," 14:122.
15. Ibid.
16. Freud, *An Outline of Psycho-Analysis*, 23:148.

The relations of an instinct to its aim and object are also open to alterations; both can be exchanged for other ones, though its relation to its object is nevertheless the more easily loosened. A certain kind of modification of the aim and change of the object, in which our social valuation is taken into account, is described by us as "sublimation."[17]

When Freud speaks of "our social valuation" being "taken into account" he hints at sublimation's service both of the ego and of the larger culture. We shall see more about this below. Thus far we have only seen that sublimation is a possible vicissitude of instinct in which the instinct undergoes a change in its aim and object. We still need a more exact definition of sublimation and some concept of its mechanism.

Freud gives a more exact definition of sublimation in his paper "On Narcissism": "Sublimation is a process that concerns object-libido and consists in the instinct's directing itself towards an aim other than, and remote from, that of sexual satisfaction; in this process the accent falls upon deflection from sexuality."[18] Thus sublimation is a process in which an instinct of object-libido has its aim diverted from its original one of explicitly sexual satisfaction to an aim remote from sexuality. Inasmuch as the aim of any instinct is satisfaction we must suppose that the aim will also be one of satisfaction but, in Freud's words, some "'finer and higher'"[19] kind of satisfaction.

Freud attempts to develop the concept of sublimation by comparing it with repression, idealization, and reaction-formation. In "On Narcissism" Freud points out that sublimation is similar to and distinct from repression. These two vicissitudes to which an instinct is subject are similar inasmuch as they both take place through the mediation of the ego, but they are not the same. Freud writes: "sublimation is a way out, a way by which

17. Freud, *New Introductory Lectures on Psychoanalysis*, 22:97.

18. Sigmund Freud, *On Narcissism: An Introduction*, in vol. 14 of *The Standard Edition of the Complete Psychological Works of Sigmund Freud*, 94. Freud characterizes libido as "the dynamic manifestations of sexuality," and as "a quantitatively variable force which could serve as a measure of processes and transformations occurring in the field of sexual excitation." Sigmund Freud, "The Libido Theory," in *An Infantile Neurosis and Other Works*, vol. 18 in *The Standard Edition of the Complete Psychological Works of Sigmund Freud*, translated and edited by James Strachey (London: Hogarth Press and the Institute of Psycho-Analysis, 1955), 255, and Freud, *Three Essays on the Theory of Sexuality*, 7:217. An "object-libido" is just this dynamic manifestation of sexuality cathected in an object as opposed to being invested narcissistically in the ego itself. Ibid.

19. Sigmund Freud, *Civilization and Its Discontents*, in *The Future of An Illusion, Civilization and Its Discontents, and Other Works*, vol. 21 of *The Standard Edition of the Complete Psychological Works of Sigmund Freud*, translated and edited by James Strachey (London: Hogarth Press and the Institute of Psycho-Analysis, 1961), 79.

those demands [of the ego] can be met *without* involving repression."[20] In sublimation the ego allows the libidinal force to be released by giving it another aim. And because in repression the instinctual impulse escapes conscious awareness and the control of the ego and "goes its own way"[21] we may conclude that sublimation is a much healthier vicissitude of an instinct than is repression.

Sublimation is furthermore similar to and distinct from idealization. In idealization, another defense mechanism of the ego, a subject unconsciously attempts to resolve instinctual tension by endowing an object with value it does not in fact enjoy. Freud explains that idealization is the process by which an object, "without any alteration in its nature, is aggrandized and exalted in the subject's mind."[22] In idealization what should be narcissistic libido is invested not in a healthily idealized self but rather in some external object, thus depleting the ego's narcissistic libido and placing the ego ideal in an external object. Because the original cause of the over-investment in the idealized object is unconscious the subject is not conscious of the over-valuing and believes the high value is a characteristic of the object itself. The subject tends to be extremely dependent on the hyper-valorized object as can be seen in the examples of an individual who idealizes a romantic interest or of a nation that idealizes its leader. But this dependency upon the idealized object creates frustration for the subject because it makes the subject appear to himself or herself as inferior to the idealized object, and the perceived inferiority frustrates the subject's instinctual satisfaction.[23]

Sublimation is similar to idealization in three respects. Both processes

20. Freud, *On Narcissism*, 14:95.

21. In "The Question of Lay Analysis" Freud remarks that the harm of repression consists in the fact that when the ego represses an instinctual impulse the ego limits "its sphere of influence. The repressed instinctual impulse is now isolated, left to itself, inaccessible, but also uninfluenceable. It goes its own way." Sigmund Freud, *The Question of Lay Analysis*, in *An Autobiographical Study, Inhibitions, Symptoms and Anxiety, The Question of Lay Analysis, and Other Works*, vol. 20 in *The Standard Edition of the Complete Psychological Works of Sigmund Freud*, translated and edited by James Strachey (London: Hogarth Press and the Institute of Psycho-Analysis, 1959), 203. And in "Inhibitions, Symptoms and Anxiety" Freud explains: "Repression proceeds from the ego when the latter—it may be at the behest of the superego—refuses to associate itself with an instinctual cathexis which has been aroused in the id. The ego is able by means of repression to keep the idea which is the vehicle of the reprehensible impulse from becoming conscious." 20:91.

22. Freud, *On Narcissism*, 14:94.

23. See ibid., 93–95, 100–101, and Freud's "Group Psychology and the Analysis of the Ego," 18:112–13.

involve a change in the subject's early object choices and instinctual aims. Sublimation and idealization both involve the separating of a drive from its first, oedipal, objects and the channeling of that drive in pursuit of other objects. And both processes operate in the social sphere, the process of sublimation, as we have noted above, being one in which the subject's social valuation is taken into account and the process of idealization requiring another to be the hyper-valorized object. Sublimation and idealization, however, can be distinguished in two ways. First, the two processes differ in regard to their effects on the instinct's ability to achieve its aim. Sublimation allows the instinct to attain its aim of satisfaction, though in a changed form; it involves a change in the goal of the instinct from crude sexual gratification to satisfaction of a higher type. Idealization, on the other hand, prevents the satisfaction at which the instinct aims by creating a great distance between the subject and the idealized object. And, second, the two processes differ in regard to the aspect of the instinct which undergoes the change. Sublimation, as we have seen, most basically concerns the instinct itself in its very aim; in sublimation the instinct directs itself to an aim other than sexual satisfaction. Idealization, on the other hand, concerns not the instinct itself but rather the object through which the instinct seeks satisfaction.[24]

The relationship between sublimation and reaction-formation is a little more complicated and not as well explained. In "Three Essays" Freud does discuss a kind of sublimation in which the diversion of "sexual instinctual forces takes place along the path of reaction formation."[25] In this case infantile sexual impulses, because of the unpleasurable feeling they arouse in the subject, "evoke the opposing mental forces (reacting impulses) which, in order to suppress this unpleasure effectively, build up the mental dams ... disgust, shame, and morality."[26] And yet Freud adds that the concept of sublimation and the concept of reaction-formation are distinguishable from each other as two different processes. "Sublimation," he writes in a footnote added to the essay in 1915, "can also take place by other and simpler mechanisms."[27] But Freud does not explain those mechanisms.

We turn our attention now to sublimation's role in artistic creativi-

24. Freud, *On Narcissism*, 14:94 and 100–101.

25. Freud, *Three Essays on the Theory of Sexuality*, 7:178 n. 2, added in 1915.

26. Ibid., 72–73.

27. Ibid., 73.

ty and cultural development in general. In the first of his "Three Essays" Freud explicitly, if simplistically, names sublimation as a source of art.[28] In the second of his "Three Essays" Freud extends the efficacy of sublimation from art to all cultural achievements. He cites the testimony of "historians of civilization" that "powerful components are acquired for every kind of cultural achievement by the diversion of sexual instinctual forces from sexual aims and their direction to new ones—a process which deserves the name of sublimation."[29] Freud himself explicitly states sublimation's role in the progress of civilization:

> Sublimation of instinct is an especially conspicuous feature of cultural development; it is what makes possible for higher psychical activities, scientific, artistic, or ideological, to play such an important part in civilized life.[30]

And while earlier in the same work Freud discusses sublimation as a means by which individual humans can avoid pain, it is clear from his examples here—"psychical and intellectual work ... an artist's joy in creating ... or a scientist's in solving problems or discovering truths"[31]—that sublimation is also a boon for civilization. And in "Leonardo da Vinci and a Memory of his Childhood" Freud calls the concepts of "the almighty and just God," under whose authority civilization—I feel compelled to note—has been able to make not a little progress, and of "kindly Nature" "grand sublimations of father and mother, or rather as revivals and restorations of the young child's idea of them."[32] So while sublimation is primarily in the service of the closed hydraulic system that is the Freudian subject, it does nevertheless serve the larger culture and civilization as well.

Throughout Freud's writings there is a certain ambiguity about sublimation which makes it resistant to thematization. We can get an idea of this ambiguity by noting two tensions in Freud's treatment of sublimation. The first tension is that Freud treats sublimation both as a result of

28. Freud writes: "The progressive concealment of the body which goes along with civilization keeps sexual curiosity awake. This curiosity seeks to complete the sexual object by revealing its hidden parts. It can, however, be diverted ('sublimated') in the direction of art, if its interest can be shifted away from the genitals on to the shape of the body as whole." Ibid., 156.

29. Ibid., 178.

30. Freud, *Civilization and Its Discontents*, 21:97.

31. Ibid., 79.

32. Sigmund Freud, "Leonardo da Vinci and a Memory of his Childhood," in *Five Lectures on Psycho-Analysis, Leonardo da Vinci, and Other Works*, vol. 11 of *The Standard Edition of the Complete Psychological Works of Sigmund Freud*, translated and edited by James Strachey (London: Hogarth Press and the Institute of Psycho-Analysis, 1957), 123.

an abnormal sexual constitutional disposition and as having an important function in normal health; the second tension is that Freud presents sublimation as having very close connections both with perversion and with artistic creativity.

Freud writes in the "Three Essays" that "it is possible … to form some idea of the mechanism of this process of sublimation,"[33] but in this very work he struggles with its ambiguity. In the summary article at the end of his "Three Essays" Freud treats sublimation as the means of achieving one of the three possible alternatives which can result from an abnormal sexual constitutional disposition. The other two alternatives are perversion and neurosis. But when sublimation is operative the same perilous disposition which can yield perversion or neurosis results in an increase in psychical efficiency. Sublimation "enables excessively strong excitations arising from particular sources of sexuality to find an outlet and use in other fields, so that a not inconsiderable increase in psychical efficiency results from a disposition which in itself is perilous."[34] Here sublimation appears in the company of perversion and neurosis as an alternative open to a sexual disposition that is abnormal.

But, on the other hand, Freud, also in the "Three Essays," presents sublimation as having an important role in normal health. He explains: "The same pathways … along which sexual disturbances trench upon the other somatic functions must also perform another important function in normal health. They must serve as paths for the attraction of sexual instinctual forces to aims that are other than sexual, that is to say, for the sublimation of sexuality."[35] So for Freud sublimation both is connected with a perilous sexual constitutional disposition and plays an important function in normal health. And for Freud sublimation is also both at the root of artistic creativity and closely related to the perversions. It is no wonder then that as late as 1930 and *Civilization and Its Discontents* Freud is still confident that in the future he would be able to systematize his theory on sublimation though unable to do so in the work at hand: "we shall certainly one day be able to characterize in metapsychological terms"[36] the special quality of satisfaction attained by way of sublimation.

33. Freud, *Three Essays on the Theory of Sexuality*, 7:178.

34. Ibid., 238.

35. Ibid., 206.

36. Freud, *Civilization and Its Discontents*, 21:79.

The second tension in Freud's presentation of sublimation is that he presents it as closely connected with art and closely related to perversion. We have seen above that Freud presents sublimation as the source of art when sexual curiosity is sublimated or directed toward the shape of the body as a whole in art and away from an exclusive focus on the genitals. And, in a larger sense, as we have seen, sublimation has fueled cultural achievements of every kind. But Freud's first use of the term "sublimate" occurs in the first of the "Three Essays," the one on "The Sexual Aberrations."

If we refer to the context in which Freud uses "sublimate," we find that the curiosity itself which would delay the satisfaction of the ultimate aim of libido in the sexual act—delay it, that is, in the lingering over the satisfaction of the preliminary aim of looking—is a temporary deflection of libidinal impulses from their normal ultimate end. This deflection is certainly normal if it is only preparatory to the fulfillment of the normal sexual aim; if, however, this preparatory deflection supplants the fulfillment of the normal sexual aim, the looking has become perversion.[37] Thus the sublimation of the pleasure of looking in the direction of art is not a perversion; rather it is something like a second order deflection of libidinal impulses: in the first order, looking at a sexual object is a deflection from the performance of the sexual act, and, in the second order, looking which is concerned with the beautiful shape of the body as whole is a deflection of the more specifically sexual looking which fixes itself upon the genitals.

Granted that sublimation benefits the arts rather explicitly and directly, but in this particular context, in which Freud is discussing "Deviations in Respect of the Sexual Aims," "Fixations of Preliminary Sexual Aims," and sexual aberrations in general, we cannot help but sense an implicit warning that sublimation has its affinity with perversions of the type which "linger over the intermediate relations to the sexual object which should normally be traversed rapidly on the path toward the final sexual aim."[38] How can sublimation function both as a source of art, a great cultural boon, and at the same stroke, because it replaces the fulfillment of the normal sexual aim, keep such close company with perversions?

Finally we must mention two drawbacks of sublimation according to Freud. First, he observes that we can prevent suffering by shifting instinctual aims so that our instincts cannot be frustrated by realities in the ex-

37. Freud, *Three Essays on the Theory of Sexuality*, 7:156–57.
38. Ibid., 150.

ternal world, but also admits that the intensity of those "'finer and higher'" satisfactions which derive from sublimation is "mild as compared with that derived from the sating of crude and primary instinctual impulses."[39] Those satisfactions that take our social valuation into account, those made possible through sublimation, do not compare in intensity to the private satisfactions at which the sexual instinct originally aims.[40]

On the general availability among people of sublimation as a way of channeling the instinctual energy of sex, Freud appears to be of two minds. On the one hand, Freud asserts that most men (he does not, I believe, intend this "men" as equivalent to "human beings") are successful in channeling large parts of the force of their sexual instincts into professional work.[41] But, on the other hand—and this would be the second drawback—Freud identifies the "weak point" of the method of sublimation as the fact that "it is not applicable generally: it is accessible to only a few people. It presupposes the possession of special dispositions which are far from being common to any practical degree."[42]

Let us conclude our consideration of Freud's concept of sublimation by noting that, *qua* psychoanalyst, he cannot account for the source of those special dispositions on which the use of sublimation depends. He writes:

> We are obliged to look for the source of … the capacity for sublimation in the organic foundations of character on which the mental structure is only afterwards erected. Since artistic talent and capacity are intimately connected with sublimation we must admit that the nature of the artistic function is also inaccessible to us along psycho-analytic lines.[43]

And it is not to any metaphysical agency that Dr. Freud turns as to the source of artistic creativity but to biology, as the lines immediately following this quotation clearly show.[44]

39. Freud, *Civilization and Its Discontents*, 21:79–80.
40. Ibid., 80.
41. "Observation of men's daily lives shows us that most people succeed in directing very considerable portions of their sexual instinctual forces to their professional activity. The sexual instinct is particularly well fitted to make contributions of this kind since it is endowed with a capacity for sublimation." Freud, "Leonardo da Vinci," 11:77–78. On female human beings' ability to sublimate, Freud says the following: "We also regard women as weaker in their social instincts and as having less capacity for sublimating their instincts than men." Freud, *New Introductory Lectures on Psychoanalysis*, 22:134.
42. Freud, *Civilization and Its Discontents*, 21:80.
43. Freud, "Leonardo da Vinci," 11:136.
44. "The tendency of *biological* research to-day is to explain the chief functions in a person's

We have seen, then, that Freud's concept of sublimation is both important and resistant to thematization, arises within the closed hydraulic system that is Freud's subject but serves cultural ends; is closely connected by way of an abnormal sexual constitution with perversion and neurosis but has an important role in normal health and in artistic creativity; is available to most men but is not applicable generally; and can be traced by psychoanalytic theory only back to the instincts which represent somatic demands, the bodily origin of sublimation being beyond the reach of psychoanalytic thought in the province of biology. Freud simply cannot account for how instinctual impulses are transfigured into works of art, cannot explain how one gets from oedipal drives to the *Oedipus Rex.* I concur with Ricoeur in thinking that it is Freud's materialism that accounts for his inability to thematize sublimation satisfactorily.

III. The Ontological Basis of Freud's Theory of Sublimation

The ontological basis of Freud's psychoanalytic thought is, of course, the thoroughgoing materialism of the age in which his mind was formed. The remarkable progress of science in the second half of the nineteenth century had led many to conclude that nothing of any importance exceeded the grasp of the natural sciences, that if science could not study something with its methodologies, so well-suited for the study of physical beings, then there was nothing real there to be studied.[45] Now Freud was a genius, and his powers of observation caused him to discover dynamisms and agencies in the human psyche and to acknowledge the reality of human creativity, the artistic making of symbols that somehow transfigure and redeem human suffering. When it came to explaining the phenomena he had observed, however, the materialism and empiricism that were the inherited categories in which he had to think confined him to what Ricoeur calls an archeology.

---

organic constitution as being the result of the blending of male and female dispositions, based on [chemical] substances." Ibid.; emphasis added. Please note that "chemical" in brackets is supplied by James Strachey, the translator and editor of The Standard Edition.

45. It was this same intellectual carbon monoxide of materialism and empiricism and the skepticism in philosophy they caused, all-pervasive in the academy, that drove a gifted young couple to consider suicide one summer day in 1901 in the Jardin des Plantes. See Raïssa Maritain, *We Have Been Friends Together: Memoirs,* translated by Julie Kernan (New York: Longmans, Green and Company, 1942), 72–78. See Barré, *Jacques and Raïssa Maritain,* 47, for the approximate date of this episode.

Freud sought the causes of the observed phenomena only by digging down to instinctual impulses arising in the id and, beneath them, to the body itself, the study of which he left to biology. A neurologist by training, he even held out hope that, in the future, the topographical system could be fixed in relation to areas of the brain.[46] Both Dalbiez[47] and Maritain[48] remark that Freud does not attempt a self-conscious philosophy but rather accepts uncritically the dominant ontological and epistemological theories of his time, materialism and empiricism. In the end, then, Freud cannot account for that which is properly human and transcendent of the instincts, that is, for the spiritual meaning in art works which, properly understood, are only partially caused by what he means by sublimation.

IV. Maritain's Theory of Sublimation and Its Ontological Basis

To Freud's materialistic and one-sidedly archeological explanation of sublimation and the art works which result from it Maritain, in broad strokes only, opposes what may be called a hylo-morphically based explanation, an explanation that takes into account not only their instinctual, that is, somatic, source but also their spiritual source. For Maritain the source of the illuminating, meaning-giving, and self-and-reality-appropriating poetic experience—which experience is "the secret life of each and all of the arts" and ordained to the art work as to its *telos*[49]—is the human spirit itself. It is the spiritual aspect of poetic experience that transfigures and redeems the instincts and accounts for the progressive, meaning-making, teleological

46. "There is a hiatus here [between the system *Cs.* and the anatomical position of that system] which at present cannot be filled, nor is it one of the tasks of psychology to fill it. Our psychical topography has *for the present* nothing to do with anatomy; it has reference not to anatomical localities, but to regions in the mental apparatus, wherever they may be situated in the body." Sigmund Freud, "The Unconscious," in vol. 14 of *The Standard Edition*, 174–75; emphasis in original.

47. "Freud has never tried to take up a frankly philosophical position. He has merely used and illustrated the evolutionary empiricism current in biological and medical circles during his education." Dalbiez, *Psychoanalytical Method and the Doctrine of Freud*, 2:286.

48. "Nothing is more unpleasant than to speak of a philosophy which does not recognize itself as such. The whole of Freudian philosophy is based upon a prejudice: the violent negation of spirituality and liberty." Maritain, "Freudianism and Psychoanalysis," 157.

49. See Jacques Maritain, *Creative Intuition in Art and Poetry* (New York: Pantheon Books, 1953), 3, and "Concerning Poetic Knowledge," in Jacques and Raïssa Maritain, *The Situation of Poetry: Four Essays on the Relations Between Poetry, Mysticism, Magic, and Knowledge*, translated by Marshall Suther (New York: Philosophical Library, 1995), 47 and 49.

aspect of human creativity, ordained as creativity is to expressing in the art work both that savory and obscure grasp of realities which the poet suffers and his or her own subjectivity grasped in those realities.[50]

And it is worth remarking that Maritain's theory of a spiritual unconscious or preconscious and of a sublimation "in quite a different sense," of which he speaks in his essay on Freud, situates the source of that poetic experience from which art works are born within human nature itself and does not require the intervention—as do Plato's theory of a separate Muse and Ricoeur's theory of the figures of Hegelian Absolute Spirit—of something beyond human nature to account for creative intuition and art.[51] For Maritain poetic experience, the source of all the arts, is grounded, in both its archeological and its teleological aspects, in an integral human nature composite of body and spiritual soul.

According to Maritain it is Freud's "negation of the autonomy of the spiritual" that leads to his reduction of all tendencies to instinct. For Freud, Maritain writes, the

> 'superior' states,—the inspiration of the poet, the love of the mystic, for instance,—are ... only transformations and masks of animal instinct, the diverted path by which a sensuality, inhibited in its normal exercise, satisfies itself in an insidious and veiled manner: all human exhilaration is specifically sensual.[52]

Freud's uncritical acceptance of the materialism of his age leaves him with no other alternative.

Maritain, however, sharing the view of the *Doctor Communis* on human nature, holds that: "the human soul, together with the matter which it informs, constitutes one substance, which is both carnal and spiritual.... Soul and matter are the two substantial co-principles of the same being, of one and the same reality, called ... [a human being]"[53] And personality is "a much deeper mystery" than mere individuality."[54] Maritain writes:

> Personality is the subsistence of the spiritual soul communicated to the human composite. Because, in our substance, it is an imprint or seal which enables it to possess its existence, to perfect and give itself freely, personality testifies to the

50. Jacques Maritain, "The Experience of the Poet," in *The Situation of Poetry*, 84.

51. See Maritain, *Creative Intuition*, 85–88, 91, and 100, on his express intention to bring the Platonic separate Muse into human nature itself.

52. Maritain, "Freudianism and Psychoanalysis," 155.

53. Jacques Maritain, *The Person and the Common Good*, translated by John J. Fitzgerald (Notre Dame, Indiana: University of Notre Dame Press, 1966), 36.

54. Ibid., 38.

generosity or expansiveness in being which an incarnate spirit derives from its spiritual nature and which constitutes, within the secret depths of our ontological structure, a source of dynamic unity, of unification from within.[55]

This view of human nature and personality gives Maritain a basis on which not only to acknowledge the role of instinctual energies in the creation of cultural objects such as works of art but also to account for their spiritual transfiguration in what Maritain means by sublimation.

In *Creative Intuition in Art and Poetry* Maritain directly opposes a "spiritual . . . unconscious or preconscious," that is, "the preconscious of the spirit in its living springs," to "the unconscious of blood and flesh, instincts, tendencies, complexes, repressed images and desires, traumatic memories . . . constituting a closed or autonomous dynamic whole."[56] The latter he identifies as the "*Freudian unconscious,*" which is "deaf to intellect, and structured into a world of its own apart from the intellect."[57] In Maritain's theory the substantial union of body and soul in the human person is so intimate that the spiritual unconscious extends to and somehow permeates the sense powers and their acts.

In the human person, Maritain states, borrowing language from Thibon, the instincts "are related to the spirit; they are made for the spirit: 'their real centre, their supreme depth, resides above organic life.'"[58] What Maritain means by poetic experience and the sublimation inherent in it are grounded in the fact that human instincts have "a secret aspiration to bathe 'in those delicate vibrations which commune with the spirit.'"[59] And Maritain asserts that the sentient powers in humans are related to the spiritual unconscious: ". . . all the sensitive powers of the soul (which are not "spiritual" in nature) and especially the imagination are involved in the spiritual unconscious, in so far as they participate in the preconscious life of the intellect or the will. The spiritual unconscious pertains primarily to the spiritual powers of the soul, but extends to the other."[60]

What precisely does Maritain mean by the spiritual unconsciousness? He treats of this most explicitly in two chapters of *Creative Intuition in Art and Poetry*. First Maritain shows how a certain spiritual unconsciousness is

55. Ibid., 41.

56. Maritain, *Creative Intuition*, 91–92.

57. Ibid., 92; emphasis in original.

58. Maritian, "Freudianism and Psychoanalysis," 156; cf. Thibon, "Mystique et Amour humain," 74.

59. "Freudianism and Psychoanalysis," 156; cf. Thibon, "Mystique et Amour humain," 75.

60. Maritain, *Creative Intuition*, 92 n. 29.

operative in all human intellectual knowing in general; next he goes on to show how poetic experience or creative inspiration is even more dependent upon unconscious operations. The first unconscious operation on which human intellectual knowing in general is dependent is the spiritual activity of the agent intellect, what Maritain calls the "Illuminating Intellect." "The Illuminating Intellect permeates the images with its pure and purely activating spiritual light and actuates or awakens the potential intelligibility which is contained in them."[61] The agent intellect is necessary to account for how the physical object known is brought to be actually intelligible, but the agent intellect only actualizes the potential intelligibilities contained in images; the agent intellect itself, however, does not know. "The Illuminating Intellect only activates, it does not know."[62] The potentially intelligible content of images is made actually intelligible in the *species impressa*, what Maritain calls "a spiritual form," an "impressed pattern," "an intelligible germ, which is received from the images by the intellect, under the activation of the Illuminating Intellect."[63] This reception in the intellect of an actually intelligible germ is, however, of itself, insufficient to account for our human intellectual knowing. The actual intelligibility of the *species impressa* must be raised to a state of actually being known.

In order for actual knowing to take place the possible intellect, the intellect that is in potency to know, having received the *species impressa* through the illuminating activity of the agent intellect, must produce the concept in which the intelligible content drawn from images is actually known and by which it, the possible or knowing intellect, is promoted to actually knowing. Maritain writes:

> [T]he intellect itself, which, having been impregnated by the impressed pattern or the intelligible germ, vitally produces—always under the activation of the Illuminating Intellect—an inner fruit, a final and more fully determined spiritual form (*species expressa*), the concept, in which the content drawn from the images is brought to the very same state of spirituality-in-act in which the intellect-in-act is, and in which this now perfectly spiritualized content is seen, is actually an object of intellectual vision.[64]

One and the same act, thanks to the agency of the illuminating intellect, promotes both the actual intelligibility of the *species impressa* to actually

61. Ibid., 96.
62. Ibid., 97.
63. Ibid.
64. Ibid., 97–98.

being known in and through the concept and the possible intellect to actually knowing.

Now Maritain's point is that although, when philosophers reflect on how we know, they can establish the necessity for and existence of the illuminating intellect and the *species impressa*, when we actually know, these necessary means of knowledge "totally escape experience and consciousness."[65] They are, in fact, "concealed in the unconscious of the spirit."[66] And there is a sense in which we are ordinarily unconscious even of the *species expressa*, the concept. The concept causes the object to be known, but in revealing the object the concept conceals itself. The concept is knowable by reflection upon how our intellects operate, but this kind of reflection does not always take place. "There can exist," Maritain writes, "unconscious acts of thought and unconscious ideas."[67]

And if these kinds of unconscious or preconscious spiritual means-by-which of knowing are present in the life of the intellect in general and in "that conceptual, logical, discursive knowledge with which poetry is on bad terms,"[68] in particular, then surely we must expect to find elements of the spiritual unconscious at play in the poetry or poetic experience that is the source of art works. Maritain extends the Thomistic treatment of human knowing to poetic experience and asserts that "if there is in the spiritual unconscious a nonconceptual or preconceptual activity of the intellect even with regard to the birth of concepts, we can with much greater reason assume that such a nonconceptual activity of the intellect, such a nonrational activity of reason, in the spiritual unconscious, plays an essential part in the genesis of poetry and poetic inspiration."[69]

According to Maritain, the poet knows, in the depths of his or her own subjectivity, the things of the world and, in so doing, knows his or her subjectivity itself. This knowing is obscure; inasmuch as it is by *affective* connaturality, it is suffering things and the roots of one's own faculties that resonate with them, under the color of emotion, more than it is cognitively grasping them. Maritain writes that in poetic experience or poetic knowledge: "what is *most immediate* … is the experience of things of the world … but what is *most principal* is the experiencing of the subject."[70] This last is, of course, an

65. Ibid., 98.
66. Ibid., 99.
67. Ibid., 98.
68. Ibid., 99.
69. Ibid., 99–100.
70. Maritain, "The Experience of the Poet," 83; emphasis in original.

objective genitive: the object experienced is the subject himself or herself. And the poet knows, is made kin to, the things of the world in all their particularities. The poet knows obscurely or suffers the "essences, quiddities, qualities, talities, haececities, ipseities with which the real and the singular abound."[71] And in these, perhaps, the poet intuitively grasps their "communication in the act of existing and in the spiritual flux from which existence proceeds, a communication which … is in things as if the secret of [their] creative sources."[72] The poet brings all this with himself or herself, known in and with them, "back to the mysterious nest of the soul," where they are "buried in the subjectivity itself."[73]

Poetic knowing is by connaturality; the poet is connaturalized "with the mystery that is scattered in things, … the invisible powers at play in the universe."[74] Poetic knowledge, Maritain writes, "proceeds not per *modum cognitionis* but by way of affective connaturality or of resonance in the subject," and in it "the emotion or inclination becomes a grasping of the real, *amor transit in conditionem objecti*."[75] In poetic knowledge "the emotion or inclination bears the real which moves the soul," that is, "the world which affects it and which it suffers in the heart of its … subjectivity."[76]

Maritain understands that in poetic experience the emotion, entering the contemplative, self-possessed soul of the poet from any source, functions as a means of knowing aspects of the real in the same way that the concept functions in more rational ways of knowing.[77] Maritain writes: "in poetic knowledge emotion carries the reality which the soul suffers—a world in a grain of sand—into the depth of subjectivity, and of the spiritual unconscious of the intellect."[78] In the depth of the spiritual unconscious the emotion that bears some reality into the poetic soul determines that soul in a specific way and, under the illuminating activity of the agent intellect, makes the soul like, connatural with, the aspects of reality it knows by means of this emotion.

For Maritain emotion in the soul of the poet makes the distinctive non-

71. Ibid., 76.

72. Ibid., 79.

73. Ibid., 76 and 74.

74. Jacques Maritain, *Distinguish to Unite or The Degrees of Knowledge*, translated under the supervision of Gerald B. Phelan (New York: Charles Scribner's Sons, 1959), 282.

75. Maritain, "The Experience of the Poet," 80.

76. Ibid., 81.

77. Maritain, *Creative Intuition*, 121–24. Maritain calls poetry "nonrational" or nonlogical" but not "antirational." Ibid., 4.

78. Ibid., 122.

rational knowing of poetry possible; the emotion is the *medium quo* of the savory, knowing in the mode of unknowing that is poetic experience.[79] He elaborates this insight in some dense lines in *Creative Intuition in Art and Poetry*:

> [I]t suffices for emotion disposing or inclining ... the entire soul in a certain determinate manner to be thus received in the undetermined vitality and productivity of the spirit, where it is permeated by the light of the Illuminating Intellect: then, while remaining emotion ... it is made into an instrument of intelligence judging through connaturality, and plays in the process of this knowledge through *likeness* between reality and subjectivity, the part of nonceptual intrinsic determination of intelligence in its preconscious activity.[80]

Maritain asserts that it is precisely because emotion serves as the *medium quo* of the savory, obscure poetic knowledge of real things—becomes, that is to say, intentional—that it is spiritualized; emotion, he writes, "is spiritualized ... conveying, in a state of immateriality, things other than itself."[81] And "it is by means of such a spiritualized emotion that poetic intuition ... is born in the unconscious of the spirit."[82]

And the spiritualized emotion which enables the poetic knowing both of things and of the poet's subjectivity is, itself, unknown or unconscious; this is knowledge not for the sake of knowing but for the sake of making. Maritain states explicitly that poetic knowledge does not know itself:

> the content of poetic intuition is both the reality of the things of the world and subjectivity of the poet, both obscurely conveyed through an intentional or spiritualized emotion. The soul is known in the experience of the world and the world is known in the experience of the soul, through a knowledge that does not know itself. For such knowledge knows, not in order to know, but in order to produce.[83]

Thus the spiritualized emotion which functions as an intentional means-by-which of poetic knowledge is as unknown directly as are the concepts by which we know more abstractively. In the very moment of poetic experience it is unconscious or preconscious. With this understanding of what Maritain means by the spiritual unconscious we can move to a consideration of how it functions in sublimation.

Maritain describes sublimation, what he calls "real sublimation," by quot-

79. Maritain, "The Experience of the Poet," 80–81.
80. Maritain, *Creative Intuition*, 122–23; emphasis in original.
81. Ibid., 123.
82. Ibid.
83. Ibid., 124.

ing Gustav Thibon. Sublimation is "'a sort of ascensional reflux of instinct toward the immaterial sources of being, a *qualitative* integration of sensitive rhythms in the pure melody of interior life.'"[84] This upward flow of instinctual energies into preconscious life of the spirit is possible, of course, because of the substantial union of the body and spiritual in a human person in which, as we have seen, the instincts are for the sake of the spiritual soul and find their true center and depth in it. Again quoting Thibon, Maritain explains that this kind of sublimation is "'accompanied by a feeling of equilibrium, of peace and of intimate plenitude, by an impression of liberation from the slavery and discordance of the inferior appetites, and by a sort of spontaneous transparency of all the depths of nature to the rays of spirit.'"[85]

Maritain calls this kind of sublimation a "final integration" of spirit and flesh.[86] He writes of "a common root of all the powers of the soul, which is hidden in the spiritual unconscious, and ... there is in this spiritual unconscious a root activity in which the intellect and the imagination, as well as the powers of desire, love, and emotion, are engaged in common."[87] It is here that in some gifted-afflicted types, in freedom from the restraints imposed by their nature on the speculative and practical uses of reason, in freedom obedient to "an inner law of expansion and generosity,"[88] and in a freedom ordained to making, poetry is born.[89] Thus Maritain concludes: "Poetry is the fruit neither of the intellect alone, nor of the imagination alone. Nay more, it proceeds from the totality of ... [the human person], sense, imagination, intellect, love, desire, instinct, blood and spirit together."[90] So for Maritain poetry integrates the spiritual and somatic aspects of our nature, and art makes that integration manifest. Thus the integration or sublimation characteristic of poetry, that heart and center of art, is grounded in Maritain's unified theory of human nature, a theory in which the lower serves the higher.

Maritain's theory of a spiritual unconscious and the sublimation in it of forces originating in the body provides both for the distinction in nature of the psychic and somatic elements and their unity in concrete experience. Thus for Maritain "the rapture of the lyrical or religious soul is in itself specifically spiritual and, therefore, specifically distinct from the an-

84. Maritain, "Freudianism and Psychoanalysis," 156; Thibon, "Mystique et Amour humain," 75.

85. Ibid., 156–57; Thibon, 75.

86. Ibid., 157.

87. Maritain, *Creative Intuition*, 110.

88. Ibid.

89. Ibid., 111.

90. Ibid.

imal instinct."[91] And he reiterates that the two "are essentially distinct and thoroughly different in nature."[92] But—distinguish to unite!—this does not mean that spiritual rapture is separated from instinct: "it is absurd to absorb the superior in the inferior, but it is unhuman to disjoin them."[93] Maritain specifically acknowledges both the distinction in nature and unity in human experience of the psychic and somatic elements. He writes that the spiritual unconscious with its higher form of sublimation and the Freudian unconscious are "at work at the same time; in concrete existence their respective impacts on the conscious activity ordinarily interfere or intermingle in a greater or lesser degree; and, I think, never—except in some rare instances of supreme spiritual purification—does the spiritual unconscious operate without the other being involved, be it to a very small extent."[94]

Now Maritain remarks, as do Dalbiez and Ricoeur, the solipsistic nature of the Freudian subject. The isolation of the subject in Freud's theory, according to Maritain, accounts for his reduction of all human tendencies to instincts arising from the body. For Maritain tendencies are specified by their formal objects, but Freud, "considering tendencies and instincts exclusively on the side of the subject, ... cannot possibly discover in them a distinction in essence."[95] This inability to specify various tendencies by their objects leads Freud to make all tendencies "flow back to the same fundamental instinct, of which they would be but transformations, or rather, different masks."[96] Maritain, following St. Thomas, can distinguish genuinely different human tendencies by their formal objects and thus recognize both bodily and spiritual tendencies and not reduce the latter to the former.

V. Conclusion

We have seen then that Freud, with his thoroughgoing materialism and reductive account of sublimation, cannot account for the specifically human creation of art, cannot provide a basis in the subject for the trans-

91. Maritain, "Freudianism and Psychoanalysis," 156.
92. Maritain, *Creative Intuition*, 92.
93. Maritain, "Freudianism and Psychoanalysis," 156.
94. Maritain, *Creative Intuition*, 92.
95. Maritain, "Freudianism and Psychoanalysis," 155.
96. Ibid.

formation of instinctual desire, for the luminous transfiguration it undergoes in poetry and art. Maritain, on the other hand, can account for both the archaeological and the teleological aspects in sublimation and ground them in human nature itself because his philosophical anthropology makes room for both the body with its instinctual drives and for the spirit with it natural élan toward meaning and transparency and for the intimate, hylo-morphic union of the two.

RAYMOND HAIN

Individuality and Personality in Maritain and Classical Hindu Philosophy

In 1998, Pope John Paul II wrote the following in *Fides et Ratio*: "In India particularly, it is the duty of Christians now to draw from this rich heritage [of religious and philosophical traditions] the elements compatible with their faith, in order to enrich Christian thought".[1] Pope John Paul II thought both that the philosophical traditions of India consisted of a "rich heritage," and that those of us who are philosophers and Christians have a duty to confront and draw upon (*depromere*) this heritage. To one who takes seriously these claims made in *Fides et Ratio*, it is difficult not to be struck by Maritain's offhand comment in *Scholasticism and Politics* that the central concept of his lectures, the concept of "personality," and the consequent distinction between "individuality" and "personality," was "a classical distinction, belonging to the intellectual heritage of humanity. And the distinction between the '*ego*' and the '*self*' in Hindu philosophy is—with other metaphysical connotations—its equivalent."[2] This seems an interesting opportunity, more than seventy years after the appearance of *Scholasticism and Politics*, to think carefully about certain aspects of the classical Hindu philosophical tradition from the perspective of Thomism, and the topic of "per-

1. §72, "Huius temporis Christianorum est, praesertim Indianorum, locupleti ex eiusmodi patrimonio elementa illa depromere quae cum illorum fide coniungi possunt, ita ut christiana doctrina ditior fiat." Both the official English and Latin versions can be found on the Vatican's website at: http://www.vatican.va/holy_father/john_paul_ii/encyclicals/index.htm.

2. Jacques Maritain, *Scholasticism and Politics*, translated and edited by Mortimer J. Adler (New York: MacMillan, 1940; Garden City, New York: Image Books, 1960), 63.

sonality," a deeply difficult topic for us today, could not be more centrally important for us. After some brief background, the purpose of this essay is to make a start at seeing how far Maritain was right, and whether this might provide philosophically fruitful resources both for thinking about Maritain's work on personality and individuality and more generally about some of the puzzles surrounding the unique characteristics of human beings.

By way of preparation, here is a brief sketch of Hinduism and classical Hindu philosophy.[3] Hinduism is the third largest religion in the world after Christianity and Islam, and is the major religious tradition of the subcontinent of South Asia. In India alone there are about one billion adherents. The oldest and most sacred texts in Hinduism are the Veda, of which there are four: the *Ṛgveda, Yajurveda, Sāmaveda,* and *Atharvaveda*. These were most likely first written down, beginning with the *Ṛgveda,* somewhere between 1500 BC and the time of the Buddha (500 BC or so), and they mostly consist of rituals and hymns. Over time, commentaries were appended to portions of the Veda, some of which were considered, along with the Veda, to be revealed, sacred texts. The most interesting of these commentaries, and the most philosophically reflective, are the *Upaniṣads* (it is in the *Upaniṣads,* for example, that the doctrine of reincarnation is first developed). Although the composition of various *Upaniṣads* continued up until the middle ages (there is a canonical list of 108), there are only thirteen principal *Upaniṣads,* compiled early as genuine appendices to the Vedic texts. The composition of these early *Upaniṣads* ranges somewhere between the seventh and eighth centuries BC until the time of Christ, during what Karl Jaspers called the "axial period" of human civilization,[4] and they are considered the traditional philosophical core of Hinduism.

The Vedantic literature, including the Veda, Upaniṣads, and other commentaries, are known collectively as "that which is heard," or revealed, and are the most sacred texts of Hinduism. A second branch of texts consist of "that which is remembered;" these are less sacred, and include stories, legends, and moral precepts. The most famous of these is the *Bhagavad-Gita,* part of a much longer Hindu epic, composed around the first century after Christ. The *Bhagavad-Gita* might helpfully be considered a kind of "New

3. For an excellent introduction to ancient Hinduism, and one to which these brief background remarks are very much indebted, see A. L. Basham, *The Origins and Development of Classical Hinduism* (New York: Oxford University Press, 1991).

4. Karl Jaspers, *The Origin and Goal of History* (London: Routledge and Kegan Paul, 1953).

Testament" of Hinduism in relation to the "Old Testament" of the Veda, and it has been the most influential Hindu text for some centuries. Our focus here will be on these classic foundational texts, the principal *Upaniṣads* and the *Bhagavad-Gita*.

Before turning to these texts, we must first note the central claims Maritain is making that should be kept in mind as we think through the Hindu texts. He reminds us in the first paragraph of the foreword that *Scholasticism and Politics* "is entirely permeated with the idea of the human person, considered in his spiritual dignity and the concrete conditions of his existence."[5] *Personality*, for Maritain, is the central theme of his lectures, and is to be sharply distinguished from *individuality*. Here is what Maritain means by individuality:

> One might say that in each of us, *individuality*, being in one that which excludes from one all that other men are, is the narrowness in being, and the 'grasping for oneself,' which, in a body animated by a spirit, derives from matter. Man, in so far as he is a material individuality, has but a precarious unity, which wishes only to slip back into multiplicity; for matter as such tends to decompose itself. In so far as we are individuals, each of us is a fragment of a species, a part of this universe, a single dot in the immense network of forces and influences, cosmic, ethnic, historic, whose laws we obey. We are subject to the determination of the physical world.[6]

Maritain means here at least that we, *as individuals*, are interested merely in ourselves. So we must, as material beings, consume food and breathe air that, as it is taken in for our own use, is no longer available for anyone else (it is, as he says, "grasped for ourselves"). The goods of the individual are private goods, and the life of the individual is, in an important sense, a private life. Personality, on the other hand, as Maritain says,

> does not refer to matter, as does the notion of individuality applied to corporeal things. It refers to the highest and deepest dimensions of being; personality is rooted in the spirit, in so far as the latter stands by itself in existence and superabounds in it. Metaphysically considered, personality, being in one's substance a signature or a seal enabling one freely to perfect and freely to give this substance, evidences in each of us that expansiveness of being which, in a corporeal-spiritual being, is linked to the spirit, and which constitutes, in the secret depths of our ontological structure, a source of dynamic unity and of inner unification. Thus, personality means interiority to oneself.... [And] [b]ecause of the very fact that I

5. Maritain, *Scholasticism and Politics*, 7.
6. Ibid., 66; emphasis in original.

am a person and that I express myself to myself, I seek to communicate with *that which is other* and with *others*, in the order of knowledge and love.[7]

This is heady language, but the core of Maritain's description is that personality consists in, as he says, an "expansiveness of spirit," an expansiveness that involves both self possession in a special way and the ability to possess what is other while at the same time not consuming that other and transforming it into oneself (and this of course makes that expansiveness potentially infinite). For the individual to possess food is for that food to be transformed into the individual himself. But for the personality to possess knowledge, or to possess another person through love, is to possess without consuming. In this sense, of course, the goods of the person, as such, are sharable goods. Instead of the food or drink of the individual, we have the knowledge of truth, or the common life of a household, which can at one and the same time be possessed by any number of persons. For Maritain, a sound philosophy of personality, of human beings as persons, is central to all the political claims he develops in *Scholasticism and Politics*, and he thinks that through such a philosophy "the genuine, vital principle of a new Democracy, and at the same time of a new Christian civilization, can be rediscovered."[8]

It is worth keeping in mind, too, that for Maritain, individuality and personality, grounded in matter and form, are not two separate things or realities within the self, but are instead two ways in which the entire self is characterized. I am wholly an individual, and wholly a person. My individuality is, therefore, something good about me, since it is a condition of my existence. Maritain's application of the concept of personality is always conditioned in part by the fact that each human person is also, and importantly, an individual.

Turning now to the *Upaniṣads* and the *Bhagavad-Gita*, is Maritain right that there is here too a clear distinction between the human being as an individual, and the human being as a person? If there is such a distinction, how might its development help, or hinder, Maritain's own distinction? This is of course an enormous question, and the present goal is no more than a thoughtful and tentative beginning. Note also that this essay does not address (nor is it meant to address) the many and complicated developments

7. Ibid., 67–68; emphasis in original.

8. Ibid., 7.

in the rich tradition of Hinduism that either parallel the *Upaniṣads* and the *Bhagavad-Gita* or come after them.[9]

First, there is certainly an important distinction within this early Hindu literature between the various parts and powers of our body and something else, something more interior and of greater importance. So, for example, we read, "This self of yours who is present within but is different from the skin, whom the skin does not know, whose body is the skin, and who controls the skin from within—he is the inner controller, the immortal."[10] This is repeated for speech, sight, hearing, even the mind, and the passage concludes with: "He sees, but he can't be seen; he hears, but he can't be heard; he thinks, but he can't be thought of; he perceives, but he can't be perceived. Besides him, there is no one who sees, no one who hears, no one who thinks, and no one who perceives. It is this self of yours who is the inner controller, the immortal."[11] One important reason that there must be this "self" (*atman* in Sanskrit, a central and admittedly difficult concept in Hindu philosophy) is that I am not identical to any particular part or power that I exercise: "If speaking is done through speech; if breathing out is done through the out-breath; if seeing is done through sight; if hearing is done through hearing; if touching is done through the skin; if thinking is done through the mind ... then who am I?"[12] Because it is true that *I* perceive, feel, and think, even though each activity is performed by a particular power, the *I* that is myself must be distinct from each power, and yet nevertheless in control of them and unifying them into one overall experiencing self. Moreover, in the *Bhagavad-Gita*, we read that "Never in the future shall we cease to exist. / Just as the embodied self / enters childhood, youth, and old age, / so does it enter another body."[13] What is striking here is that just as you must have a unifying self to draw together your various powers into one experience at any one time, likewise you need a unifying self over and above your different powers and parts across

9. For an excellent introduction to some broader philosophical issues in classical Hindu philosophy as well as other Asian philosophies (though by no means from a Thomistic perspective), see Joel Kupperman, *Classic Asian Philosophy* (New York: Oxford University Press, 2001).

10. *Upaniṣads*, translated by Patrick Olivelle (New York: Oxford University Press, 1996), *Bṛhadāraṇyaka Upaniṣad* 3.7.21, p. 43. All references to the *Upaniṣads* will be by the name of the *Upaniṣad*, chapter, section, and division, as well as the page reference to Olivelle's translation.

11. *Bṛhadāraṇyaka Upaniṣad* 3.7.23, p. 44.

12. *Aitareya Upaniṣad* 1.3.11, p. 197.

13. *The Bhagavad-Gita*, translated by Barbara Stoler Miller (New York: Bantam, 1986), 2.12–13, p. 33. All references to the *Bhagavad-Gita* will be by teaching and verse number, as well as the page reference to Miller's translation.

time as well; there must be something common that is at the same time other than childhood, youth, and old age.

If it is clear that there must be a "self," surely what Maritain supposes is the "person," it is much less clear what this self is like. Here is a passage somewhat more explicit than the similar one mentioned above. This is the response of a sage to a man asking about the nature of the self: "You can't see the seer who does the seeing; you can't hear the hearer who does the hearing; you can't think of the thinker who does the thinking; and you can't perceive the perceiver who does the perceiving. The self within all is this self of yours."[14] For this reason, the *Upaniṣads* repeat many times that we must use negative language when speaking of the self. Here is one representative passage: "About this self (*atman*), one can only say 'not ——, not ——'. He is ungraspable, for he cannot be grasped. He is undecaying, for he is not subject to decay. He has nothing sticking to him, for he does not stick to anything. He is not bound; yet he neither trembles in fear nor suffers injury. Look—by what means can one perceive the perceiver?"[15] If our very self must be something over and above our body and its powers, as well as our mind and its powers, by what power will we be able to detect it? And even if our self were capable of apprehending the "self," how could it turn back on itself and perceive itself, as if the eye could see that which is seeing?

Despite this tendency towards negative anthropology, there are also some positive characterizations of the self. The self is, for example, what is most important to a person: "This innermost thing, this self (*atman*)—it is dearer than a son, it is dearer than wealth, it is dearer than everything else."[16] And although the self is never identified with any part of the body or the lower sense powers, it is sometimes identified with "breath." "This very breath is the self consisting of intelligence; it is bliss, unageing, and immortal.... He is the ruler of the world. He is the sovereign of the world. He is the lord of the world. One should realize: 'He is my self (*atman*).'"[17] In one sense, this is fitting, since it is our breath that makes the difference between a living body, one in whom the self is present, and a dead body in which the self is absent: "A man continues to live after his speech leaves him, for we see people who are dumb. A man continues to live after his sight leaves him, for we see people who are blind. A man continues to live after his hearing leaves him, for we see people who are deaf. A man continues to live after his mind

14. *Bṛhadāraṇyaka Upaniṣad* 3.4.2, p. 39.
15. Ibid., 4.5.15, p. 71.
16. Ibid., 1.4.8, p. 15.
17. *Kauṣītaki Upaniṣad* 3.8, p. 220.

leaves him, for we see people who are imbeciles. And a man continues to live after his arms are cut off and his legs are cut off, for we see such people. But only the breath, you see, is the self consisting of intelligence. When it grasps the body, it enables the body to get up."[18]

The self is also both extremely small and unimaginably expansive. It exists "as measuring the size of a span and as beyond all measure."[19] "This self (*atman*) of mine that lies deep within my heart—it is smaller than a grain of rice or barley, smaller than a mustard seed, smaller even than a millet grain or a millet kernel; but it is larger than the earth, larger than the intermediate region, larger than the sky, larger even than all these worlds put together."[20]

Eventually, the self is identified with *Brahman*, the other deeply difficult concept in Hindu philosophy. *Brahman* is the source of all that exists, and in some sense it *is* all that exists. Here is a series of passages revealing that the self is all things and is eventually *Brahman* itself: "This self (*atman*) of mine that lies deep within my heart—it contains all actions, all desires, all smells, and all tastes; it has captured this whole world; it neither speaks nor pays any heed. It is *Brahman*. On departing from here after death, I will become that."[21] *Brahman*, too, is rarely characterized as anything positive, but in one rare passage it is identified with knowledge: "Who is this self (*atman*)? ... It is *Brahman*.... It is everything that has life—those that move, those that fly, and those that are stationary. Knowledge is the eye of all that, and on knowledge it is founded. Knowledge is the eye of the world, and knowledge, the foundation. *Brahman* is knowing."[22]

The Hindu self, therefore, has much in common with Maritain's "personality." The self is to be distinguished from the body and its many powers. It is what is most dear about us, and what we must through asceticism come to know best of all. It is expansive and in a sense all things, a reminder, of course, of Aristotle's phrase that the soul can become all things.[23] And it is most fundamentally, at least according to one text, the activity of *knowing*. But an important absence, for Maritain, is any substantive discussion of love. Love occasionally appears, but it is never identified with our higher activities, or with *Brahman*, nor is it an important means to or part of our eventual union with *Brahman*.

On the other hand, the notion of individuality contained in these texts

18. Ibid., 3.3, p. 216.

19. *Chāndogya Upaniṣad* 5.18.1, p. 146.

20. Ibid., 3.14.3, p. 124.

21. Ibid., 3.14.4, p. 124.

22. *Aitareya Upaniṣad* 2.3.1–3, pp. 198–99.

23. *De Anima* 3.5, 430a14–15.

seems to be precisely what Maritain has in mind in his own use of the term. The contrary to the self is most immediately the body, the corpse that is left over after death, or even the individuality of the body and its powers that cannot in themselves give us access to anything greater than themselves. According to the *Bhagavad-Gita*, "As the mountainous depths / of the ocean / are unmoved when waters / rush into it, / so the man unmoved when desires enter him / attains a peace that eludes / the man of many desires. // When he renounces all desires / and acts without craving, / possessiveness, / or individuality, he finds peace."[24] And elsewhere, "An agent called pure / has no attachment or individualism, / is resolute and energetic, / unchanged in failure and success."[25] Our individuality requires attachment to the material things of this world, and to respond authentically to the inner self requires a detachment from such things, a detachment that implies the recognition that these things, while perhaps necessary, are purely means and are of no value in themselves.

In general, therefore, Maritain was right to point out that the distinction between individuality and personality is present in Hindu philosophy, and that it has implications very similar to those he himself intended. But of course one must not ignore some of the obvious stumbling blocks in the way of any straightforward combination of Maritain's Thomistic philosophy with Hinduism. The *Upaniṣads* and the *Bhagavad-Gita* also speak of reincarnation; the self inhabits first one body and then another, limited neither to human bodies nor even to living beings. And the ideal state, release from the cycle of reincarnation, implies a submersion of the self in Brahman that wipes away any real distinction between ultimate reality and the self. These difficulties, along with the absence of love, are all, I think, rooted in the relationship between the self and the individual. Maritain wished to defend the unique and important character of the self, and here Hinduism is very sympathetic. But the most interesting absence in these classical Hindu texts is any account of individuality as a necessary principle of the human person. It turns out that Maritain's reminder that personality and individuality are linked as form and matter is as important to politics, to the life of the city, as the careful development of personality itself. Here are three important and related themes for us to consider: reincarnation with the eventual goal of dissolution into Brahman; the political difficulties rooted in the four traditional social classes of Hinduism; and, the absence of a deep and developed account of love.

24. *Bhagavad-Gita* 2.70–71, p. 42.

25. Ibid., 18.26, p. 139.

As in ancient Greek philosophy, the roots of Hindu philosophy leave open an interpretation of the self that could eventually lead to a version of hylomorphism.[26] The word for "self" is originally simply the word for "living body" (every translator of the *Upaniṣads* must make important interpretative decisions about when the word *atman* means simply "body" and when it means the "self"), and the connections between the self and "breath" remind us that ψυχή meant "breath" for the Greeks before it meant "soul." Despite the suggestive character of these aspects of early Hindu philosophy, a strong dualism eventually emerged as dominant. The self therefore merely inhabits the body, and its primary goal is to escape embodiment and achieve unification with *Brahman*.

Because the self merely inhabits the body, individuality is not essentially part of that self. This makes reincarnation possible, of course, but it also makes perfectly plausible a recognition that the self is most truly a mere aspect of *Brahman* (a reminder of arguments in the West about whether or not there is only one human intellectual power, or if each unique human being possesses his or her own independent intellectual power[27]). Without the individuality of matter, it is much harder to say what *distinguishes* one self from another. Aquinas must have had something like this in mind when he wrote in the *Summa Theologiae* that "if anyone says that the intellectual soul is not the form of the body he must first explain how it is that this action of understanding is the action of this particular man."[28]

More importantly for the political implications in which Maritain was

26. The many parallels between classical Hindu philosophy and classical Greek philosophy have interested scholars for a long time. Recently, Thomas McEvilley has made a persuasive empirical case that there was significant and fruitful interpenetration of Hindu and Greek thought throughout the classical period. See his masterful *The Shape of Ancient Thought: Comparative Studies in Greek and Indian Philosophies* (New York: Allworth Press, 2002).

27. Aristotle's *De Anima* gave rise in the West to serious controversy over the nature of the intellectual principle in human beings, in part because Aristotle's text is obscure in places. For example, Ibn Rushd argued in the twelfth century that an intellectual power that could do what Aristotle said it could (that is, perform an operation independently of matter and continue to exist separated from all matter) must be different from the human soul that was the substantial form of the body, though it made possible that soul's knowledge. That is, there must be only one genuinely intellectual power, and each individual human being somehow shares in the knowledge made possible by that power. For an excellent consideration of Aquinas's attempt to interpret Aristotle in a way that avoids Ibn Rushd's interpretation see Anton Pegis, "Some Reflections on *Summa Contra Gentiles* II, 56," in *An Etienne Gilson Tribute*, edited by Charles J. O'Neil (Milwaukee, Wisconsin: Marquette University Press, 1959).

28. St. Thomas Aquinas, *Summa Theologica*, translated by Fathers of the English Dominican Province, vol. 1 (Notre Dame, Indiana: Christian Classics, 1981), I, q. 76, a. 1.

interested, if one's body is not truly part of one's self, then what happens to the body is not immediately relevant to one's life. So the *Bhagavad-Gita* emphasizes detachment not only from desire, but from all action and its implications: "Disciplined by understanding, / one abandons both good and evil deeds; / so arm yourself for discipline— / discipline is skill in actions. // Wise men disciplined by understanding / relinquish the fruit born of action; / freed from these bonds of rebirth, / they reach a place beyond decay."[29] It is only the inner self that matters, and the actions of the body and its condition are restricted by our duty but have no essential value. It should not surprise us, then, that Hindu culture could reconcile itself to the existence of a class of "untouchable" human beings, people who possessed a self as great as the self of anyone else (or any*thing* else), but whose individuality trapped them at a lower level of existence. If this lower level of existence is not truly part of myself, and what happens to it does not in itself help or harm me (it is how I respond to such things that matters most), then you do no disservice to my true self by treating my body with contempt.

It is now also perhaps easy to see why love might play such a small role in early Hindu philosophy. It is not clear that there is, in the end, anything to love. I do not love something *merely* because it has a self, an aspect of *Brahman,* since this is true of all existing things. Love that is completely diffuse is no longer an interesting form of love. Nor do I love *Brahman* itself, in the end, for I am myself *Brahman.* Love requires an other (one that can be possessed without being consumed), and if all in the end is *Brahman,* there is nothing left to love. (Note, by the way, that Aristotle's god too, though a knower, doesn't seem much of a lover; the Christian God *is,* of course, but then the Christian God has a real plurality of "others," the Persons of the Trinity.)

Let us conclude with a provocative claim. Maritain was most worried about a flattening of the human person, perhaps at the hands of materialism, that would limit our dignity by emptying human knowing and human loving of any real significance (and it is a striking fact that we face today in the West both skepticism about the significance of knowing and loving, and practical difficulties with human relationships, our treatment of the young, old, and disabled, and so on). And here, saving the import-

29. *Bhagavad-Gita* 2.50–51, p. 39.

ant exception of authentic human love, classical Hindu philosophy is very sympathetic to Maritain. But reflecting on classical Hindu philosophy also reminds us that our material individuality is just as important as personality to a proper and politically fruitful understanding of the human person. Emphasizing personality at the expense of individuality is as dangerous as emphasizing individuality at the expense of personality. Perhaps, after all, a proper understanding of human dignity, a dignity that blossoms most of all in the flowers of knowledge and love, requires hylomorphism.

FEDERICO TEDESCO

From Maritain to Aquinas

Beyond the Polarity between Individual and Person

"One would never discover the limits of the soul [phychēs], should one traverse every road—so deep a measure [logon] does it possess."

—Heraclitus[1]

"No man can ever feel his own identity aright except his eyes be closed; as if darkness were indeed the proper element of our essence."

—Melville[2]

"Dieu mon Dieu je me tiens devant toi dans ma détresse.... Je suis à toi je suis à toi—mais que suis-je. Je ne veux me connaître qu'en ta lumière qui vivifie."

—Raïssa Maritain[3]

I. Introduction

In his introduction to *Scholasticism and Politics*, Maritain notes that all the texts in this collection, although originating from different perspectives, converge upon the notion of person: "However varied the topics dealt with may be, the general purpose, which makes the organic unity of the volume, is easily perceptible. It is entirely permeated with the idea of the human person."[4] It is interesting to observe that even the epistemological observa-

1. Heraclitus, *Fragments*, edited by T. M. Robinson (Toronto: University of Toronto Press, 1991), 33 n. 45.

2. Herman Melville, *Moby Dick* (New York: Random House, The Modern Library, 1926), 53.

3. Raïssa Maritain, "Procession, in Id.," in *Poèmes et Essais* (Paris: Desclée de Brouwer, 1968), 77–78.

4. Jacques Maritain, *Scholasticism and Politics*, translated and edited by Mortimer J. Adler (New York: Image Books, 1960), 7.

tions he makes in the second chapter ultimately contribute to the theory of man as person. A more effective understanding of *Scholasticism and Politics,* and Maritain's thought in general, therefore requires a detailed examination of the meaning that he ascribes to the concept of person.

It is well known that Maritain defines the notion of person starting from the metaphysical concept of subsistence: "The first metaphysical root of personality is what is called subsistence"[5]; and in *The Person and the Common Good* he specifies that "Personality is the subsistence of the spiritual soul communicated to the human composite."[6]

Through an analysis of Maritain's subsistence theory, I will begin by showing that it implies—in spite of the author's intentions—a semi-dualistic conception of human nature that is expressed most noticeably by the polarity between individual and person. One could argue that, by defining the metaphysical personality as "the subsistence of the spiritual soul communicated to the human composite," Maritain gets trapped by the very sin of angelism that he attributes to Descartes in *Three Reformers.* Secondly, I will show how Aquinas' personalism solves the antinomies that lead Maritain to develop the above-mentioned polarity, in a way that does not, however, threaten the marvelous unity characterizing human nature as such. In fact, although matter and spirit belong to entirely different planes of being,[7] they come together in man to create what Aquinas, in *On Being and Essence,* calls an *essentia quaedam.*[8] From this perspective, man is the entity in whose essence the communion between the world of matter and that of spirit is realized. An effort to introduce even the smallest polarity between the body and the intellective soul would imply a destruction of this communion and therefore a refusal to recognize both the essence of the human being and his purpose in the world.

5. Jacques Maritain, *Distinguish to Unite or The Degrees of Knowledge,* translated by Gerald B. Phelan (Notre Dame, Indiana: University of Notre Dame Press, 2002), 245.

6. Jacques Maritain, *The Person and the Common Good,* translated by John J. Fitzgerald (Notre Dame, Indiana: University of Notre Dame Press, 1972), 41.

7. "Sic igitur substantia intellectualis et corpus, quae seorsum existentia essent diversorum generum species, prout uniuntur, sunt unius generis ut principia." *Summa Contra Gentiles* (SCG) II, chap. 69. The Latin text is from the Leonine edition, vol. 13.

8. See M.-R. Rolland-Gosselin, *Le "De ente et essentia" de S. Thomas d'Aquin* (Le Saulchoir: Revue des sciences philosophiques et théologiques, 1926), 42–44; Cajetan, *Commentary on "Being and essence"* (Milwaukee, Wisconsin: Marquette University Press, 1964), 295–99.

II. Maritain's Theory of Subsistence

As we have seen, Maritain argues that, from a metaphysical point of view, personality must be defined in terms of subsistence. The specific problem then becomes understanding what kind of subsistence defines the person as such in Maritain's thought. In fact, Aquinas and his commentators always distinguish between two degrees of subsistence when addressing the question of the person.[9] Broadly speaking, the notion of subsistence refers to the mode of being (*modus essendi*) according to which something exists *in itself*. Consequently, it is not possible for an accident to fall within the class of realities which subsist, since an accident is, by definition, a reality which exists *in something else* as its property. Hence, the general notion of subsistence excludes the relation of inherence that defines the mode of being of accidents and designates the aptitude of existing in itself: "Subsistence refers to a certain mode of being, namely that of existing in itself, and not in something else, as accidents do."[10] Unlike an accident, a part does not inhere in the suppositum of which it is part, and therefore, not existing in something else as its accidental property, it is said to exist in itself and by itself. This way of being of the substantial part is thus the first degree of subsistence, and it corresponds to what could be called the weak connotation of the perseity concept: "But for a thing to exist in itself, it suffices sometimes that it be not inherent, as an accident or a material form; even though it be part of something."[11]

At a higher level, however, the notion of subsistence excludes not only the relation of inherence, but also that of partiality, in such a way that, strictly speaking, the only one that can be called subsistent is the suppositum, or in other words the individual substance that is complete in its own nature. In this connection Aquinas points out that "This particular thing [hoc aliquid] can be taken in two senses: firstly, for anything subsistent,

9. See St. Thomas Aquinas, *Summa theologiae* (ST) I, q. 75, a. 2, ad 1. See also Cajetan commentary on ST III, q. 2, a. 2; Johannes a Sancto Thoma, *Naturalis Philosophiae* I, q. 7, a. 3, in vol. 2 of *Cursus Philosophicus*, edited by Reiser (Torino: Marietti, 1930–37); Magistri Petri de Bergamo, *Tabula Aurea*, vol. 2 in Doctoris Angelici Divi Thomae Aquinatis, *Opera Omnia*, vol. 34 (Paris: Vivès, 1880), 219–220, *sub nome* "subsistentia."

10. "Subsistere autem dicit determinatum modum essendi, prout scilicet aliquid est ens per se, non in alio, sicut accidens." *Super I Sententiarum*, vol. 1 of *Opera Omnia*, 7 vols., edited by Roberto Busa (Stuttgart-Bad Canstatt: Fromman-Holzboog, 1980), d. 23, q. 1, a. 1; see also SCG I, chap. 25 and Franciscus de Sylvestris Ferrariensis's commentary on this text available in the Leonine edition.

11. ST I, q. 75, a. 2, ad 2.

secondly, for that which subsists, and is complete in a specific nature. The former sense excludes the inherence of an accident or of a material form; the latter excludes also the imperfection of the part."[12]

Both Cajetan and John of St. Thomas retain the theory of degrees of subsistence and develop it very precisely. In his comments regarding a text from the third part of the *Summa*, Cajetan writes that it is necessary to distinguish the notion of existing by itself from the notion of existing separately: "Aquinas used the word 'separately', in order to make the young theologians aware that there is a distinction between the mode of 'existing in itself' and that of 'existing in itself separately.'"[13] Everything that does not inhere in something else exists in itself, and this therefore includes any kind of substance, either complete (the suppositum) or incomplete (a part of the suppositum). But, only the substance that is complete in its own nature can be said to exist separately, which therefore refers exclusively to the suppositum: "no substance which is part of something else can exist in itself separately, given that it does not exist apart from the whole it belongs to."[14] So, for instance, the hand I am writing with, which exists in itself, cannot exist separately from the body of which it is an integral part.

In the same way, John of St. Thomas teaches in numerous texts of the *Cursus Philosophicus* that it is necessary to distinguish between on the one hand the "subsistentia terminativa et hypostatica" that applies only to a suppositum and, on the other hand, the simple property of existing in itself, that as such can apply equally to the parts of the substance, such as the hand or the rational soul.[15] In fact, in the *Cursus Theologicus* the author explains that there are exactly two formal effects of subsistence: the first

12. "Hoc aliquid [that is the individual substance] potest accipi dupliciter, uno modo, pro quocumque subsistente, alio modo, pro subsistente completo in natura alicuius speciei. Primo modo, excludit inhaerentiam accidentis et formae materialis, secundo modo, excludit etiam imperfectionem partis." ST I, q. 75, a. 2, ad 1. This and all other Latin quotations of the *Summa* are from the Leonine edition. See also *Quaestio de anima*, a. 1. The expression "hoc aliquid" is the literal translation of the Greek expression *tode ti* by which Aristotle refers to the individual substance (*prōte ousia, synolon*). Since the individual substance is as such indefinable (see *Metaphysics* 7.10, 1036a1–6), the only way to refer to it is to use an ostensive definition. In fact, *tode ti* means "this thing right here."

13. "Apposuit Auctor ly separatim, ut sciant novitii discernere inter per se existere, et per se separatim existere." ST III, q. 2, a. 2.

14. "Per se separatim existere, nulli substantiae quae est pars ulterius convenit: quia non existit separatim a suo toto." Ibid.

15. See *Cursus Philosophicus* I, q. 7, a. 3. Concerning John of Saint Thomas see John Deely, "Editorial Afterword," in *Tractatus de signis: The Semiotic of John Poinsot*, edited by John Deely (Berkeley: University of California Press, 1985), 394–514.

confers upon an individual in the genus of substance what the author calls the "modus existendi per se," and the second grants this same substantial individual the "modus existendi incommunicabiliter."[16]

Why is it so important to maintain this distinction between the two meanings of the subsistence concept? It is important because, while the second subsistence degree necessarily implies the first, the first degree does not imply the second in any way.[17] There could therefore be a case of a being that, although existing in itself, nonetheless cannot be said to have a separate form of existence. This is due to its incompleteness, the fact that it does not have the *modus existendi incommunicabiliter* discussed by John of St. Thomas. In order to advance from the first degree of subsistence to the second one, what exists in itself must achieve the completeness required by its own essence. That is to say, it must be integrated with the whole to which it belongs by its very nature. At this point it must be noted that this is precisely the case of the rational soul.[18] The rational soul possesses existence in itself, but it only achieves the second degree of subsistence when it becomes incorporated into a matter that is properly set out to receive it. Rather than communicating its own subsistence to the human composite, the intellective soul only receives its full subsistence from within this sublime composite. This is why Aquinas, when referring to the strong meaning of perseity, describes the human soul as a "quasi subsistens": "Therefore, as the human soul is a part of human nature, it can indeed be called 'this particular thing,' in the first sense, as being almost subsistent [quasi subsistens]; but not in the second, for in this sense, what is composite of body and soul is said to be 'this particular thing.'"[19] In fact, according to Aquinas' conceptual lexicon "that is rightly said to subsist 'per se,' which is neither inherent in the above sense, nor part of anything else. In this sense, the eye or the hand cannot be said to subsist 'per se.'"[20]

At this point it must be noted that the theory of subsistence degrees

16. Johannes a Sancto Thoma, *Cursus Theologicus*, vol. 4 (Paris: Desclée, 1931–64), q. 32, disp. 34, a. 1, n. 22.

17. Ibid.

18. See *Cursus Philosophicus*, t. II: *Nat. Phil.*, I, q. 7, a. 3.

19. ST I, q. 75, a. 2, ad. 1. Concerning the meaning Aquinas ascribes to the Latin adverb "quasi," see M.-D. Chenu, *Introduction a l'étude de Saint Thomas d'Aquin* (Paris: Vrin, 1954), 102: "Un *quasi* permet de ne pas perdre le bénéfice d'un rapprochement abstraitement inexact."

20. "Proprie et per se subsistens dicitur quod neque est predicto modo inhaerens, neque est pars. Secundum quem modum oculus aut manus non posset dici per se subsistens." ST I, q. 75, a. 2, ad 2.

plays a fundamental role in Thomistic personalism.[21] As a matter of fact, it is only through the recognition of weak and strong meanings of the subsistence concept that it is possible to affirm the perseity of the rational soul without simultaneously falling into a form of semi-dualism. The human soul does exist in itself in the sense that it does not inhere in the body it animates; nonetheless, however, it needs to unite with the body in order to achieve the ontological perfection that is the only route to gaining the second degree of subsistence. That is why Aquinas, in *Commentum in libros Sententiarum,* writes that "man is a person not only because of the soul, but because of the soul and the body, since these are the causes of his subsistence."[22]

Nowhere in Maritain's work can there be found a distinction between degrees of perseity[23]. This means that the author's personalism, based as it is on a theory of subsistence that conflates the weak and strong meanings of perseity, gives rise to a form of semi-dualism. As a matter of fact, there is an argument that appears in all of Maritain's writings about the person, an argument that curiously enough survived the process of revision that drove the author to write a second version of the IV appendix to *Les degrés du savoir.* This argument holds that "the body subsists with the subsistence of the soul"[24] or, in a slightly different formulation, "Personality is the subsistence of the spiritual soul communicated to the human composite." [25] Now, if the body subsists with the subsistence of the soul, then, in accordance with the principal that one does not give that which one does not have, the rational soul possesses by itself what John of Saint Thomas calls *subsistentia terminativa seu hypostatica.* However, this argument clearly implies that the rational soul is a suppositum even before being united with the body that it is destined to animate. In both the first and second editions of the fourth appendix of *The Degrees of Knowledge,* Maritain himself does in fact argue that the formal effect of subsistence is that of transforming the substantial

21. See Norman Kretzman, "Philosophy of Mind," in *The Cambridge Companion to Aquinas,* edited by Norman Kretzmann and Eleonore Stump (New York: Cambridge University Press, 2009), 133–36; Robert Pasnau, *Thomas Aquinas on Human Nature: A Philosophical Study of "Summa theologiae" I, qq. 75–89* (Cambridge: Cambridge University Press, 2002), 48–57.

22. "Non tantum ab anima habet homo quod sit persona, sed ex ea et corpore; cum ex utrisque subsistat." *Super III Sententiarum,* disp. 5, q. 3, a. 2, ad 2. The Latin text is from the Busa edition.

23. Cf. Mirella Lorenzini, "Sussistenza e razionalità nell'antropologia di J. Maritain," in *Divus Thomas* 1 (1992): 164–86.

24. Maritain, *The Degrees of Knowledge,* 457.

25. Maritain, *The Person,* 41.

essence into a *principium quod,* that is to say, into a suppositum: "to exercise the existence the essence must be completed by subsistence and thus become a supposit."[26] So, if the rational soul is a suppositum because the soul itself enjoys the second degree of subsistence, it is clear that the soul's union with the body is necessarily accidental. Hence, it is not possible to maintain at one and the same time that the person is "composé d'âme et de corps" and that it subsists "de la subsistance de l'âme,"[27] unless the composition postulated has a purely accidental character.

I would also point out that Maritain's subsistence theory, failing as it does to take into account the degrees of perseity, falls not only into a semi-dualistic conception of human nature but also into nonsense. In fact, if the rational soul itself is complete *in ratione substantialitatis,* then it is clear that the rational soul enjoys the *subsistentia terminativa seu hypostatica.* In that case, it would be nonsense to argue that the rational soul communicates its own perseity to the human compound. As Maritain himself acknowledges, the formal effect of the second subsistence degree is precisely that of impeding such communication.

The semi-dualistic logic implicit in Maritain's subsistence theory clearly manifests itself in the negative evaluation that the author assigns to corporeity. In *The Degrees of Knowledge,* he argues that the life of the body is so alien to the spiritual sphere of the person that it effectively represents a contamination for the person: "Personality . . . suffers many checks in the psychological and moral register. There it runs the risk of contamination by the miseries of material individuality."[28] Likewise, in *De Bergson à Thomas d'Aquin* Maritain, on the one hand, recognizes the role of the body in the ontological genesis of the human person but, on the other, argues that corporeity imposes upon ontological personality what he calls a "diminution."[29] In *The Rights of Man and Natural Law,* Maritain, considering instincts and passions, ends up acknowledging that there is a dimension in man that is not properly human, but rather animal: "I should like to point out once again that if a sound political conception depends above all on concentrating on

26. Maritain, *The Degrees of Knowledge,* 461.

27. Maritain, *La philosphie morale. Examen historique et critique des grands systèmes,* vol. 11 of Jacques et Raïssa Maritain, *Oeuvre Complètes,* edited by Jean-Marie Allion, Maurice Hany, et al. (Fribourg Suisse-Paris: Éditions Universitaires-Éditions Saint Paul, 1991), 495.

28. Maritain, *The Degrees of Knowledge,* 247.

29. Maritain, *De Bergson à Thomas d'Aquin,* vol. 8 of Jacques et Raïssa Maritain, *Œuvre Complètes* (Fribourg Suisse: Éditions Universitaires; Paris: Éditions Saint Paul, 1989), 104.

the human person, it must at the same time bear in mind the fact that this person is an animal gifted with reason, and that the part of animality in such a set-up is immense."[30] The concept of "animal gifted with reason" (*animal doué de raison*) or, more precisely, the way this notion is used, leads one to think that rationality befalls human nature in a kind of accident, as if it were something that one *has* and not something that one *is*. However, the concept of rational animal used to designate the human way of being indicates something quite different. Seeing as the intellective soul is the *principium essendi* of human beings, it is not added to a preexisting form in order to confer on man yet another competence. Owing to its perfection, the intellective soul absorbs within itself all the functions that humans share with the animal and vegetable worlds, generating these functions by itself.[31] Man's sensitivity, since it is transfigured by the intellective soul from which it flows and toward which it is oriented, cannot therefore be compared to the sensitivity of animals.[32] When human beings engage in nourishing or reproduction, these activities are imbued with truly intelligible values, subject as they are to the attraction of intelligent life. The same is true in relation to passions: when entering into the human domain, rage and lust become obedient to reason.[33] Although they in themselves lack *logos,* they nonetheless become fit to hear its voice and follow its lead.[34] However, this does not mean that the rational soul exerts a despotic form of dominion over man's passions. Rather, since the passions have sense as their guide, and sense has the human suppositum as its subject, they in themselves follow that which appeals or repels sense.[35] The fact that the passions do present a certain resistance to the political domain of reason does not imply, however, that they are in themselves deaf to the voice of intelligence. On the contrary, it must be said that human passions remain deeply obedient to this voice even when they happen to choke it off. Now, this fact is sufficient to radically distinguish human passions from the passions to which animals are subject. From an on-

30. Maritain, *The Rights of Men and Natural Law,* translated by Doris C. Anson (New York: Charles Scribner's Sons, 1943), 55.

31. See ST I, q. 76, a. 3.

32. "Omnes potentiae animae, sive subiectum earum sit anima sola, sive compositum, fluunt ab essentia animae sicut a principio." ST I, q. 77, a. 6. "Sensus est propter intellectum, et non e converso. Sensus etiam est quaedam deficiens partecipatio intellectus: unde secundum naturalem originem quodammodo est ab intellectu, sicut imperfectum a perfecto." ST I, q. 77, a. 7.

33. See St. Thomas Aquinas, *De Veritate,* q. 25, a. 4; ST I, q. 81, a. 3.

34. See Aristotle, *Nicomachean Ethics* 1.6, 1098a3–5.

35. See ST I, q. 81, a. 3.

tological point of view, therefore, there is no opposition between rationality and animality in human nature, and this is due to the fact that no exclusively animal component exists within humans.

However, it would seem that Maritain received his inspiration for developing the subsistence theory restricted to the human person from the passage of *Cursus Theologicus* where John of St. Thomas examines the example of the rational soul as elaborated by philosophers who, like Suarez, argue that the subsistence of the material suppositum is the result of the partial subsistence of its two component parts.[36] In order to demonstrate that the perseity of the soul in a state of separation is not partial even though it is imperfect, John of St. Thomas joins Maritain in arguing that the subsistence of the person is already provided entirely within the soul itself. He therefore writes that "the same subsistence which is in man is in the soul."[37] Yet, in contrast with Maritain, John of St. Thomas is quick to clarify that, even if all of man's subsistence is provided by his intellective soul, it is still not completely expressed within the soul until the soul joins with the body it was destined to animate:

> Yet, if we do not admit in the body a partial subsistence, and yet the soul nevertheless subsists separately, it is necessary to say that the entire subsistence of man is given in the soul. However, it is not completely expressed until the soul joins with the body: the soul subsists perfectly in the composite, as here it cannot be joined and referred to something else.[38]

The participation of the body is necessary to the genesis of the person in this version of the theory of perseity degrees as well. This is clear from the fact that, according to this theory, the separate soul cannot be considered a person even though it has all the subsistence of the human composite. This is precisely because it does not have a completely expressed subsistence: "Thus, the separated soul is not a person, as it does not possess a perfect subsistence."[39]

36. See *Cursus Theologicus*, vol. 1, q. 3, disp. 4, a. 2, n. 18.

37. "Eadem tamen subsistentia quae est in homine, est in anima." Ibid.

38. "Si vero in corpore non admittimus partialem subsistentiam, et tamen anima subsistit separata, necessario dicendum est totam subsistentiam hominis dari in anima : sed non totaliter explicari in anima, sed in communicatione ejus ad corpu : ibique subsistere incommunicabiliter, quatenus non est amplius explicabilis et communicabilis in aliud." Ibid.

39. "Ideoque anima separata non est persona, quia non est ibi subsistentia modo incommunicabili." Ibid. It is interesting to note that, in the corresponding passage in *Cursus Philosophicus* (*Phil. Nat.* I, q. 7, a. 3), John of St. Thomas follows a line of reasoning that is diametrically opposed

No matter what point of view we use to examine Maritain's subsistence theory, it is clear that his theory leaves out all those distinctions that the Thomistic school considered indispensable to effectively describe that borderline entity that is the rational soul. This simplification nonetheless gives rise to a theoretical model in which the person, rather than being the boundary between the immaterial and corporeal worlds, appears to be a kind of angelic entity condemned to dealing with matter. From this point of view, the polarity between individual and person is none other than the conceptual expression of the division in human nature brought about by a subsistence theory based on a semi-dualistic logic. According to Maritain, corporeity is in fact so foreign to the essence of person that they become polar opposites.[40] For Aquinas, however, there is no such thing as person until the rational soul brings the light of intelligence into matter properly set out to receive it.[41] Viewed in the light of subsistence theory, the individual-person polarity cannot be considered, as suggested by Jacques Croteau and others in terms of a pair of concepts that have the function to capture fundamentally different aspects of the same human reality.[42] The individual-person polarity, on the contrary, is the necessary outcome of a subsistence theory that, failing to take into account the degrees of perseity, inevitably falls into semi-dualism.

Moreover, it must be noted that, even from a logical point of view, the individual-person polarity does not function. In fact, the notion of individual is a concept of second degree (*secunda intentio*), and as such it refers to a property of a concept of first degree (*prima intentio*).[43] Hence, the notion

to that developed in *Theologicus* in order to prove the same thesis. In fact, the author notes there that the intellective soul's subsistence cannot be partial because the intellective soul is completely excluded from the second degree of perseity: "Quare anima humana non habet subsistentiam, quae compleat et constituat suppositum, etiam quando est separata, quia adhuc est communicabilis et unibilis." This much more concise and clear line of reasoning proves that there is no need to postulate that the soul should possess the same level of subsistence as a composite, although not fully realized. The same thing applies to the author's argument in *Phil. Nat.*, IV, q. 9, a. 2, ad 1.

40. "[T]he human being is caught between two poles; a material pole, which, in reality, does not concern the true person but rather the shadow of personality or what, in the strict sense, is called *individuality*, and a spiritual pole, which does concern *true personality*." Maritain, *Person and Common Good*, 33; emphasis in original. See also Maritain, *Scholasticism and Politics*, 63.

41. *Super III Sententiarum*, d. 5, q. 3, a. 2, ad 2.

42. See Jacques Croteau, *Les fondements thomistes du personnalisme de Maritain* (Ottawa: Editions de l'Université d'Ottawa, 1955), 55; Vittorio Possenti, *Una filosofia per la transizione. Metafisica, persona e politica in J. Maritain* (Milano: Editrice Massimo, 1984), 87.

43. "Sed individuum dupliciter potest significari: vel per nomen secundae intentionis, sicut

of individual is a logical concept like that of genus, species, and so on. In contrast, the *nomen personae* is a metaphysical concept, and as such it refers to a certain kind of reality, namely a complete substance which possesses a rational nature (*rationalis naturae individua substantia*).[44]

Considering the problems to which the individual-person polarity gives rise, it is easy to understand why so many Thomists have strongly criticized it.[45]

III. From the Metaphysics to the Theology of the Human Person

Having established the subtle but crucial distinction between Maritainian and Thomistic anthropology, it must be shown that the tensions implicit in the metaphysical concept of the person can be overcome only on the condition of admitting the postulate of divine providence.[46]

Although the individual-person polarity implies a much less sophisticated subsistence theory than the one developed by Aquinas, Cajetan and John of St. Thomas, and although this polarity falls into an objectionable semi-dualism, it is nonetheless necessary to recognize that the problem that led Maritain to introduce this polarity is in fact real, and cannot in any way be circumvented by a philosopher who means to use the concept of

---

hoc nomen individuum vel singulare, quod non significat rem singularem, sed intentionem singularitatis; vel per nomen primae intentionis, quod significat rem, cui convenit intentio particularitatis; et ita significatur hoc nomine persona; significat enim rem ipsam, cui accedit intentio individui." *Super I Sententiarum*, d. 23, q. 1, a. 1.

44. "Il faut bien comprendre tout d'abord que ces deux termes, et les notions qu'ils expriment, ne se trouvent pas sur le même plan de pensée. 'Individu' désigne un concept logique … 'Personne' au contraire signifie un concept métaphysique." *Le "De ente et essentia" de S. Thomas d'Aquin*, edited by M.-D. Rolland-Gossellin (Paris: Vrin, 1948), 124.

45. See Pedro Descoqs, "Individu et personne," in *Archives de philosophie* 24, no. 2 (1938): 18–30; Étienne Gilson, *L'esprit de la philosophie médiévale* (Paris: Vrin, 1944), 203–205; Julio Meinvielle, *Critica de la concepción de Maritain sobre la persona humana* (Buenos Aires: Ediciones Nuestro Tempo, 1948), 26–35; Cornelio Fabro, *L'anima. Introduzione al problema dell'uomo* (Rome: Editrice Studium, 1955), 182–83; Ugo Degl'Innocenti, "Individuo e persona," *Aquinas* 3 (1959): 390–93; Joseph de Finance, *L'ontologia della persona e della libertà in Maritain*, in *J. Maritain oggi*, edited by Vittorio Possenti (Milan: Vita e Pensiero, 1983), 156–73; M.-D. Philippe, *Les trois sagesses* (Les Sables d'Olonne [Vandée]: Éditions du Jubilé, 2008), 206–207.

46. See Federico Tedesco, "Da Maritain a Tommaso d'Aquino o dalla metafisica alla teologia della persona," in *Il peso e la leva*, edited by Luca. S. Maugeri (Bologna: Pardes, 2013), 35–71; "De Maritain à Thomas d'Aquin ou de la métaphysique à la theologie de la personne humain," in *L'action*, edited by J. Ferrari, R. Formisano, M. Malaguti (Paris: Vrin, 2013), 469-72.

person in a meaningful way. The notion of person based on the metaphysics of substance seems, in fact, to hide at least two antinomies. The first antinomy may be formulated as follows:

a. Thesis: The notion of person designates a whole that cannot be reduced to the physical universe as a part.

b. Antithesis: The notion of person designates a reality that constitutes a part of the physical universe.

The second antinomy can instead be expressed as follows:

c. Thesis: The notion of person designates an entity that engages in self-determination following a sovereign act of intelligence.

d. Antithesis: The notion of person designates an entity that is subject to determination by the physical universe.

The notion of person implies the idea of a whole (a), because it refers to an individual who engages in self-determination beginning from a sovereign act of intelligence (c): "in a more special and perfect way, the particular and the individual are found in the rational substances which have dominion over their own actions; and which are not only made to act, like others; but which can act of themselves [per se agunt]."[47] In other words, the human person is a totality insofar as it is an individual whose rational nature allows him to enjoy autonomy, in the sense that it is the human person himself to decide his own ends.[48] This is the reason why Aquinas attributes a *triplex incommunicabilitas* to the person as such.[49] Likewise, John of St. Thomas intends to express the same idea when in the *Cursus Theologicus* qualifies the person as completely "incommunicabilis."[50]

On the other hand, however, the concept of person implies the notion of a completeness that man cannot achieve in any way without the body.

47. ST I, q. 29, a. 1.

48. "The free act of the human person, considered in its pure and secret intimacy as a free act, is not of this world. By its liberty, the human person transcends the stars and all the world of nature." Maritain, *The Person*, 20; see also Maritain, *Neuf leçons sur les notions premières de la philosophie morale*, vol. 9 in Jacques et Raïssa Maritain, *Œuvre Complètes* (Fribourg Suisse: Éditions Universitaires—Paris: Éditions Saint Paul, 1990), 805.

49. See *Super III Sententiarum*, d. 5, q. 2, a. 1, ad 2.

50. *Cursus Theologicus*, vol. 1, q. 3, disp. 4, a. 2. "The free act of the human person, considered in its pure and secret intimacy as a free act, is not of this world. By its liberty, the human person transcends the stars and all the world of nature." Maritain, *The Person*, 20. See also Maritain, *Neuf leçons*, 805

Now, since his body makes man a part of the physical universe (b), that is to say a slave to what we could call the determinism of matter, it also seems to destroy the liberty (*incommunicabilitas*) produced by the exercise of his intelligence (d): "each of us is a fragment of a species, a part of the universe [b], a unique point in the immense web of cosmic, ethnical, historical forces and influences—and bound by their laws. Each of us is subject to the determinism of the physical world [d]."[51]

Thus we see very clearly why Maritain sought to develop the notion of person in such as a way as to erase the body's contribution as much as possible. For the Thomisitic school, man should in fact be simultaneously an irreducible totality endowed with autonomy, and a functional part bound by the determinism of the physical universe. In this regard, it is interesting to note that Aquinas, on the one hand, writes that the notion of part is incompatible with the concept of person: "ratio partis contrariatur personae"[52]; on the other hand, he employs the notion of part as the fundamental concept of the argument with which he proves that the Angels (and men) love God more than themselves *naturali dilectione*.[53] How can these antinomies be resolved without resorting to the individual-person polarity?

In order to understand the depth of the problem we must take a closer look at the paradoxes generated by the metaphysical notion of person. It is said that the capacity to engage in self-determination beginning from an act of sovereign intelligence belongs to the essence of a person. In fact, the person must be defined in terms of self-possession and self-mastery, in so far as the person, thanks to his intellect, holds himself in his own hands.[54] And yet, man does not himself decide the time and place of his birth, nor does he decide to which genealogical line he will belong. Nonetheless, these factors are extremely important in determining the life of a human being, imposing insurmountable limits on his liberty. For instance, being born an Athenian citizen in the fifth century BC or a Jew in 1940s Germany obviously determines an entirely different set of opportunities for develop-

51. Maritain, *The Person*, 38; "Mais encore la personne humaine est engagée dans toutes les misères et les fatalités de la nature matérielle, des servitudes et des besoins du corps, de l'hérédité, de l'ignorance, de l'égoïsme et de la sauvagerie des instincts." Maritain, *De Bergson à Thomas d'Aquin*, 84.

52. Cf. *Super III Sententiarum*, d. 5, q. 3, a. 2.

53. Cf. ST I, q. 60, a. 5. However, Aquinas was completely aware of the ambivalent role played by the body in the ontological completion of the human person; see ST Suppl. III, q. 93, a. 1.

54. See Maritain, *Person and Common Good*, 40.

ment. Likewise, being born in a certain neighborhood rather than another or being educated in a certain family rather than another, fundamentally affects a person's freedom and imposes limits that are very difficult to overcome.

And yet, while the fact that man cannot choose the incorporation of his soul—the fact that he cannot decide which world sequence in which to exist—does indeed involve a radical limit on the individual's ability to engage in self-determination, it does not, however, involve the suppression of his liberty. Although man is thrown into a world sequence not of his choosing and incorporated into living matter with specific genetic predispositions, nonetheless he is still able to decide (within the realm of these insurmountable limits) where to go and who to be.

However, it must be recognized that, even within the world sequence to which man is subject, he cannot exercise his own liberty properly. In fact, self-determination should not be understood as the ability to become anything, but rather (as Maritain reminds us), as the freedom to become exactly what one is as an individual.[55] It is, however, clear that in order to realize one's individual nature, it is necessary to understand that nature and its potential for development. The problem is that the radical knowledge of the self is precisely one of those things that lies beyond the range of human intelligence.[56] As Maritain notes in a wonderful page from *Existence and the Existent*, my subjectivity as such is unknown not only to others but also to myself. But, if it is impossible to achieve radical self-understanding, then self-determination, strictly speaking, does not exist either. Yet if there is no such thing as self-determination in the sense of the freedom to become who we are, then neither is there such a thing as the person.

Why is radical self-understanding denied to man? Because man cannot properly grasp the causes that his individuality depends on. And what are these causes? Aquinas always denied that matter could be the proper cause of the individuation of the rational soul.[57] Due to the *remota causa removetur effectus* principle, in fact, the soul in this case would lose its own individuality once separated from its body. In an important text from the second book of *Summa Contra Gentiles*, Aquinas relates the principle of

55. Ibid., 44.

56. Maritain, *The Degrees of Knowledge*, 469–72.

57. See *Super I Sententiarum*, d. 8, q. 5, a. 2, ad 6; *De ente et essentia*, 4; SCG II, chap. 75; ST I, q. 76, a. 2, ad 2; *Quaestio de anima*, a. 1, ad 2.

individuation with the cause of being, and explains that, if the existence of a form depends on matter, then its individuation depends on matter as well; if on the contrary the existence of a form does not depend on matter, then its individuation does not exactly depend on matter, even if it is produced at the same time as the multiplication of matter: "if the being of the form depends on matter, its multiplication, as well as its unity, depends on matter. But if this is not the case, then the form will have to be multiplied in accordance with the multiplication of the matter, that is to say, together with the matter and in proportion to it; yet not in such a manner that the unity or multiplicity of the form itself depends upon the matter. It has been shown, however, that the human soul is a form not depending in its being on matter. It therefore follows that souls are multiplied in accordance with the multiplication of bodies, yet the latter will not be the cause of the multiplication of souls."[58]

It could be said therefore that the rational soul as a *quasi-subsistens* form receives its individuality *in* matter but not *by* matter. In fact, it ultimately depends on the cause of the rational soul's incorporation, and therefore on God.[59] It is in fact God who decides in which matter to incorporate a soul, simultaneously deciding in which world sequence this soul will end up opening the eyes of its intelligence.

The role of God in the individuation of the rational soul has been, as far as I know, nearly completely neglected by philosophers. And yet the antinomies generated by the notion of person can be overcome only by acknowledging the role of God in the individuation of the rational soul. If God is in fact the cause of the soul's incorporation, then the fact that an individual belongs to a certain world sequence and genealogical lineage is completely determined by a providential or teleological principle. To admit that earthly matters are ruled by a providential principle would involve arguing that everything that happens to man is included within the eternal design that God uses to guide man towards his final end. From this perspective, all the violations that man continually suffers as a result of his

58. SCG II, chap. 81; see also St. Thomas Aquinas, *De unitate intellectus*, chap. 5.

59. "Ad secundum dicendum quod unumquodque secundum idem habet esse et individuationem. Universalia enim non habent esse in rerum natura ut universalia sunt, sed solum secundum quod sunt individuata. Sicut igitur esse animae est a Deo sicut a principio activo, et in corpore sicut in materia, nec tamen esse animae perit pereunte corpore; ita et individuatio animae, etsi aliquam relationem habeat ad corpus, non tamen perit corpore pereunte. " *Quaestio de anima*, a. 1, ad 2.

being subject to the physical universe appear themselves to be subject to God's prudence. The necessities of nature, the fatalities of matter, the very randomness that rules the majority of human matters, no longer seem to imply the negation of the person, but rather appear to be the steps of the exodus through which God guides man from the radical misunderstanding of himself to the knowledge of his reason of being within a specific world sequence.[60] By introducing man in the secret of his own individuality, God gives man the liberty to become exactly who he is, and thus God confers on man that unique autonomy that distinguishes a person as such from an ontological point of view. Divine providence is, therefore, the ultimate necessary condition for man's liberty rather than that which prevents him from exercising it.

An analysis of the antinomies implicit in the metaphysical notion of person shows that the possibility of using this notion in a way that makes sense depends on first admitting the postulate of divine providence. In short, this means that there are persons only if God exists.

60. Concerning the notion of the exodus of reason, see Federico Tedesco, "The Paradoxes of Evil as the *Rationis Exodus in Deum*," in *Aquinas and Maritain on Evil*, edited by James G. Hanink (Washington, D.C.: American Maritain Association Press, 2013), 3–12.

II

FREEDOM, MORALITY, AND CIVIL SOCIETY

TERRY HALL

Dirty Hands in Politics?

Maritain's Answer to Machiavelli

My purpose in this essay is to make clear Jacques Maritain's assessment of Machiavelli's central argument in *The Prince.*[1] In a sea of scholarship on the Florentine's great work, Maritain's essay stands out in its ability to get right to the heart of the challenge posed by this remarkably brief yet remarkably forceful—one might even say, aggressive—book.[2] Succinctly put, Maritain's most telling response to Machiavelli's claim to present the "effectual truth" (*verita effettuale*) of political rule is to distinguish between the ethical horizon of understanding and the political horizon of understanding. What is perhaps most fruitful about Maritain's critique of Machiavelli is his insistence on the insufficiency of criticizing Machiavelli only from within the first horizon, the ethical. The ethical criticism is telling as far as it goes, but it does not, Maritain thinks, go far enough. At the deepest level, Machiavelli's teaching is a political teaching. The most fundamental engagement with the Florentine philosopher must therefore occur within the larger horizon of political, in contrast to moral, philosophy. In order to bring out this contrast we must turn first to the moral evaluation of Machi-

1. All quotations from *The Prince* are from the translation by Harvey C. Mansfield, 2nd ed., (Chicago and London: University of Chicago Press, 1998). For an accessible Italian text, see Mark Musa's bilingual edition of *The Prince* (New York: St. Martin's Press, 1964).

2. Nietzsche picks up on the brisk intensity and forcefulness of *The Prince* when he comments on its tempo: "[Machiavelli] cannot help presenting the most serious matters in a boisterous *allegrissimo* ... long, difficult, hard, dangerous thoughts and the *tempo* of the gallop and the very best, most capricious humor." See Friedrich Nietzsche, *Beyond Good and Evil: Prelude to a Philosophy of the Future,* translated by Walter Kaufmann (New York: Vintage Books, 1966), §28, pp. 40–41.

avelli's argument in *The Prince*. Prior to doing so, however, we must sketch the main lines of his teaching.

I. Machiavelli's Teaching

In a well-known formulation, Leo Strauss once remarked on Machiavelli's established reputation as a teacher of evil.[3] To understand how he acquired this reputation is not difficult. In the famous chapter fifteen of *The Prince*, Machiavelli says bluntly that if a prince wants to preserve his power and his rule he must "learn to be able not to be good, and to use this and not use it according to necessity." A prince who fails to use the not-good when doing so seems the only means of preserving his rule will, Machiavelli says, "learn[s] his ruin rather than his preservation."[4] To be sure, Machiavelli teaches that sometimes the political situation dictates not using conduct that is not good, or that on some occasions a ruler must exercise virtue, or more precisely, the appearance of virtue. Machiavelli teaches that evil is sometimes politically necessary while at other times good is politically necessary. "Necessity" here means "political necessity," viz., that which in the particular circumstances must be done in order to preserve one's rule. In other words, a prince must be prepared to employ what the tradition has called virtue as well as what the tradition has called vice, depending on the situation at hand. The human condition (*le condizione umane*), Machiavelli says, does not permit a ruler to be virtuous all the time, and when it does not, vice or evil is not just permissible but necessary. Machiavelli teaches that the pre-modern understanding of virtue as a *habitus*, a settled disposition of one's character, must be abandoned. The reason is that habituation to virtue in its pre-Machiavellian sense would constrain the freedom of action Machiavelli espouses.

But Machiavelli goes even further and reverses the meaning of these terms, virtue and vice, as the tradition has understood them. The last sentence of chapter fifteen says:

> And furthermore one should not care about incurring the fame of those vices without which it is difficult to save one's state [*lo stato*]; for if one considers everything well, one will find something that appears to be virtue, which if pursued would be one's ruin, and something else appears to be vice, which if pursued results in one's security and well-being.[5]

3. Leo Strauss, *Thoughts on Machiavelli* (Glencoe, Illinois: Free Press, 1958), 9.

4. *The Prince*, 61.

5. Ibid., 62. In a footnote on this same page, Mansfield notes that some manuscripts have

Thus prior to Machiavelli, honesty and mercy are simply or absolutely virtuous and good, dishonesty and cruelty (murder, for example) simply or absolutely vicious and evil. According to Machiavelli, such virtues are not actually virtues—that is, they are not absolute, unconditional virtues—because they sometimes produce political ruin; and such vices are not actually vices—likewise, are not always vices—because they sometimes preserve political power. Vice that is politically necessary falsely appears, to the naive, as vice, when it is actually virtue. Likewise, virtue that is detrimental to political necessity falsely appears, again to the naive, as virtue. What Machiavelli teaches, then, is a revaluation of values: Machiavellian *virtù* is, in Leo Strauss' crisp formulation, a combination of traditional virtues and traditional vices, the precise mix of which depends on political expediency.[6] Thus Machiavelli does not caution the prince against cruelty per se, only against cruelty badly used; cruelty well used he recommends. This distinction and the recommendation which follows on it he makes on the condition that it is permissible (or "licit") to speak well (or good) of evil (*se del male é licito dire bene*)—which permission Machiavelli immediately grants himself when he goes on to say that cruelty well used, or good cruelty or good evil, is that which is done at once, quickly, and then not persisted in. Bad cruelty or bad evil, is stupid cruelty insofar as it is persisted in after its political usefulness has passed. Machiavelli hopes that his politically ambitious readers will be ruled by these new modes and orders in place of the old modes and orders of traditional morality. In this way Machiavelli can be said to be a teacher of evil.

Machiavelli rests his teaching of evil on its prospects for success. Learn how not to be good, he says, and you will achieve success in ruling; you will hold onto and expand your power. Because men are not good, absolute moral rectitude in a ruler is a recipe for failure in ruling. "[I]f all men were good," the Florentine maintains, "this teaching would not be good; but because they are wicked and do not observe faith with you, you also do not have to observe it with them."[7] In a world of avaricious, evil-will-

"infamy" instead of "fame." Thus Mark Musa in his bilingual edition follows the former texts and prints *infamia* for the Italian and "infamy" for the English. See Musa's edition at 128–129. Machiavelli's point is not, I think, altered depending on the translation, for what he is concerned with is how the action appears to others who—mistakenly—follow the older teaching about virtue and vice, good and evil. Machiavelli intends not to save but to overcome this appearance.

6. "The judicious alteration of virtue and vice is virtue (*virtù*) in his meaning of the word." Leo Strauss, "Machiavelli," in *History of Political Philosophy*, 3rd ed., edited by Leo Strauss and Joseph Cropsey (Chicago: The University of Chicago Press, 1987), 301.

7. *The Prince*, 69.

ing men, political success comes only to those who are prepared to overcome evil with evil. Machiavelli praises the Carthaginian general Hannibal for his "inhuman cruelty" (*le mirabili azioni di Annibale … sua inumana crudeltà*),[8] which Machiavelli identifies as the primary cause of Hannibal's success. The most trenchant reply to those who would blame Machiavelli as a teacher of the necessity of evil in politics is, "It works, does it not?"

II. Maritain's Moral Response to Machiavelli

Maritain's critical evaluation of Machiavelli is aimed, not just at Machiavelli, but more widely at Machiavellianism. Machiavellianism identifies those Machiavelli has inspired and so brings into focus the issue of the Florentine's influence beyond the scope and time of fifteenth-century Italian politics. Perhaps Machiavelli is not quite so radical or intemperate or unrestrained as those who later have acted under the influence of his teaching. But Machiavelli has supplied the justification and rationale for a style of political conduct that refuses to eschew the notion of necessity and expedience he defended and thus refuses to admit any moral limitations on what a ruler may do to preserve the state he rules and to expand his power. Perhaps Machiavelli would have withheld praise of, for example, Hitler or Stalin, as he did of the Sicilian tyrant Agathocles on grounds of the latter's "savage cruelty and inhumanity [and] his infinite crimes" (*sua efferata crudeltà e inumanità, con infinite scelleratezze*).[9] The fact remains that, as Maritain notes, Hitler read Machiavelli avidly and learned from him a vital political lesson: "The reading of these unequalled pages, [Hitler] said, was like a cleansing of the mind. It had disencumbered him from plenty of false ideas and prejudices. It is only after reading *The Prince* that Hitler understood what politics truly is."[10]

8. Ibid., 67.

9. Ibid., 35. It is well to note that the discussion of Agathocles occurs in the chapter dealing with rulers who attained their principality "*per scelera*": through crimes, by which Machiavelli seems to mean especially heinous immorality. We should also note that Machiavelli withholds unqualified praise from Agathocles on the same grounds and in the very same terms that he later accords unqualified praise to Hannibal, namely for his inhuman cruelty. And yet: after appearing to say that Agathocles went too far in his cruelty, a few paragraphs later he holds up the Sicilian tyrant as a model of a man who used cruelty well and achieved success because of it. See *The Prince*, 37–38.

10. Jacques Maritain, "The End of Machiavellianism," in *The Range of Reason* (New York: Charles Scribner's Sons, 1952), 144. Maritain is here quoting from Hermann Rausching's book,

Hitler, Stalin, Mussolini, Mao, Pol Pot, Kim Il Jong: these are examples of what Maritain calls absolute Machiavellianism, in contrast to what he terms conservative or moderate Machiavellianism. The latter is content to use injustice within certain limits, "reasonable limits," let us say.[11] It is akin to Machiavelli's "cruelty well used" principle, since it is willing to confine injustice within at least some limits. Absolute or unrestrained Machiavellianism accepts no limits to the kind and range of political actions but is committed to "*boundless* injustice, *boundless* violence, *boundless* lying and immorality [as] normal political means, and which draws from this boundlessness of evil an abominable strength." Absolute or total Machiavellianism, Maritain concludes, "causes politics to be the art of bringing about the misfortune of men."[12] Otherwise morally scrupulous men when caught in extreme situations—what Machiavelli calls "necessity"—can succumb to limited Machiavellianism fortified by the belief that they can revert to moral behavior when the crisis has passed. Absolute Machiavellians have no need of appeals to necessity as a reason to cross moral boundaries. For them putatively normal situations are extreme situations. They have learned how not to be good permanently. Such learning is part of their character. They have habituated themselves to evil. With such men, no appeal to morality can find a purchase.

What are the grounds for the appeal to morality as a check against conservative Machiavellianism? There are at least three. First, there is the foundational moral principle itself that good must always be done and pursued and evil must always be avoided.[13] Adherence to this principle rules out recourse to conservative Machiavellianism. Second, one can point out that adherence to moral principle perfects the human person while rejection of it impairs the person.[14] Taken together both constitute what Maritain calls "the moral conscience."

Hitler M'a Dit, published in 1940. Lest one try to take refuge in the conviction that men such as Hitler or Stalin were mere aberrations of Machiavelli, one would do well to reflect on Leo Strauss's comment about "how easy it is, after a few centuries of Machiavellianization of Western thought, to give Machiavelli's teaching an air of perfect respectability." See Leo Strauss, *What is Political Philosophy?* (Chicago: The University of Chicago Press, 1988), 43.

11. Ibid., 143.

12. Ibid., 145; emphasis in original.

13. I give the principle in the form that Aquinas uses as the first precept of the natural law. "Hoc est ergo prium praeceptum legis, quod bonum est faciendum et prosequendum, et malum vitandum." *Summa theologiae* I-II, q. 94, a. 2.

14. "Society, properly speaking—human society—is a society of persons. In so far as a city

> Confronted with *any* temptation of Machiavellianism, that is, of gaining success and power by means of evil, moral conscience answers and cannot keep from answering, just as when it is tempted by any profitable fault: It is never allowed to do evil for any good whatsoever.[15]

A Christian, Maritain says, can be checked by the prospect of deforming and thus endangering his immortal soul should he succumb to the Machiavellian temptation in its conservative form. The man of conscience knows that politics does not supply the final end for human persons, which can be found only on a level that transcends the political. To come to such a pass that he must choose between continued participation in politics and preserving fidelity to morality is not, for him, the calamity it is for either form of Machiavellianism. Rather than do evil, the Christian prince can always abdicate. He can wash his hands of politics.[16]

A slight digression is in order here. Maritain cautions against setting up a false alternative: either dirty hands or clean hands, that is, either to be willing to do evil or to consign oneself to the view that politics itself is inherently evil and thus to be avoided altogether. This "clean hands" posture Maritain designates "hypermoralism." Both alternatives he judges to be extreme positions and as such neither represents a solution to the political problem. If Maritain counsels political men to avoid dirty hands, he also does not think they must wear white gloves. He acknowledges that political leadership often involves rough stuff. "[O]ne can respect justice," he says, "and have brains at the same time, and manage to be strong."[17] It is "a lie" that the just man is altogether meek and mild and doomed to failure in the political arena.[18] Although he supplies no examples of hypermoralism,

---

deserves this name, it is a *city* [emphasis added] of persons. And why does the person demand for himself life in society? He demands this, first, by virtue of the very *perfections* which are inherent in him, and because of the fact of this being open to the communications of knowledge and love, of which I have spoken, and which require an entrance into relation with other persons." Jacques Maritain, *Scholasticism and Politics*, translated and edited by Mortimer J. Adler (Garden City, New York: Image Books, 1960), 71.

15. Maritain, "The End of Machiavellianism," 145; emphasis in original.

16. As Thomas More did when he resigned his office of Lord Chancellor rather than sanction King Henry's desire to divorce one wife and take another. This in spite of the danger of plunging England into new civil wars as lethal as the previous Yorkist conflicts. For a dramatic re-enactment, see Robert Bolt, *A Man for All Seasons* (New York: Vintage Books, 1990). Bolt's play can be read as a brilliant gloss on Maritain's essay.

17. Jacques Maritain, *Man and the State* (Chicago: University of Chicago Press, 1951), 57.

18. Ibid, 60; cf. 59 where Maritain forthrightly acknowledges that "power and coercion [are] inherent in social life," while adding that they must be controlled by "the form and regulations

accounts of political life abound with them. Perhaps the most celebrated is Henry Stimson's remark that "gentlemen do not read other gentlemen's mail." Stimson made this comment when, as Herbert Hoover's Secretary of State in the 1920s, he explained why he eliminated the US Cipher Bureau, whose charge was to intercept and decrypt messages sent by foreign governments. Such surveillance is not an evil act.[19]

The third moral check consists in reminding would-be Machiavellians that the ever-present danger even of limited Machiavellianism is that it can be a slippery slope to absolute Machiavellianism. Every lapse into evil makes the next opportunity for evil easier to embrace. To facilitate the embrace, Machiavelli speaks about *learning* how not to be good.[20] This might seem puzzling counsel in a book dedicated to Lorenzo de' Medici and that holds up Cesare Borgia as the very exemplar of a successful and praiseworthy prince. Surely, such men already know and thus do not need to learn how not to be good, for in the doing they are quite practiced. Machiavelli's dictum is not so much about action as about conscience, a potential impediment to action. Learning how not to be good involves not just being willing to contemplate and then to do the evil action, but, more fundamentally, quieting the voice of conscience so as to clear the way for the evil action. This the Machiavellian can and must learn to do. A dramatic depiction of this phenomenon occurs in Robert Bolt's play dealing with the life of Thomas More. Seeking to suborn the morally weak Richard Rich, Thomas Cromwell leads Rich step-by-step into providing information to be used against More. Encumbered by his conscience at the beginning of the interrogation, Rich eventually produces the damaging information, to which Cromwell responds, "There that wasn't too painful, was it? And you'll find it easier the next time."[21] And so Master Rich does, blithely committing rank perjury at trial in order wrongly to convict More of treason.

---

of human reason spurring human freedom." I am grateful to my colleague John Hittinger for reminding me of these passages in *Man and the State* concerning Machiavelli's "lie."

19. See the brief account published on-line by the National Security Agency, "Pearl Harbor Review—The Black Chamber," at http://www.nsa.gov/about/cryptologic_heritage/ center_crypt_history/pearl_harbor_review/black_chamber.shtml; accessed October 13, 2010.

20. *The Prince*, chapter 15.

21. Bolt, *A Man for All Seasons*, 76.

III. Maritain's Political Response to Machiavelli

As pertinent as the foregoing might be, it does not constitute an answer to Machiavelli at the political level. Unswerving moral rectitude might save one's soul, but it might also deliver one's country into the hands of unscrupulous Machiavellians. Clean hands might be what morality requires, but are not dirty hands what politics sometimes requires? Might not dirty hands be the price of political survival? The ruler's soul might be immortal but, as Maritain trenchantly points out, "the Body Politic has no immortal soul."[22] When a regime dies it dies completely. It is to this question of the choice between dirty and clean hands—the choice between success achieved by Machiavellianism and defeat brought about by the unwavering commitment to (traditional) virtue—that Maritain devotes his most discerning analysis.

If the choice faced by a political community is between success at the political level and sinning against God and man, Maritain's counsel is to accept defeat of one's country. He formulates the point thus:

> No doubt—to imagine a thoroughly extreme example—a nation or a state could and should accept destruction, as did the legion of Mauritius, if its citizens were summoned to choose between martyrdom and apostasy.

However, he goes on to say that

> such a case would not be a political case, it would be a case of sacrifice of political life itself to divine life, and a witnessing, in some way miraculous, of the superiority of the order of grace over the order of nature.[23]

In such an extreme instance, one has left the realm of politics altogether, so that the challenge posed by Machiavellianism—that it is successful politically—is no longer relevant: What Maritain appreciates, but Machavelli does not, is that the realm of politics is not ultimate, but penultimate. What Maritain has to show is that Machiavellianism is not, *pace* Machiavelli, *politically* successful, that instead of preserving the political community it inevitably destroys it. Establishing this point requires noticing the temporal dimension of political association as it relates to the end of politics. To an analysis of the end of the individual human person we must add an analysis of political life, which concerns the proper end of the temporal association

22. Maritain, "The End of Machiavellianism," 147.
23. Ibid.

of persons in the plural. We must bring into clear focus the notion of the common good in its temporal dimension and dynamics.

Maritain argues that political evil *does not* succeed.[24] He arrives at this conclusion by demonstrating that absolute Machiavellianism, Machiavellianism without limits, destroys political association inasmuch as it destroys civic life. That is, it not only corrupts the ruler, it corrupts the polity itself. It might be "successful" on a particular occasion and for a time. Over the long term, however, it inevitably undermines the common good which is the proper end of political community. The unmitigated power of evil, Maritain maintains,

> destroys itself by destroying that good which is its subject. The inner dialectic of the successes of evil condemn them not to be lasting. The true philosophical answer consists, therefore, in taking into account the dimension of time.... [T]he illusion [of Machiavellianism is the illusion] of *immediate success*.[25]

The common good is achieved insofar as it is distributed to all and insofar as all contribute to its achievement. Its achievement is the fruit of a lengthy unfolding in the way that the growth of a healthy forest fructifies (Maritain's term) and consolidates over generations. Justice, friendship, civility, peace, trust and the appropriate level of material prosperity are all components of the political common good. These all nourish the soil of political life, enabling men not merely to live, but to live well. In the older sense found in classical political philosophy, virtue enables men to live together in comity. Machiavellianism, however, plants bad seeds that sprout virulent growths. This may be conducive to the more or less immediate physical security of the Machiavellian state. In the long run, however, Machiavellianism inclines toward the aggrandizement and empowerment of the one or the few and not the many. That is the classic intention and outcome of tyranny.

> [T]he tragedy of totalitarian States seems to us especially manifest in the fact that, requiring for themselves the total devotion of the person, yet having no respect for the person and its inner reserves, they fatally seek a principle of human exaltation in the myths of external greatness; in an effort toward prestige and external power, never to be achieved. And this inevitably leads to war and to the self-destruction of the civilized community.[26]

24. Ibid., 148.
25. Ibid., 148–149; emphasis in original.
26. Maritain, *Scholasticism and Politics,* 82–83.

One remembers that Machiavelli states that the only art (*sola arte*) that is of concern to the prince is the art of war, which art he should in fact exercise more in time of peace than in time of war (*e nella pace vi si debbe più esercitare che nella guerra*).

One especially clear way of appreciating the force of Maritain's argument is to focus attention on the phenomenon of trust. Trust is essential to the social co-operation that is indicative of the common good and therefore of political activity that seeks such a good. Trust is an inevitable casualty of Machiavellianism. Absolute Machiavellianism renders trust between fellow citizens and between citizens and rulers dangerous, indeed toxic. In Machiavellian regimes, informers and secret police flourish. Betrayal of and violence to persons flourish. We see this in miniature in the context of Machiavelli's praise of Cesare Borgia in the seventh chapter of *The Prince*. Borgia was able to conquer the Romagna for himself by employing an especially cruel henchman, Remirro d'Orco. In the end, to deflect hatred of himself for what he had unleashed on the inhabitants of that province, Borgia had Remirro executed and his bloody corpse displayed in the public square. One cannot trust a prince who acts in that way. One can only fear him. The assault on trust is presented on a much larger scale in Stalin's Gulag, in Nazi Germany, in the pages of Orwell's *1984* (where betrayal and distrust are the central themes) and elsewhere. Solzhenitsyn captures the sense of futility men experience when living under Machiavellian pseudo-politics in the title of one of his books—*From Under the Rubble*—and in the title of one of its essays, "As Breathing and Consciousness Return."[27] Under Machiavellian "rule" one is forced to live amidst rubble, where breathing and consciousness, human life itself, are stifled. This is what Maritain means when he says that Machiavellianism does not succeed at the political level. *Pace* the Florentine's confidence that his political philosophy preserves states, in fact it eventually ruins them.

To be sure, Maritain is far from sanguine about the eventual failure of Machiavellian policies. He emphasizes that "eventually" might mean a long time, during which this kind of polity continues to function after a fashion. He notes that Mussolini maintained his rule for twenty years.[28] European

27. Alexander Solzhenitsyn et al., *From Under the Rubble*, translated by A. M Brock et al. (Boston: Little, Brown and Company, 1975).

28. Maritain, "The End of Machiavellianism," 149 n. 1. Maritain describes Mussolini as a "wretched disciple of Machiavellianism" and notes that Il Duce wrote a preface to an Italian edition of *The Prince*.

and Soviet communism endured for an even longer time, although Maritain predicted (in 1941!) that in time it would in fact fail.[29] He acknowledges that on the temporal level and in the life of societies there are no iron-clad assurances. States ruled by justice, by an anti-Machiavellian temper, may well go down to defeat. Triumphant states ruled by evil may in fact continue to exist for generations. States ruled according to justice, however, do not fail *because of* justice.[30] Justice, for Maritain, does not cause evil or injustice. Just societies fail, when they do, as a result of a complex of other causes. Evil societies succeed, when and for as long as they do, for the same reason: "Any long-range success of Machiavellianism is never due to Machiavellianism itself, but to other historical factors at play."[31] To identify these external causes and factors may be difficult:

> [T]he temporal good in which the state's justice bears fruit, the temporal evil in which its iniquity bears fruit, may be and are in fact quite different from the immediate results which the human mind might have expected and which the human eyes contemplate. It is as easy to disentangle these remote causations as to tell at a river's mouth which waters come from which glaciers and which tributaries.[32]

No matter how long such regimes endure, Maritain's point is that they remain, to one degree or another, failed states. They fail politically insofar as they suffocate human flourishing. North Korea may successfully manage hereditary successions far into the future. Such "success," however, is a failure by any properly political standard. North Korea is more accurately described as an administrative unit than as a political community. The Kim administration endures, yes, but bodies and souls captive to it rot. As Thomas More puts it, "[W]hen statesmen forsake their own private conscience for the sake of their public duties … they lead their country by a short route to chaos."[33] Maritain amends this dictum by acknowledging that the road to chaos might be rather long while insisting, with Robert Bolt's More, that even so chaos will almost certainly be Machiavellianism's ultimate outcome.[34]

29. Ibid.
30. Ibid., 150.
31. Ibid., 158.
32. Ibid., 149.
33. Bolt, *A Man for All Seasons*, 22.
34. For a more expansive presentation of the themes discussed in this essay, I refer the interested reader to Fr. James Schall's excellent chapter on Maritain's Machiavelli essay, "Justice, Brains, and Strength: Machiavelli and Modernity in Political Philosophy," in *Jacques Maritain: The Philosopher in Society* (Lanham, Maryland: Rowman and Littlefield, 1998). Fr. Schall and I are in substantial agreement on how to interpret Machiavelli as well as Maritain's understanding of Machiavelli.

PETER PAGAN AGUIAR

The End of Democracy

Authority or Freedom from Truth?

I. The Political Implications of Freedom without Truth

In his essay, "Democracy and Authority," Jacques Maritain distinguishes between "anarchic democracy" and "organic democracy," and shares some critical observations regarding the former.[1] Maritain's essay can help one understand why our own political union is perceived by many to be disintegrating with alarming rapidity. As seen in the growing TEA Party movement and its many critics in the mainstream news media and in the federal government, deep socio-political fissures are developing, and there have been various calls for greater calm and civility in public discourse. Yet one may question whether sound political discourse can flourish within a society that discourages a universal and uncompromising commitment to objective truth, within a technocratic regime that fosters a thoroughly pragmatic approach to human existence and exhibits clear signs of a crisis of metaphysical reason.

Among the politically indispensable truths emphasized by Maritain—truths that are widely disputed today—are truths concerning God and authority, freedom and man's inherent dignity. As he advances his line of argument, Maritain mentions various ecclesiastical documents, including Pius XI's *Divini Redemptoris* (*On Atheistic Communism*). Citing a specific passage from that papal document, Maritain highlights certain key truths

1. Jacques Maritain, *Scholasticism and Politics*, translated and edited by Mortimer J. Adler (Garden City, New York: Image Books, 1960), 94–103.

about man, including the immortal nature of man's soul and his supernatural vocation in Christ. The truths expressed in that passage are especially significant today, particularly in view of the politically divisive legalization of elective abortion, which is based on an influential conception of freedom. The idea of freedom to which I refer is promoted in judicial decisions like that of *Planned Parenthood v. Casey*, in which the joint opinion asserted that liberty consists in

> the right to define one's own concept of existence, of meaning, of the universe, and of the mystery of human life. Beliefs about these matters could not define the attributes of personhood were they formed under compulsion of the State.[2]

If, on the basis of public reason rather than blind acceptance of unregulated judicial fiat, citizens could arrive at a broad consensus regarding the nature and purpose of human life, much could be achieved in terms of ending the ongoing disintegration of "organic democracy" and reversing the decline toward a thinly veiled totalitarianism. If, however, the question of life after death exceeds the limits of public reason, as many now believe in an increasingly anti-metaphysical climate of opinion, would it be possible on the basis of a purely temporal political good to remedy this country's deteriorating social climate? In what follows I aim to address that question and the question of what speculative reason may rightly hold regarding immortality and the inherent dignity of the human person from the moment of conception.

The particular stance one adopts on the metaphysical question of life after death will have a deep impact on one's understanding of the political common good. If we assume for the sake of argument that there is no life after death, or that it is impossible to establish that man's rational soul is immortal, how are we to answer questions like the following: What is the ultimate meaning of human existence? What is the final purpose of society? Moreover, are the answers to such questions purely arbitrary, or should they be treated as purely arbitrary if there is significant disagreement in the various responses to such questions posed within a pluralistic society such as our own? If we cannot use reason to discover the truth on such fundamental issues, on what basis are we to proceed forward?

Can a politically sound society develop on the basis of a morality of ob-

2. Supreme Court Justice Sandra Day O'Connor's majority opinion in *Planned Parenthood of Southeastern Pennsylvania v. Casey*, 505 US 833 (1992).

ligation without relying on any deep metaphysical commitments? In a morality of obligation, as the term is employed here, the rightness or wrongness of human acts depends on whether or not the acts conform to the accepted laws of human conduct or rules of practical reason. If the ultimate measure of a man's free acts is human legislation established within the boundaries of the autonomous State to which he belongs, one could hardly condemn the acts of foreign citizens who, in their own foreign territories, conducted themselves strictly in accord with the laws established within the political boundaries of their own sovereign States. Such condemnation could not be justified without reference to a legal order above and beyond the more limited political boundaries of each of the distinct sovereign States. As Alan Dershowitz suggested in a debate with Alan Keyes,[3] our evaluation of the rightness and wrongness of human acts would vary from one sovereign State to another, reflecting the diversity of legal codes. There would be no universal and binding code of human conduct outside of a unified global State. Even if there were a unified global State ruled by an individual or group of individuals, it would still seem legitimate to question whether one ought to submit to their legislative dictates in all cases, even when they decide arbitrarily not to grant to a particular group of individuals the same rights and privileges bestowed upon another, essentially similar, group of individuals. In such cases, why should I always submit to their authority if they assert that the ultimate source of all authority is to be found in their will or in the will of the majority? Would an appeal to force suffice?

If one assumes that the path of reason is closed to us, it would seem that the question of how we should live together in society must be resolved on the basis of unbridled power. The law of force would be the supreme norm of conduct within human society. Yet social relations based on the law of force appear subhuman. Relatively few serious thinkers argue in earnest that human life in society must in essence be reducible to the hedonic life of lower animals seeking primarily if not exclusively to avoid pain and to gratify their sensory appetites, and those who do argue in support of such a view need not be taken very seriously. It is difficult if not entirely futile to engage in rational philosophical discourse those committed to the animalistic pursuit of sensual pleasure above the life of speculative reason ordered to truth for truth's sake, which life is intrinsically relational in character.

3. *Does Organized Religion Hold Answers to the Problems of the 21st Century?* http://www.keyesarchives.com/transcript.php?id=147.

II. Reason, Faith, and the Slide toward Totalitarianism

To say that the life of speculative reason is inherently relational in character is to say that rational animals are social by nature, and beings which are completely devoid of reason are not truly social by nature. Those who abandon reason altogether and give themselves over to a life of unregulated passion are not fit to participate actively in a society of free moral agents.

Some will object that there are societies of subhuman or non-rational animals, but that is to use the term "society" in an improper or analogous sense, unless there is no radical existential difference between human persons and other animals, such as baboons. To be sure, there are those who, like the author of *The Descent of Man*, fail to appreciate the ontological gap between man and subhuman animals. This failure, which is often reinforced by professional educators and journalists, is reflected in purely naturalistic theories of anthropogenesis. Such theories seek to offer a comprehensive explanatory account of the human person—a substantial unity of body and rational soul—without reference to any higher immaterial or supernatural cause beyond the methodological limits of modern natural science. Yet the assumption that modern natural science could arise on the basis of nothing more than purely natural material causes is dubious at best. The naturalist assumption is by no means a self-evident philosophical principle, although in modern science methodological naturalism is clearly a fruitful working assumption. When this scientific assumption is elevated to the level of a universally applicable philosophical principle, however, we have reason to question such an elevation favored by proponents of scientism. Natural science might one day explain in full the behavior of subhuman organisms, but why should we concede that it is within the competence of modern science to explain in full the ordinary social interactions between free moral agents capable of making and observing laws? Why should we grant that natural science provides the epistemological template or prototype for either economic or political theories? It is not obvious why we should accept the absolute explanatory supremacy of modern natural science, such that all other ways of knowing, including ethics and metaphysics and theology, are treated as subordinate to natural science.

So we may direct our attention away from those who cling to the ancient opinion that might makes right to the many who recognize, whether explicitly or implicitly, that the inherently social path of reason is not closed to human persons. Recognizing that unbridled power is not the ultimate measure of what is and what is not good rational action, one might be inclined to identify this ultimate measure with the authoritative dictates of a purely practical reason, without appealing to any speculative or metaphysical claims pertaining to natural teleology or the universal tendencies inscribed within nature. In view of the various disagreements among citizens at the level of purely practical reasoning, whose practical reason should we follow? Moreover, practical reason does not proceed without some end in view, an end *presupposed*, not established, by practical reason. A faulty end, furthermore, will entail misdirected practical reasoning. Additionally, if one holds that the last end of human action in society is purely arbitrary, the unbridled will to power resurfaces as the ultimate norm of human conduct, which leads to the idea of anarchic democracy discussed by Maritain. From there we eventually slide into some form of totalitarianism. The true final end of human action must be discovered not by the will to power, nor by practical reason left to itself, but by speculative reason, which is naturally directed to the pursuit of truth for truth's sake. Apart from truth, the will to power seems virtually inescapable in the political arena. Once the true final end of human action in society is identified, one is better equipped to address the question of the ultimate ground of political authority.

If we must proceed along the path of speculative reason, but assume that the range of reason without the aid of faith does not extend beyond the sphere of goods within man's reach prior to death, what are we entitled to say about the ultimate point of human life in society? And what role does religion play in such a scenario? If one pauses to consider the writings of Jean-Jacques Rousseau, one will find that he had some remarkable things to say about such matters. He suggested that religion has a useful role to play in society, but the sort of religion he favored was not revealed religion. In his treatment of "Civil Religion" in *The Social Contract*, Rousseau writes:

> Jesus came to set up on earth a spiritual kingdom, which, by separating the theological from the political system, made the State no longer one, and brought about the internal divisions which have never ceased to trouble Christian peoples.[4]

Concerning this religion "of the Gospel," as he puts it, he says:

4. Bk. 4, chap. 8, "Civil Religion": http://www.constitution.org/jjr/socon_04.htm.

By means of this holy, sublime, and real religion all men, being children of one God, recognize one another as brothers, and the society that unites them is not dissolved even at death.

But this religion, ... so far from binding the hearts of the citizens to the State, it has the effect of taking them away from all earthly things. I know of nothing more contrary to the social spirit.

We are told that a people of true Christians would form the most perfect society imaginable. I see in this supposition only one great difficulty: that a society of true Christians would not be a society of men....

Christianity as a religion is entirely spiritual, occupied solely with heavenly things; the country of the Christian is not of this world. He does his duty, indeed, but does it with profound indifference to the good or ill success of his cares. Provided he has nothing to reproach himself with, it matters little to him whether things go well or ill here on earth. If the State is prosperous, he hardly dares to share in the public happiness, for fear he may grow proud of his country's glory; if the State is languishing, he blesses the hand of God that is hard upon His people....

Set over against [Christians] those generous peoples who were devoured by ardent love of glory and of their country, imagine your Christian republic face to face with Sparta or Rome: the pious Christians will be beaten, crushed and destroyed....

But I am mistaken in speaking of a Christian republic; the terms are mutually exclusive. Christianity preaches only servitude and dependence. Its spirit is so favourable to tyranny that it always profits by such a regime. True Christians are made to be slaves, and they know it and do not much mind: this short life counts for too little in their eyes.[5]

Needless to say, Christians would reject such a caricature of revealed religion. They would admit, however, that if the temporal sovereign demands of them anything opposed to the law of God, they must obey God rather than man. That is precisely what worries those who reject revealed religion as divisive. Those who endorse Rousseau's line of thought would have each individual accept the rule of the "general will," which can easily be manipulated by those who occupy the seats of political and economic power. Such thinking makes it easier to accept something like the Roman understanding of the intimate relation between State and religion, with religion serving the purely temporal aims of the State. When religion is so subordinated to the temporal aims of the secular State, the stage is set for the rise of totalitarian political regimes, a twentieth-century example of which was Stalin's

5. Ibid.

Russia, which was anything but tolerant of revealed religion. Founded on atheistic materialism, Stalin's totalitarian regime did not recognize the authority of objective truth within man's reach.

III. The Redemption of Democracy

Turning from a Rousseauian vision of the city of man to that of Aristotle, whose writings exhibit remarkable confidence in the power of speculative reason, Plato's celebrated student may provide us with a less problematic naturalistic view of political life in society. This is especially so inasmuch as his writings seem, at least according to some interpretations, compatible with a deistic cast of thought, and because it is plausible to hold that Aristotle was not entirely clear on the immortality of individual human souls, although he did appreciate the profound cognitional difference between man and non-rational animals. From a strictly Aristotelian perspective, the ultimate point of human life in society is *eudaimonia* or happiness properly understood, a life of moral and intellectual virtue that does not extend beyond the grave. In the primary sense *eudaimonia* is the intellectual life of philosophical contemplation, but in the secondary sense *eudaimonia* is the active life of political virtue.[6]

Aristotelian *eudaimonia* might appeal to some, but one may still question whether *eudaimonia* as an exclusively temporal good is truly sufficient vis-à-vis natural human desire. Is the desire for a good beyond this transitory realm of existence, a desire for perfect or everlasting happiness, fully consistent with man's rational nature, or is such a desire a manifestation of serious psychological imbalance to be cured by means of some form of psychotherapy? Can a finite good that does not extend beyond this life suffice to ground a sound theory of human action? Must one resort to a theory of human action rooted ultimately in man-made laws and duties?

If there is no life after death, then the innate desire for everlasting happiness would appear to reflect no small psychological disorder, inasmuch as such a desire would be contrary to the dictates of reason. In that case any organized religion that promulgates the doctrine of life after death should be set aside as false if not socially harmful. To show that the innate desire for everlasting happiness contradicts the dictates of reason, however,

6. Aristotle, *Nicomachean Ethics* (NE) 10.7: http://classics.mit.edu/Aristotle/nicomachaen.10.x.html.

one would need to establish, not simply take for granted, that man's rational soul, like the souls of plants and animals educed from the potentiality of matter, cannot survive the disintegration of the human body. No such demonstration is to be found in the works of Aristotle.

If man's soul were educed from the potentiality of matter, man's soul could not survive the dissolution of the body, and the desire for everlasting happiness would be strictly irrational, surely no more rational than the dream of traveling to the moon simply by flapping one's arms like a duck!

But is it truly reasonable to maintain that man's rational soul is educed or derived from the potentiality of matter, that the human soul is not radically different than the material souls of plants and animals? Aristotle does recognize the ontological gap, but he is less than clear on the immortality of each individual rational soul.[7] Surely the operational status of a rational soul separated from its body is hard to imagine. Without reference to infused species or ideas, it is difficult to avoid the conclusion that the separated rational soul would be inactive at the level of intellective cognition. The absence of intellective activity, however, would not necessarily imply complete annihilation at the more fundamental level of substantial being. Without infused ideas, the cognitional hiatus of the separated rational soul would not be entirely dissimilar to the cognitional state of the soul of an unborn human embryo who has not yet formed any universal concepts based on sense experience.

In this connection one might add that the inherent dignity of the separated rational soul and that of the unborn human embryo would seem morally equivalent if, as seems reasonable to maintain, no substantial change occurs between the moment of conception and the moment of death at some point after birth. This innate dignity of the rational soul, which is the first act of an organic body having life in potency, would be reflective of the source from which it derives, and this source cannot be material. For an effect cannot be ontologically superior to its total cause, and an immaterial or spiritual effect is ontologically superior to a material cause. Since an immaterial effect cannot be educed from the potentiality of matter, given the ontological disproportion between matter and spirit, the immaterial effect must be traced back to an immaterial efficient cause capable of producing something from nothing. Such an efficient cause may properly be called "God," the uncaused cause of all participated being.

7. Aristotle, *De Anima* 3.5: http://classics.mit.edu/Aristotle/soul.3.iii.html.

If we admit the absolute need for this uncaused cause, then the admission of God's existence, upon whom we depend for our very existence, and in whose image we are all made, has implications concerning man's inherently relational or social nature. We are not mere creatures of the State, and we ought not be treated as such. As rational creatures made in the image of God, we must act together in solidarity for the sake of the common good, consistent with our inherent dignity as persons made to know the truth about ourselves and about our ultimate destiny as truth seekers capable of transcending the spatial and temporal cognitive boundaries of sensory perception.

If the natural desire for a good beyond the limits of space and time is strictly consistent with our rational nature, political action cannot fully be explained or justified solely on the basis of some yearning for one or another set of perishable goods. The ultimate end of human action in society is a transcendent good that alone can set to perfect rest man's natural desire. And a natural desire cannot be in vain, inasmuch as potency is unintelligible apart from its proportionate act. This transcendent good, for whom man was created in His image, a good which responds to man's innate moral and spiritual aspirations, cannot properly be denied or ignored in serious public discourse without dire political consequences.

Of course, we must avoid a radical unification of Church and State. For such a unification would end up smothering either the secular order, as in theocracy, or the sacred, as in atheistic totalitarianism. Interestingly, as the historical record clearly testifies, both theocracy and atheistic totalitarianism are characterized by the frequent exercise of unholy and lethal force, and countless violations of the right to religious liberty. We must render to Caesar what belongs to Caesar, and render to God what belongs to God, while admitting that Caesar's temporal authority is derived from and subordinate to a higher Authority. When a lower authority issues a legislative mandate contrary to the Eternal Law, the lower authority fails to act within the proper boundaries of his participated authority. In such cases we must not render obedience unto Caesar, since he has failed to exercise his limited authority in conformity with and for the sake of the universal good of society, which cannot be separated from God.

We must also avoid introducing a radical separation between the secular and the sacred, between culture and religion. A radical separation of these two interrelated domains of action would encourage a form of interior disintegration akin to multiple personality disorder, inasmuch as one would be torn between the love of two separate masters. Such interior division is unsustainable, and one will end up hating one or the other. A proper integration of our interior and social existence is possible only if one recognizes that the love of one is subordinate and ordered to the love of the other—the unparticipated Source of every wholesome love, which is essential Goodness. The thesis of incommensurability of basic goods, including life, play, human friendship and religion, is metaphysically dubious. All lower or participated goods must be traced back to their transcendent Source, essential Goodness, without which no truly free and morally sound democratic order would be possible.

Without a deep and widely shared commitment to the way of truth, including metaphysical truth, the demise of "organic democracy" is unavoidable. If we are to recover genuine freedom for excellence and reverse the decline toward "anarchic democracy" ending in tyranny, modern man must submit himself to the authority of the Truth that became flesh so that we might be elevated and united forever within the fullness of Truth.

DENIS A. SCRANDIS

Maritain and Ratzinger on the Crisis of Modern Times

This essay examines two assessments of the "crisis of modern times," one from Jacques Maritain in 1938 and the other from Joseph Cardinal Ratzinger some 67 years later in 2005. Although separated by the most destructive war in human history and the collapse of fascist socialism and Soviet communism, the crises of Western culture described by these two men are remarkably similar. In fact, the emerging rationalist-inspired humanism that Maritain described in 1938 (a form of Marxism) seems to be the cultural hegemon in Ratzinger's account of our own secular Western culture.

I. Maritain's "Integral Humanism and the Crisis of Modern Times"[1]

Maritain's intention in this essay is to present the "concrete logic of historical events in a philosophy of culture" and not to present a mere logic of ideas in a metaphysics, say, of Hegelian or Marxist inspiration.[2] Maritain's short essay described four kinds of humanism, namely, the humanism of pagan Greece and Rome, the anthropocentric humanism of the European Enlightenment, an emerging Marxist humanism, and his own (Christian) Integral Humanism.

Classical Greek Humanism tended to "make man more truly human"

1. Jacques Maritain, "Integral Humanism and the Crisis of Modern Times," in *Scholasticism and Politics*, translated and edited by Mortimer J. Adler (Garden City, New York: Image Books, 1960).

2. Ibid., 11.

and to "manifest his original dignity" by "enabling him to participate in everything, which can enrich him in nature and history." It demanded that man develop his powers, his creative energies, and his life of reason. It used technology to make the forces of nature into "instruments of his freedom."[3] It was open to nature and God.

"Anthropocentric humanism" refers to a historical series of philosophies that grew out of René Descartes' revolutionary teachings, which tried to correct problems inherent in the Cartesian foundation, and that yielded a genealogical line of humanisms. It is also known as the Age of Enlightenment. Descartes conceived of man as a union of two mutually exclusive substances, namely, of thought (or consciousness) and extension (or body). As a result, human thought or knowledge of the world was cut off from the other substance, that is, thought or knowledge was cut off from the world. Man as understood by Descartes could no longer learn about the world of nature through his senses. With the realm of nature situated beyond thought (in extension), rationalistic or "Enlightenment" philosophers struggled in the face of the burgeoning age of scientific discovery to explain all of human knowledge in terms of thought. Hence "anthropocentric humanism" and modern philosophy conceived of human nature as self-enclosed or self-sufficient, excluding every thought that was not innate to itself as possessing no reliable cognitive value.[4]

Disbelieving in God and in extra-mental realities, anthropocentric humanism demanded a development of reason apart from the Gospel. It isolated human reason from its supra-rational life, namely, from prayer, worship, grace, sin, repentance, and asceticism. It also forgot the irrational in man in whose recall Marx, Nietzsche, and Freud would glory.

Now, anthropocentric humanism sought something other than personal perfection. It claimed that it itself could make and deliver a better future.

> Enormous promises have been made to man, ever since the day of Descartes, in the prediction that progressive enlightenment will automatically bring about a complete felicity of release and repose, an earthly beatitude.[5]

It promised progressive enlightenment and a beatitude that atheists could enjoy. But, having abandoned God and divine and natural law for moral self-sufficiency, man no longer recognized human goods and lost track of

3. Ibid., 11–12.
4. Ibid., 12.
5. Ibid., 13.

his soul.[6] This anthropocentric humanism gave way to various counter-humanisms from Kierkegaard, Nietzsche, and others.[7]

According to Maritain, counter-humanisms emerged in opposition to anthropocentric humanism.

> The irrational tidal wave is in reality the tragic wheel of rationalistic [or anthropocentric] humanism; it reacts against a humanism of reason closed up in itself, but it does so by making man open to the powers from below, and shutting him off from higher communications and the spirit which liberates, and walling the creature up in the abyss of animal vitality.[8]

Man reacted against the humanism of reason enclosed within itself. Yet, cut off from all thought of transcendent being and of a life of friendship with God, the rebellion was limited to accomplishing only material objectives. So, contrary to anthropocentric humanism and arising from the principle that "man alone, and through himself alone, works out his salvation," counter-humanism constructed "a lived religion. The purest case of this tendency [was] that of Marxism."[9] In our own day, this dominant statist political philosophy assigns to government the remedy of all economic, social, and political inequities. This is Marxist humanism.

Marxist salvation was purely and exclusively temporal. It was accomplished without God since God did not exist. Moreover, it was against God in that it was "against whatever in man and [whatever in] the human milieu [was] the image of God."[10] Thus a school teaching virtue, a hospital delivering services mercifully, and even a pious Christian addressing all humanity in charity would draw animus from this atheism. This Marxist "salvation demanded the organization of humanity into one body whose supreme destiny [was] not to see God but to gain dominion in history."[11] It was radically atheistic. Maritain said that this politically oppressive force was more aptly called "anti-Christ" than "anti-Christian" since it was more opposed to the presence and action of Christ in human history than it was opposed to church teachings.[12]

Finally, the fourth kind of humanism is Maritain's Christian "Integral Humanism." It must reassume the work of classical Greek humanism. It must remake anthropology by rehabilitating the creature, especially isolat-

6. Ibid.
7. Ibid., 14.
8. Ibid., 15.
9. Ibid., 16.
10. Ibid.
11. Ibid.
12. Ibid., 21.

ed man. There must be a new anthropology centered on man in his openness to the world and to God. This anthropology must discover in the spiritual order the ways by which God finds His way into men so that man will find himself in God.[13] Man's vertical movement toward eternal life must be pursued along with his horizontal movement through history.[14]

Integral Humanism will care for the masses, not just the elite. It will care for their right to work and to live a spiritual life. It will have an awakening of the religious conscience, especially an awakening of liberty and its creative forces. It will thus bring them to a mature culture.[15] It places hope in a political ideal of brotherly love to direct the work of authentic social regeneration while pagan civilizations place hope in force alone.[16] In the realm of action, spiritual values should hold the first place.[17] The liberty of the Christian must be safe-guarded. Maritain concluded his essay with the speculation that the terrestrial efficacy of the Gospel and of reason, which he called the hope of man, might succeed at that time (in 1938) after a "long night" of some four centuries.[18]

II. Ratzinger's *Christianity and the Crisis of Culture*

Two years before becoming pope and during the debate over the European Union (EU) Constitution, Joseph Cardinal Ratzinger wrote *Christianity and the Crisis of Culture.*[19] It describes the current culture of Western Europe and its secular attitudes, which were on display during the constitutional debate. Ratzinger's discussion does not invoke Maritain's four-part division of humanisms. Ratzinger combines Maritain's post-Cartesian humanisms into one movement, namely, into Enlightenment culture. And, Ratzinger suggests a distinctively Christian alternative culture based upon St. Benedict of Nursia's *Rule,* whereas Maritain articulated his Christian Integral Humanism.

According to Ratzinger, Western culture faces several dangers. These include destructive technologies and weapons of mass destruction as well as terrorists who seek to use them.[20] There are genetic engineers who desire

13. Ibid., 18.
14. Ibid., 18–19.
15. Ibid., 28.
16. Ibid., 29.
17. Ibid., 30.
18. Ibid., 31.
19. Joseph Ratzinger, *Christianity and the Crisis of Culture,* translated by Brian McNeil (San Francisco: Ignatius Press, 2006).
20. Ibid., 25.

to re-make man in images of their own choice. There are further questions concerning the distribution of wealth as Marxist-socialist redistributionism dominates European politics. And there are fears of a clash of cultures.[21] Yet, Ratzinger says that the truest and gravest danger facing Western culture is not something technological and powerful but a certain moral confusion and weakness. Our need is not for new weapons technology but for a public morality fortified by the moral strength of man.

> Moral strength has not grown in tandem with the development of science; on the contrary, it has diminished because the technological mentality confines morality to the subjective sphere. Our need, however, is for a public morality, a morality capable of responding to the threats that impose such a burden on the existence of us all. The true and gravest danger of the present moment is precisely this imbalance between technological possibilities and moral energy.[22]

What do we have instead? To what kind of public morality does Enlightenment secularism turn for security? Our "technological mentality" relegates moral thought to the realm of the merely subjective.[23] This yields a moral weakness, which gives rise to a new public moralism that pays lip service to notions of "justice," "peace," and "conservation" in vague politicizing discourse. This new public morality cares more for a political utopia than for the dignity of the individual.[24] It despises man in the name of grandiose objectives and reduces the core message of Jesus to slogans of political moralism.[25]

In the debate over the EU's constitution, the secularists ignored reference to God and to Europe's Christian roots, a rejection which showed the extent of this culture's godlessness. The Enlightenment's secular agents insist, for example, that merely mentioning Europe's Christian origins would offend Muslims and Jews. (The avoidance of this possible offense to Muslims was just one of their grand objectives.) Yet, Muslims and other non-Christian religionists feel threatened, not by references to Europe's foundation in Christian morality but by "the cynicism of a secularized culture that denies its own foundations."[26]

Now Enlightenment culture is substantially defined by what is known as the rights of liberty. Liberty is a fundamental value and the criterion for all other values. Although one has freedom of expression, one should not

21. Ibid., 26–27.
22. Ibid., 27.
23. Ibid.
24. Ibid., 28.
25. Ibid., 29.
26. Ibid., 33.

question official prescriptions defining liberty.[27] Some rights clash. While women have a right to abortion, their unborn have no right to life. The church's inability to ordain female priests is politicized as misogynist. God's condemnation of homosexual activity is deemed politically incorrect.[28]

This radical culture was born of the Enlightenment and its advocates would like to apply it to constitute an official European identity.

> But according to the thesis of the laicist Enlightenment culture of Europe, it is only the norms and substance of this same Enlightenment culture that can determine the identity of Europe, and it follows that every state that accepts these criteria can belong to Europe. Ultimately, it is unimportant to know on *which* framework of roots this culture of liberty and democracy is planted.... For these [Christian roots] are dead roots that do not form part of today's identity. Accordingly, this new identity, which is defined exclusively by the Enlightenment culture, entails that God has nothing whatever to do with public life and with the foundations of the state.[29]

God is thus to have nothing to do with the foundation of the European Union and with its public life.[30]

This Enlightenment culture claims to be universal and complete and Ratzinger challenges both claims.[31] European Enlightenment culture cannot be universal or apt for all mankind while it is rejected by Europe's Muslim populations. And it cannot be complete in itself since its lack of spiritual values motivates its rejection. Ratzinger sees a coming clash of cultures between this radical secularism and the great historical cultures.[32]

> The real antagonism typical of today's world is not that between diverse religious cultures; rather, it is the antagonism between the radical emancipation of man from God, from the roots of life, on the one hand, and the great religious cultures, on the other. If we come to experience a clash of cultures, this will not be due to a conflict between the great religions.... The coming clash will be between this radical emancipation of man and the great historical cultures.[33]

Ratzinger does not expect the conflict to fall between Islam and Christianity, but between Islamic radicalism and European secularism.

Enlightenment culture as a modern culture believes that reason originates from the irrational.[34] It is Christianity's view that the world comes

27. Ibid., 34.
28. Ibid., 35.
29. Ibid., 37; emphasis in original.
30. Ibid.
31. Ibid., 38.
32. Ibid., 44.
33. Ibid.
34. Ibid., 49.

from reason, namely, from the *Logos*. "Christianity has understood itself to be the religion of the *Logos*, to be a religion in keeping with reason."[35] Ratzinger believes that Enlightenment philosophy's attempt "to shape human affairs to the total exclusion of God leads us more and more to the brink of the abyss, toward the utter annihilation of man." Ratzinger believes non-believers of goodwill should follow Pascal's advice to act as if God exists and to live lives consistent with God's love and justice.[36]

The thrust of the Enlightenment's attack is not just at Christianity, its doctrines and history. The attack is against individual witness in the public square. Thus Ratzinger says:

> Our greatest need in the present historical moment is people who make God credible in this world by means of the enlightened faith they live.... We need men who keep their eyes fixed on God, learning from him what true humanity means. We need men whose intellect is enlightened by the light of God, men whose hearts are opened by God, so that their intellect can speak to the intellect of others and their hearts can open the hearts of others. It is only by means of men who have been touched by God that God can return to be with mankind.[37]

Yet, how can men of today break out of their cultural mold and become living exemplars of God-centered living? Ratzinger says: "It is only by means of men who have been touched by God that God can return to be with mankind."[38] Specifically he recommends we follow Benedict of Nursia (the founder of Western monasticism and Pope Benedict XVI's namesake) who purified himself and brought God to the men of Europe.[39]

III. The Agreement of Maritain and Ratzinger on the Crisis of Modern Times

Both Maritain and Ratzinger describe Western culture as being in a state of crisis. Maritain sketched the philosophical development of the (rationalist-Marxist cultural) crisis, and Ratzinger reports how present-day Enlightenment advocates (heirs of Maritain's Marxists) redefine European culture as an atheistic political and social union, which he says is headed for destruction. Do these two thinkers describe the same culture in terms of different perspectives? It seems so.

35. Ibid., 47.
36. Ibid., 51.
37. Ibid., 52.
38. Ibid.
39. Ibid., 53.

Maritain prefaced his discussion of humanism with a reminder of the original goal of making man more truly human by perfecting his powers, especially his reason. After such a noble start and against such a project, Descartes redefined man in a way that cut him off from the natural world, from God, and ultimately from himself. Skepticism and relativism followed. An earthly beatitude was said to lie ahead. Although Ratzinger did not sketch the history of modern philosophy in *Christianity and the Crisis of Culture*, his *Regensburg Lecture* (2006) offers a complementary account of the Enlightenment's destructive influence on theology.[40] Maritain concluded his treatment of anthropocentric humanism observing that "modern" man had lost track of his soul, and, in the ensuing state of crisis, articulated counter-humanisms, especially that of Marx.

Post-World War II Europe institutionalized socialist and Marxist economic concepts. Whereas Maritain hoped in 1938 for a society that would allow the truly poor to work with dignity, the socio-economic system in Ratzinger's time struggles under an exceedingly expensive system of redistributive social justice that features health and vacation benefits, early retirement, and life-long pensions for members of the so-called "working class."

Ratzinger's analysis of Enlightenment culture focuses on the skepticism and relativism that come out of it. Ratzinger regards moral relativism as the greatest danger facing Western culture. Our secular mentality confines moral judgment to the realm of personal opinion, and our weak "public moralism" cares more for a political utopia than for the dignity of the individual.

According to Maritain, Marxist humanism kept its predecessor's materialism, its isolation from transcendent being, and its notion of progress. Progress, however, became a form of salvation in which the state will remedy all inequities. Progressives demand the organization of humanity into one body, namely, their own, in order to gain dominion in history.

The European Union's constitutional debate redefined European culture as a godless, universal, and complete culture that is capable of absorbing other cultural entities that will embrace Enlightenment principles. This coincides with the goal of Marxism as Maritain understood it, namely, the organization of humanity into one body (as was happening in the Soviet

40. See Joseph Ratzinger, "The Regensburg Lecture," reprinted in James V. Schall, *The Regensburg Lecture* (South Bend, Indiana: St. Augustine's Press, 2007).

Union) in order to gain dominion in history. Maritain did not speak of a clash between Western culture and non-Western culture. For him, the imminent clash was to be within Western culture, namely World War II. Ratzinger identifies a coming clash that will be between European secularism and the great religious cultures. In fact, fundamentalist Islamic elements that wage jihad against the West draw upon the anti-Western (or anti-secular) antipathy that is widespread throughout Islam.

Maritain's consideration of the Christian solution to the cultural crisis is developed at length in his work *Integral Humanism*.[41] Maritain wants to resume the ancients' task of perfecting man in body and soul. He wants to rehabilitate the notion of creature, which has been eviscerated by modern philosophy. He wants a new anthropology centered on man in his openness to the world and to God. Although Ratzinger does not speak of recasting the philosophical consideration of man in *Christianity and the Crisis of Culture*, he does call for rehabilitating speculative philosophy and theology in his *Regensburg Lecture*.

Maritain observed that the thrust of our cultural Marxism is more anti-Christ than anti-Christian since it opposes the presence and action of Christ in human history more than it opposes Church teachings. Hence, anti-Christ Marxism opposes any individual manifestation of Christ in the public square, be it the Christian graduate student of youth counseling who refuses to teach the "validity" of the homosexual lifestyle or the Catholic pharmacist who refuses to make available for public use the RU-486 abortifacient. Ratzinger recognizes the importance of this witness, which he calls our "greatest need."[42]

Maritain calls for the spiritual renewal of the masses, society, and culture within a mature conscience. Maritain also seeks to discover the ways by which God finds his way into men so that man will find himself in God. Ratzinger believes our greatest need is people who make God credible in the world by living lives of enlightened faith. Both men agree that the recovery of our culture from its secular crisis lies in heroic Christian witness. Both the philosopher and the theologian agree generally on the nature, cause, and cure of the crisis of modern times.

41. Jacques Maritain, *Integral Humanism*, translated by Joseph W. Evans (New York: Charles Scribner's Sons, 1968).

42. See n. 37 above.

CORNELIA A. TSAKIRIDOU

Perceptions of Islam

Pope Benedict XVI and Jacques Maritain

IN MEMORY OF ANTHONY O. SIMON

I. Introduction

For my own experience made me feel that the most abandoned of people in the most symbolic metaphysical sense of the most sublime negative way are the Muslims.... I felt that their temporary exile was the prefiguration of the penitential life of hermits, of solitaries who would sanctify all Muslim generations, fulfilling for them at the sacrifice of Kurban, obtaining by the brotherly compassion the coming of Mercy.[1]

These words, spoken in 1959 during France's colonial war with Algeria by its most distinguished Islamicist, Louis Massignon, suggest a different perception of Islam from the one presented thirty-six years later by Pope John Paul II (Karol Wotjyla). The pope argued that "Islam is not a religion of redemption" because it does not believe in a crucified and resurrected God. Since Jesus is only a prophet "not only the theology but also the anthropology of Islam is very distant from Christianity."[2] In casting Jesus as one of the messengers and beloveds of God, Islam puts a distance between

1. Louis Massignon, *Testimonies and Reflections: Essays of Louis Massignon*, edited by Herbert Mason (Notre Dame, Indiana: University of Notre Dame Press, 1989), 22.

2. John Paul II, *Crossing the Threshold of Hope*, translated by Jenny McPhee and Martha McPhee (New York: Knopf, 1995), 92–93. See also Mahmoud M. Ayoub, "Pope John Paul II on Islam," in *A Muslim View of Christianity: Essays on Dialogue by Mahmoud Ayoub*, edited by Irfan A. Omar (New York: Orbis Books, 2007), 243.

humanity and divinity that only ecstasies and miracles can bridge. The divine word is spoken and heard; it does not become flesh.[3]

The Catholic approach to Islam is defined by this tension between the openness of Massignon (1883–1962) and the insistence of John Paul II on difference. It is a creative and perhaps unavoidable tension, nowhere more evident perhaps than in Pope Benedict XVI's 2006 Regensburg address, "Faith, Reason and the University: Memories and Reflections."[4] The speech was widely criticized for containing stereotypical views of Islam that perpetuate an image of Muslim intolerance, violence, and irrationalism. Yet, nothing said on that occasion was new or inconsistent with Catholic teaching as expressed in papal and conciliar documents. The pope reiterated the Church's position on interreligious dialogue and presented ideas developed in previously published work. His controversial quotation from a medieval dialogue between a Byzantine emperor and a Muslim scholar, in which the emperor described Islam as a destructive religion that proselytizes by war, was a common theme in medieval debates between Christians and Muslims.

In 2000, *Dominus Iesus* clarified Catholic doctrine on interreligious dialogue. It affirmed *Nostra Aetate,* which recognized the dignity of all religions, seeing in their teachings reflections "of that truth which enlightens all men."[5] Subtitled "On the Relations of the Church to Non-Christian Religions," *Nostra Aetate* was composed in consultation with the prominent French Dominican scholar of Islamic theology Fr. (Abuna) George Chehata Anawati (1905–94). A native of Egypt, Anawati had dedicated his entire life to Muslim-Catholic dialogue and was the founder of the *Institut Dominicain d'Études Orientales* in Abbasiya. He belonged to a group of exceptional Catholic scholars, led by Massignon, who in the first half of the twentieth century came to know and study Islam in the Middle East and North Africa, during a period of war, decolonization and regional tensions.

For the most part, these scholars delved into Islam while remaining convinced of the spiritual and intellectual superiority of Catholicism. Al-

3. "Jesus … came to humanity as the Word of God to heal and to save, to carry the process of divine revelation in history further." Mahmoud Ayoub, "The Miracle of Jesus: Muslim Reflections on the Divine Word," in *A Muslim View of Christianity,* 115.

4. http://www.vatican.va/holy_father/benedict_xvi/speeches/2006/september/documents/hf_ben-xvi_spe_20060912_university-regensburg_en.html.

5. http://www.vatican.va/roman_curia/congregations/cfaith/documents/rc_con_cfaith_doc_20000806_dominus-iesus_en.html; http://www.vatican.va/archive/hist_councils/ii_vatican_council/ documents/vat-ii_decl_19651028_nostra-aetate_en.html (article #2).

though consistent with intellectual trends influenced by colonialism, their work was part of a monumental period in French Catholic thought that deserves to be examined in its own terms. The same applies to Benedict's Regensburg address. The political, social, and ideological dimensions of the controversy it created should not be allowed to overshadow the theological and philosophical significance of its arguments.[6] Ironically, Benedict's speech, delivered to the faculty of the university where he once taught, warned about the decline of theology in Western universities.

Yet, Regensburg presented theology as an intellectual achievement rather than as the reasoned expression of the human encounter with God. The pope rightly argued that the separation of reason and faith limits their scope. But the emphasis he placed on rationality needs qualification. Reason, theological reason especially, must venture outside its own normative parameters, to think and speak in the ambiguous and paradoxical voice of the ascetic and the mystic—to proclaim orthodoxy from the margins.[7] This movement defines the thought of Jacques Maritain (1882–1973). A convert to Catholicism, Maritain renewed and poeticized Thomistic philosophy, and inspired the French Catholic encounter with Islam in the first half of the twentieth century. A close friend of Massignon, he gave him valuable counsel whenever his ventures in Islamic theology and Arab culture clashed with Catholic teaching and philosophy.[8] In the 1920s and 1930s, the two helped Georges Anawati discern a vocation in the Dominican Order.[9]

This paper explores the relationship between reason and theology in Benedict's thought, discusses his views of interreligious dialogue and Islam in the context of Catholic and Muslim responses to modernity, and compares them with those of Maritain, the philosopher who gave the most integral Catholic response to the challenges faced by Christianity in an increasingly secular and multi-religious world.

6. Karen Armstrong, "We Cannot Afford to Maintain these Ancient Prejudices About Islam," *The Guardian*, September 18, 2006; http://www.guardian.co.uk/commentisfree/2006/sep/18/religion.catholicism.

7. Mahmoud Ayoub, "The Idea of Redemption in Christianity and Islam," in *A Muslim View of Christianity*, 91, 95.

8. Jacques Keryell, "Louis Massignon-Jacques Maritain et leur disciple, Louis Gardet," in *Louis Massignon et ses contemporains*, edited by Jacques Keryell (Paris: Éditions Karthala, 1997), 113.

9. David Burrell et al., "Georges Chehata Anawati (1905–1994)," in *Medieval Scholarship: Biographical Studies in the Formation of a Discipline*, vol. 3, edited by Helen Damico (London: Routledge, 2000), 131.

II. An Incarnational Rationality

Benedict's principal argument in Regensburg was that theology can enrich and enlarge the scope of reason. The controversy stemmed from his reference to Byzantine-Muslim polemics, specifically the debate between Byzantine emperor, Manuel II Paleologos (1391–1425) and a Muslim theologian (*muderris*) in Ancyra (Galatia). Since the advent of Islam, and particularly in Anatolia under Seljuk and Ottoman rule, Orthodox Christians and Muslims, whether sultans or simple soldiers, showed great interest in the theological and moral issues that were dividing the two religions. Manuel and the *muderris* met in Anatolia between 1390 and 1391 while Manuel was an honorary hostage in the court of Sultan Bayezid I. Manuel's criticism of Islam as a violent and destructive religion in that context shows that the criticism was not offensive to his Muslim interlocutor.[10] War was very much a common experience and theological debates reflected that fact. Manuel's interpreter was a Greek convert to Islam.[11] According to Speros Vryonis, Christianity and Islam "were both conscious of their exclusive, 'true' and unique nature. The political defeat of the one or the other necessarily required a religious explanation, for political victory of a Muslim or Byzantine state would seem to imply the 'truth' of Islam or Christianity."[12]

Even though it invoked the history of Muslim-Christian dialogue, Benedict's reference to Paleologos was not central to his argument. A discussion of contemporary Muslim literature on modernity would have been more helpful. But by no means was his choice of this example a condemnation of Islam. Ratzinger's theology and the judicious way in which he has consistently approached other religions, makes this an untenable position. It is important to keep in mind that in Regensburg the pope was addressing three groups: secular critics of religion, Christians who believe that religion is a matter of personal sentiment and cultural expression, and advocates of

10. Speros Vryonis Jr., *The Decline of Medieval Hellenism in Asia Minor and the Process of Islamization from the Eleventh through the Fifteenth Century* (Berkeley: University of California Press, 1971), 428. Manuel was a trained theologian, intellectual and academic reformer. He visited England and debated Sorbonne theologians on Latin doctrine. Steven Runciman, *The Great Church in Captivity* (Cambridge: Cambridge University Press, 1968), 115–16, 102–103; http://www.ccel.org/ccel/pearse/morefathers/files/manuel_paleologus_dialogue7_trans.htm.

11. Vryonis, *The Decline of Medieval Hellenism*, 461.

12. Ibid., 421–22.

a type of ecumenism that calls for unity on the basis of a common spiritual essence or truth from which all religions spring.

In his 2004 book, *Truth and Tolerance: Christian Belief and World Religions,* Ratzinger criticizes Karl Rahner's view that divine grace is extra-sacramentally and extra-ecclesially present in non-Christians who unconsciously live in the spirit of Christ (the "anonymous Christian"), and Sarvepalli Radhakrishnan's vision of a universal spiritualism (rooted in the Hindu metaphysics) in which all religious differences will be nullified.[13] He argues that differentiation is essential to the nature and development of religions and consistent with the dynamics of religious movements: "Religion demands the making of distinctions ... between different forms of religion and distinctions within a religion itself, so as to find the way to its higher points."[14] Ratzinger notes the Qur'an's emphasis on the unity of God, the variety and diversity of Muslim sects, theological schools and devotions, and Islam's claims to universality. Some of its "forms" have a "proximity to the mystery of Christ."[15] Others reflect "sick and degenerate forms of religion," like violence and ritualism, that affect not only Islam but also Hinduism (e.g., caste system) and Christianity (e.g., Crusades).[16]

Ratzinger's theology rests on a sacramental, incarnational rationality. The mystery of a Triune God informs reason; it does not bring it to absurdity and rupture. His view of Islam stems from Christian Logo-centricity: the internalization in religion of reason in a depth unforeseen by philosophy. Christianity is revolutionary because "it insisted that it was not one religion among others but represented the victory of perception and knowledge over the world of religions,"—what Justin Martyr (d. 167) called "vera philosophia."[17] In Christianity, "the enlightenment can become part of religion, because the God of the enlightenment has himself entered into religion."[18] Knowledge replaces "poetry and politics: the two great sources of religion."[19]

For Ratzinger, this relationship to reason and universality is exclusive to Christianity. Despite its appeal to philosophical monotheists, Judaism could

13. Joseph Cardinal Ratzinger, *Truth and Tolerance: Christian Belief and World Religions,* translated by Henry Taylor (San Francisco: Ignatius, 2004), 16–17, 24–25; Karl Rahner, *Later* Writings, vol. 5 of *Theological Investigations,* translated by Karl-H Kruger (Baltimore, Maryland: Helicon Press, 1966), 131. See also Karl Rahner, *Jesus, Man and the Church,* vol. 17 of *Theological Investigations,* translated by Margaret Kohl (New York: Crossroad, 1981), 39–50.

14. Ibid., 204.

15. Ibid., 54.

16. Ibid., 204.

17. Ibid., 170–71.

18. Ibid., 173.

19. Ibid., 170.

not overcome its confinement to a particular people (a proselyte would never entirely belong). Islam is not mentioned in this context but it would seem that what prevents it from reaching this universality, despite its trans-national and trans-cultural character, is the fact that it remains poetical and political.[20] Muslim modernists like India's Sayyid Ahmad Khan (1817–98) and Pakistan's Abu'l-A'la Mawdudi (1903–79), have also attributed a transcending rationality to Islam that makes it compatible with modernity and enables it, as Mawdudi argued, to transcend those aspects of modernity tainted by imperialism and colonialism.[21]

What does a meta-religious and meta-poetic Christianity imply? "The Christian," Benedict writes, "denies that mystical experience has sole validity and teaches the absolute value of the divine call that has been made audible to Christ."[22] Christianity offers a lucid and sober taste of God, the "rational intoxication" of the sacraments—a God who offers himself *in ecclesiam* to all those who seek him.[23] It has no need for "the passionate power ... which catches us up and turns us, at least for a moment, into gods, helps us for a moment to sense the pleasure of infinity and to forget the misery of finite existence."[24]

This prudent approach seems to overlook the radical, charismatic marginality of the saint who *lives* in and beyond what the temporal church dogmatizes. Benedict is not interested in the deconstruction of theological discourse or in questioning its attachment to the temporal structures of rationality. The saint is a model of moderation. In *Christianity and the Crisis of Cultures,* he writes that when theology is not "anchored" to "the realism of the saints," it "degenerates into an empty intellectual game and also loses its character."[25] Communication with Jesus is a "personal act" of faith, which becomes complete only when we participate in the life of the Church and share ourselves with others.[26] This sober vision of the spiritual life lacks the intensity that accompanies the human encounter with God.

20. Ibid., 171. Fazlur Rahman, *Islam and Modernity: Transformation of an Intellectual Tradition* (Chicago: The University of Chicago Press, 1982), 139–40.

21. Jacques Waardenburg, "Some Thoughts on Modernity and Modern Muslim Thinking About Islam," in *Islam and the Challenge of Modernity,* edited by Sharifah Shifa al-Attas (Kuala Lumpur: International Institute of Islamic Thought and Civilization, 1996), 331–34.

22. Ibid., 31.

23. Ibid., 128.

24. Ibid., 128–29.

25. Joseph Cardinal Ratzinger, *Christianity and the Crisis of Cultures,* translated by Brian McNeil (San Francisco: Ignatius, 2006), 109.

26. Ibid., 113.

Maritain also distinguished between philosophical and mystical language and rejected metaphysical mysticism (arguing that its wisdom belongs to the natural order). But he also approached philosophy and theology as deeply existential endeavors, infused with sudden insights, with poetry, art, and a passionate love of God that challenged, enriched, and revitalized the human intellect.[27] He wrote about the influence of mystical experience on ontology: "The intellect may well receive, after the manner of a sudden revelation, a knowledge of that which constitutes the proper object of the third level of abstraction ... at the sight of something or other—a blade of grass, a windmill—a soul may know in an instant that these things do not exist by themselves and that God exists."[28]

Not surprisingly, Maritain's thought became the background against which a number of French Catholic scholars and religious made the study of Islamic mystical theology their vocation. In his study of Catholic renewal in France, Gérard Cholvy describes Maritain as "the great thinker who undertook to define the immersion of the Christian in the world."[29] So eager was Maritain to see a Catholic overture to Islam and so inspired by the work of Massignon, that in *The Degrees of Knowledge* he wrote: "What we would like to see develop is a comparative theological mysticism working towards the discernment of various depths in properly spiritual values and towards a recognition of God's visitations; for nowhere is He left without witnesses."[30]

Maritain's poeticization of reason anticipates contemporary critiques of religious logocentricity, the prescription by ideologies (institutions) of exclusive patterns of transcendence with which orthodoxy is identified. Mohammed Arkoun (1928–2010), the noted critic of Christian and Muslim modernities, has looked at Islam from this standpoint. For Arkoun, only the prophetic and mystical aspects of religion can help deconstruct and emancipate reason and bring language and thought to a creative and com-

27. "Philosophical language proposes to speak of reality without touching it, mystical language seeks to divine reality as if by touching it without seeing it." Jacques Maritain, *Distinguish to Unite or The Degrees of Knowledge*, translated by Gerald B. Phelan (Notre Dame: University of Notre Dame Press, 1995), 347 n. 42; see also 304–305. See also Cornelia A. Tsakiridou, "When Art Fails Humanity: Jacques Maritain on Jean Cocteau, Modernism and the Crisis of European Civilization," in *The Renewal of Civilization: Essays in Honor of Jacques Maritain*, edited by Gavin T. Colvert (Washington, D.C.: American Maritain Association, 2010), 152–73.

28. Maritain, *The Degrees of Knowledge*, 296–97.

29. Gerard Cholvy, "Le renouveau catholique en France au temps de Massignon," in *Louis Massignon et ses contemporains*, 37.

30. Maritain follows Aquinas ST II-II, q. 2, a. 7, ad 3; Maritain, *The Degrees of Knowledge*, 292; see also 290–91 n. 70.

municative surge.[31] Arkoun, who is familiar with both Ratzinger and Maritain, would have been an interesting thinker to consider in Regensburg.

Indeed, the history of religious syncretism and conversion shows that entrance to the religion of the other is through the tangible worlds of worship, devotion and imaginative engagement (i.e., legend, folklore) rather than through the appropriation of concepts and doctrine.[32] Ascetics, mystics, and religious eccentrics appear in that framework. Yet, contrary to what Arkoun has suggested, such phenomena are not incompatible with orthodoxy. They actually challenge and renew religious institutions. The "holy fools" in Eastern Orthodoxy are one example. Another example is the hymnographies of great theologians like St. John Damascene, St. Thomas Aquinas, or St. Bonaventure which take theological language and infuse it with the music and vivid imagery of devotion. Mystics like St. Symeon the New Theologian and St. John of the Cross stood precariously close to God, on the margins of what their times understood as orthodoxy (but never outside it).[33] They took theological language and gave it the intimacy, intensity, and paradox that define the mystic's encounter with God. For Symeon the personal experience of God is the only true theology.[34]

Maritain understood this tension and tried, through his interpretation of Thomism, to integrate mystical experience with Catholic orthodoxy. His thought reaches beyond Ratzinger's emphasis on the unique rationality of Christian revelation. It suggests that in Christian theology *logos* is poeticized and paradox elucidated (but never completely). From this perspective, it was easier for Maritain than it is for Ratzinger to engage Islam's distinctive vision of God and its great ascetics and mystics, figures like Rabia (c. 713–c. 801), Mansur al-Hallāj (c. 858–922) and Jalāl ad-Din Rumi (1207–1273).

III. Converging Humanisms?

Philosophy typically questions the validity of principles and intuitions that are preternaturally or supernaturally reached. It challenges continu-

31. Mohammed Arkoun, *Islam: To Reform or to Subvert?* (London: Saqi Books, 2006), 164–65.

32. Vryonis, *The Decline of Medieval Hellenism*, 351–402.

33. St. Symeon the New Theologian, *Life, Times and Theology*, vol. 3 of *On the Mystical Life: The Ethical Discourses*, edited by Alexander Golytzin (Yonkers, New York: St. Vladimir's Press, 1997), 7–53.

34. Symeon does not share Augustine's confidence in "the mind's capacity for searching the divine mysteries." Ibid., 9–10.

ities established in the context of tradition, and the interpretation of history, Scripture and religious law. Being thus inherently progressive and modernizing, philosophy appears to challenge religion. As many who have tackled modernity and religious reform have discovered, the relationship between revelation, dogma, and the demands of reason is not always a harmonious one.[35] Maritain was one of the most important Catholic thinkers to engage modernity. The Socratic paradigm was central to his understanding of philosophy as a Christian endeavor.[36]

Like Maritain, Benedict gives a special place to Socrates not only for his commitment to truth but also for the negative and divine wisdom that inspired him to question the norms of Athenian society.[37] The Regensburg address concludes with a passage from the *Phaedo* (90c-d) where Socrates dismisses the relativist's distrust of reason as self-serving, frivolous, and indifferent to the "the truth of beings" and the pursuit of wisdom. In citing this text, Benedict is taking a jab at the postmodern suspicion of reason. For Benedict, misology is ironically the consequence of Enlightenment rationalism—a notion as we shall see that Maritain also embraces. In *Truth and Tolerance*, Benedict criticizes the postmodern view of language as a system of signs in which reality is only conventionally (culturally) embedded. Truth becomes a function of signification and a construct. He cites the *Phaedrus* (274b-275d) where an Egyptian king, Thutmose of Thebes, explains that rather than elucidate reality, a system of written signs will dominate and displace it.[38] Where the Socratic legacy is invoked, rationality is never abstract: philosophy is to be practiced existentially, as a way of life. This is where thought is at once universalized and personalized. Thus, from a Christian standpoint, the Socratic method ultimately points to an incarnational view of reason.

35. Ratzinger, *Truth and Tolerance*, 144; Fazlur Rahman, "Islamic Modernism: Its Scope, Method and Alternatives," *International Journal of Middle Eastern Studies* 1 (1970): 324–25. "It is not an accident that in the entire gamut of Islamic modernism the only serious student of philosophy the Muslim world can boast of is Muhammad Iqbal." Rahman, *Islam and Modernity*, 73; see also 46–47, 95–96, 148–49.

36. Jacques Maritain, *The Peasant of the Garonne: An Old Layman Questions Himself about the Present Time*, translated by M. Cuddihy and E. Hughes (New York: Holt, Rinehart and Winston, 1968), 17. See also Cornelia A. Tsakiridou, "Redeeming Modernism: Jacques Maritain and the Catholic Vocation," in *The Vocation of the Catholic Philosopher: From Maritain to John Paul II*, edited by John P. Hittinger (Washington, D.C.: American Maritain Association, 2010), 98.

37. Ratzinger, *Truth and Tolerance*, 145–46.

38. Ibid., 188–89.

Maritain's humanism redefines modernity by infusing human reason with divine grace. In *Scholasticism and Politics,* he argues that due to its supernatural ordination, the philosophy of Aquinas can engage a variety of faiths and religions in an authentic and vital dialogue with the fundamental truths of Catholicism.[39] The truths of Catholicism are understood dynamically. For Maritain, Thomism is spiritual and intellectual labor, the work of Providence freely and creatively working through human reason, opening new horizons for understanding reality and humanity. The philosopher in this case is a visionary and pioneer, a mystic and humble reformer. Like Socrates and his *daemonion,* he listens to voices that speak from the past but have a timeless resonance. Benedict too, as we shall see, argues that when enriched by Christian revelation, reason expands the limits of human knowledge.

The idea of a universal, trans-cultural philosophical method rooted in Christian revelation and theology has parallels in Islam where, starting in the nineteenth century, progressive and modernizing thinkers like Muhammad 'Abduh, Sayyid Ahmad Khan, and Murtaza Mutahhari saw Islam as an exemplarily rational religion.[40] The reflection of a spiritual rationality in the Qur'an and Sunnah has been suggested more recently by Seyyed Hossein Nasr and Osman Yahya, respectively.[41] They view the sacred text as the ideal form and ultimate source of all religious experience—concealed in time and revealed to those who reach a certain level of holiness and esoteric knowledge (*gnosis*). According to the Sudanese reformer and visionary Mahmoud Taha, a prophetic and dynamic Islam, hidden in the sayings of the Prophet and the early Mecca revelations, provides the universal paradigm for individual and social liberation.[42] For Taha, Islam perfects itself in time. Since it is not confined within the particularities of a given era, it cannot close its vision to change.[43] The Persian advocate of an Islamic modernity Jamāl al-Din al-Afghani (1838–1897) and his Egyptian disciple

39. Jacques Maritain, *Scholasticism and Politics,* translated and edited by Mortimer J. Adler (London: Geoffrey Bless, 1954), 186–87.

40. Jacques Waardenburg, "Some Thoughts on Modernity and Modern Muslim Thinking About Islam," in *Islam and the Challenge of Modernity,* 329–36.

41. Ibid., 337–38.

42. Mahmoud Mohamed Taha, *The Second Messsage of Islam,* translated by Abdullahi Ahmed An-Naim (Syracuse, New York: Syracuse University Press, 1987), 43–47.

43. "[T]he perfection of Islamic Shari'a lies in the fact that it is a living body, growing and developing with the living, growing and developing life, guiding it steps, and charting its way toward God, stage by state." Ibid., 39; see also 10–12, 62–77.

Muhammad 'Abdu (1849–1905) also argued for an Islamic rationality that would reform and reinvigorate Muslim societies.[44]

But reason here does not freely engage reality. It emanates from the sacred text and immediately asserts the universality of its scope.[45] This is perhaps why 'Abdu is not willing to see a separate secular sphere, writing characteristically (in a phrase that recalls the title of one of Maritain's books) that Islam's "motto is … to subordinate Caesar to God and to hold him accountable for both his deeds and misdeeds."[46]

IV. The Range of Christian Reason

Maritain embraced Pope Leo XIII's 1879 encyclical *Aeterni Patris,* which sought to revive Thomism as Catholicism's premier philosophy. He was also influenced by Pope Piux X's 1907 encyclical *Pascendi Domini Gregis,* which condemned modernism as a heresy for reducing religion to an immanent, esoteric, and irrational phenomenon. Maritain's response was that Thomism was the true modernism. In Aquinas he saw a philosophy that could bear on contemporary realities (intellectual, social, political) in both a critical and creative way.[47] Maritain was confident that he was living in a time when new vistas of intellectual and spiritual communion with other peoples and faiths were emerging. To counter the evils of Western modernity, it was essential to recognize error and seek the truth across all cultures and religions, with an open mind and a profound regard for the human person, centered on the passion and mystery of Christ.

Maritain believed that secular thought and the ideologies it generated in the first half of the twentieth century were indebted to the intellectual and spiritual legacy of Christianity. He placed the most significant ideological movements in Europe (e.g., communism, fascism) in a specific religious-intellectual paradigm and emphasized the unconscious energies that religion,

44. Majid Fakhry, *A History of Islamic Philosophy* (New York: Columbia University Press, 1983), 336–37.

45. For an opposite view, see Arkoun, *Islam: To Reform or to Subvert?,* 203: "After the thirteenth century, Islamic thought eliminated all references to its own philosophical legacy.… Sunni and Shi'i thought never paid serious attention to the modern European development of philosophy until the nineteenth century. The recent expansion of the fundamentalist interpretation of Islam shows that modern philosophy remains totally alien to contemporary Islamic thought."

46. Fakhry, *A History of Islamic Philosophy,* 346.

47. Tsakiridou, "Redeeming Modernism: Jacques Maritain and the Catholic Vocation," in *The Vocation of the Catholic Philosopher,* 99–100.

through eschatology, contributed to their emergence and force. He recognized and criticized the impact of colonialism on non-European cultures, and allowed for mutual influence and growth. And much like contemporary Muslim philosophers, he rejected a positivist, abstract and functionalist rationality as detrimental to the human person and society.[48]

His incisive analysis of the collusion of reason and power in European society, anticipates Edward Said's critique of Orientalism and Arkoun's deconstruction of western and Islamic philosophical and theological orthodoxies. Using his political writings (discussed below) we can better understand how the ideologies, produced in the context of the secularization of European thought, affected, through colonialism, numerous nations and cultures and helped shape their identities and histories.

Benedict's approach is far less concerned with ideological and cultural realities. He argues that a "single rationality" permeates all fields of human knowledge. Interreligious dialogue is the critical and rigorous exchange of ideas on core theological issues. The philosophical legacy of Hellenism is essential to (and encompassed by) Christian revelation and an antidote to irrationalism in religion. In Regensburg he recognized this problem in both Christianity and Islam. He mentioned the Cordoban theologian Ibn Hazm (994–1064), who saw God as "absolutely transcendent … and not bound up with any of our categories"—a conception that excludes the intelligibility of the divine nature. Also present in the Christian tradition, radical hiddenness and incommunicability render divine discourse authoritarian and arbitrary. Christianity accepts God's unreachable majesty, but mediates it with the Incarnation, the ultimate expression of divine humility in the person of the Son and *Logos*. Thus, rather than impose his will, God invites human beings to discover it in reasoned communion.

This appears to be an indirect criticism of Islam. Since Muslims reject the divinity of Christ, reasoned communion with God is not possible. There is room for objections here and a call for a more contextual argument. In mystical Islam God places his word (*kalimāt Allah*) right in the heart of those who love him and strive to know him intimately (ascetics like Rabia, al-Hallāj, Shibli and Niffari).[49] Muhammad's *hadith* ("God puts

48. Mehmet S. Aydin, "An Islamic Evaluation of the Modern Concept of Rationality," in *Islam and the Challenge of Modernity*, 88.

49. Annemarie Schimmel, *Mystical Dimensions of Islam* (Chapel Hill, North Carolina: The University of North Carolina Press, 1975), 38–97. Cf. Vatican Council II, "*Nostra Aetate*," [Dec-

His face in front of the face of His servant at prayer") suggests an intimate encounter with God, though by no means implying an incarnation.[50] *Logos*, the central concept in Benedict's discussion of the integral presence of reason in the Christian conception of God, has some Qur'anic equivalents (e.g., *kalimāt Allah, qawl*) worthy of comment consistent with the view of the Qur'an as the uncreated Word of God.[51] Mention of these aspects, coupled with references to modernists like al-Afghani, who argue that religion is inseparable from progress, might have made Benedict's call for reasoned dialogue resonate with Muslim audiences.[52]

On the other hand, Benedict was right not to open the range of reason too widely. Maritain makes this mistake occasionally in his eagerness to engage other religions and Christian churches. For example, he compares Sufi mysticism with the natural (philosophical) mysticism of Plotinus, but makes no references to Islamic mystical theology.[53] He comments on anti-rational tendencies in Russian Orthodox Christianity, but does not consider Orthodox views of rationality.[54] He praises Vladimir Soloviev but overlooks doctrinal errors in his sophiological ideas. Convinced of the supremacy of Catholicism, Maritain was not afraid to open the Church to other voices even if that led him to the drawing of superficial differences or similarities.[55] He saw the life of ideas as a life of solidarity with those individuals and traditions that define wisdom in transcendent terms as an essential human quest—beyond

laration on the Relation of the Church to Non-Christian Religions] (1965), no. 3. Diane Steigerwald, "Le Logos: clef de l'ascenscion spirituelle dans l'ismaélisme," *Studies in Religion/Sciences Religieuses* 28 (1999): 179–80.

50. Muhammad Abdel Haleem, *Understanding the Qur'an: Themes and Style* (London: I. B. Tauris, 1999), 114.

51. Qur'an 9:31–32. "When We will something to happen, all that We say is 'Be,' and it is." Ibid., 16:40. "If all the trees on earth were pens and all the seas, with seven more seas besides, [were ink,] still God's words would not run out: God is almighty and all wise." Ibid., 31:27. All English quotations of the Qur'an are from *The Qur'an: English Translation and Parallel Arabic Text*, translated by M. A. S. Abdel Haleem (Oxford: Oxford University Press, 2010). See also Mahmoud M. Ayoub, "Towards an Islamic Christology, II: The Death of Jesus, Reality or Delusion," *The Muslim World* 70, no. 2 (1980): 94, 112; "The Word of God in Islam", *Greek Orthodox Theological Review* 31, nos. 1–2 (1986): 73. For Ayoub, the Qur'an is the Word of God but it is not God.

52. Fakhry, *A History of Islamic Philosophy*, 335.

53. Jacques Maritain, "The Natural Mystical Experience and the Void," in *Understanding Mysticism*, edited by Richard Woods (New York: Image Books, 1980), 493.

54. Jacques Maritain, *Integral Humanism: Temporal and Spiritual Problems of a New Christendom*, translated by Joseph E. Evans (New York: Charles Scribner's Sons, 1968), 104.

55. "There is only one Church of which Christ Himself is the Head with the Pope for the Vicar on earth." Jacques Maritain, *The Things That Are not Caesar's*, translated by J. F. Scanlan (New York: Charles Scribner's Sons, 1931), 176–77. Maritain, *The Degrees of Knowledge*, 7.

philosophy or metaphysics. For Maritain, dialogue was grounded less in conceptual distinctions and more in the recesses of the human soul.

Maritain was influenced by the thought of Massignon and Louis Gardet (1904–1986), but he was also influenced by the life of Fr. Charles (of Jesus) de Foucauld (1858–1916), the French aristocrat and hermit of the Sahara. He embraced de Foucauld's idea that Muslims can be redeemed through conversion to Christianity, a conversion left entirely to the freedom of the individual and the intervention of divine grace.[56] The ambiguities of this conception are evident. In his study of the colonialist underpinnings of de Foucauld's Algerian mission, Fergus Fleming concludes that "the interests of Christianity and colonialism were so closely intertwined that he saw little difference between the two."[57]

It would be a mistake to attribute de Foucauld's views only to colonialist ideology. A former officer of the French army, de Foucauld lived an eremetical life in Nazareth, Morocco, and later among the Touareg of Algeria until his assassination (he was beatified by Benedict in 2005). His view of Islam changed during his years in Algeria. In 1908, facing, like the Order of the White Fathers that had preceded him, negligible conversions and resistance from the local population, he expressed sympathy for the Muslims whose lives he shared but said this about Islam: "Mohammedanism cannot stand up in the face of education—history and philosophy expose its errors, and it falls like night before day."[58] Years later, Massignon saw his tragic death as a form of atonement, a spiritual affirmation of his earlier love for Islam, the Arabic language and the solitary life of the desert that had inspired both men to rediscover God and Catholicism.[59]

V. Christian Modernity and Islam

During his 2010 visit to Scotland, Benedict cautioned about the dangers of marginalizing religion in European society.[60] "As we reflect on the

56. Charles de Foucauld, *Spiritual Autobiography of Charles de Foucauld*, translated by J. Holland Smith, edited by Jean-Francois Six (New York: P. J. Kenedy and Sons, 1964), 161, 175, 181. On Massignon's relationship with de Foucauld, see Massignon, *Testimonies and Reflections*, 21–31.

57. Fergus Fleming, *The Sword and the Cross: Two Men and An Empire of Sand* (New York: Grove Press, 2003), 141–45.

58. De Foucauld, *Spiritual Autobiography*, 181.

59. Hugues Didier, "Louis Massignon et Charles de Foucauld," in *Louis Massignon et ses contemporains*, 101.

60. September 16, 2010; http://www.vatican.va/holy_father/benedict_xvi/encyclicals/documents/ hf_ben-xvi_enc_20090629_caritas-in-veritate_en.html.

sobering lessons of atheist extremism of the twentieth century, let us never forget how the exclusion of God, religion and virtue from public life leads ultimately to a truncated vision of man and of society and thus to a 'reductive vision of a person and his destiny'."[61] This statement builds on two themes that are present in all of his writings. The first is that the Incarnation humanized reason and gave it genuine universality. The second is that religious experience and thought are the sine qua non of humanism. For Benedict, the Catholic Church is the intellectual and spiritual foundation of civil society.[62] The freedoms enjoyed in European societies today by peoples of all faiths draw from this tradition while the evils suffered in World War II and in the Cold War stem from the rejection of its values.

These ideas echo what Maritain wrote in 1936: "Western humanism has religious and transcendent sources without which it is incomprehensible in itself.... [T]he sources of Western humanism are both classical and Christian."[63] European ideologies owe their absolutes, values and eschatology to Greek philosophy and Christian theology. Soviet communism "is a religion, and a most imperious religion ... an atheistic religion for which dialectical materialism is dogma and of which Communism as a regime of life is the ethical and social expression."[64] It deifies the state and its institutions. It subjects human dignity to civil authority and treats it as a relative rather than an absolute value.

Benedict's approach to Islam is based on the conception of Europe as a socio-cultural and ideological space, dominated by Christianity. Though non-European in its origin, Christianity "took on its most efficacious cultural and intellectual form" in Europe, in the very space that now opts to marginalize its influence on its institutions and future.[65] In earlier writings, this European Christianity claims a geographic specificity and a cultural universality. Christianity replaces the abstract universalism of the Enlightenment with its own incarnational universality. This idea is used to explain how, starting with the Enlightenment, progress came to be seen as

61. http://www.catholicherald.co.uk/news/2010/09/16/papal-visit-2010–popes-holyrood house-speech-full-text/; See also Benedict XVI, *Caritas in Veritate* (2009), no. 29.

62. "The dialogue between those outside the Church and us Catholics, us Christians, is a matter of great urgency, and we must at all costs remain faithful to this basic principle of living a faith that proceeds from the *Logos*, from creative reason, and is therefore open to all that is truly rational." Ratzinger, *Christianity and the Crisis of Cultures*, 50.

63. Maritain, *Integral Humanism*, 4–5.

64. Ibid., 36.

65. Ratzinger, *Christianity and the Crisis of Cultures*, 29.

the a-historical and a-religious transformation of human communities and nations. Benedict uses modern Turkey as an example. The utopian vision of its founder, Kemal Atatürk, sought "to plant on Muslim soil the secular attitudes that had matured in the Christian world of Europe" ("and one may of course ask whether this is in fact possible").[66] True modernity belongs to Christianity in an essentialist, exclusive way. Only a nation that is genuinely Christian is truly modern. Other modernities, both inside and outside Europe, are bound to fail.

Objections may be raised to his claim on historical grounds. Nationalist experiments in the Middle East in the first half of the twentieth century created their own mythologies and historical revisionisms, and many failed for a variety of reasons. The remedy for Enlightenment universalism may rest with the development of local and regional modernities that integrate a country's religious traditions while relating selectively to western institutions and norms. And modernity is not a monolithic phenomenon. As Fazlur Rahman has noted, secular nationalist and Islamist visions in modernizing nations (e.g., Turkey, Egypt) may appear incompatible but are actually aligned in their genesis and formation: "Turkish nationalism, of which the firebrand Atatürk was an embodiment, had already incorporated Islam as its integral constituent."[67] Kemalism's rigorous secularism not only helped create modern Turkey but has inadvertently shaped Turkey's present-day Islamist politics.

Yet, Benedict's argument that modernity is essentially Christian deserves serious consideration. So does his idea that Christianity remains a vital but dormant force in European culture. Inherently robust, it is to be distinguished from what he describes in *Truth and Tolerance* as "defective forms of religious practice" that give a false impression of religious vitality.[68] The following observation is instructive: "the mere spread of religious phenomena, or of those resembling religion, is not the same as the flourishing of religion.... Even the illusion that in the place of a worn-out Christianity the Asiatic religions or Islam are a rising force is deceptive."[69]

The influence on religion of ideological movements is rightly implied here, as is the tendency, particularly in European and American societies,

66. Ibid., 36.

67. Rahman, *Islam and Modernity*, 54; see also 53. See also Cornelia A. Tsakiridou, "Nationalist Dilemmas: Halide Edib on Greeks, Greece and the West," *New Perspectives on Turkey* 27 (2002): 1–34.

68. Ratzinger, *Truth and Tolerance*, 143.

69. Ibid.

to treat religion as a matter of feeling and taste, a sort of spiritual commodity. But not all interest in other religious traditions is superficial in that way. We cannot exclude the presence of moral and spiritual qualities in Islam and Buddhism that resonate more clearly with certain contemporary realities and are for that reason thoroughly genuine. On the other hand, given a general distaste for substance in popular culture, religions which articulate certain values from a geographical and social distance (exotic) may be more attractive because they require less of a moral or spiritual commitment from their Western adherents. Benedict is right to be cautious. Statements like "to what extent the new surge forward of the Islamic world is fuelled by truly religious forces is equally open to question" should be understood in that context.[70] In the absence of redemptive ideologies like communism or socialism, Islam's call for justice can be particularly appealing to people facing political and economic oppression.

For Benedict, Muslims are allies in the struggle against secularism: "The Muslims, who so often tend to be mentioned in this context [i.e., European civilization's Christian identity], feel threatened, not by the foundations of our Christian morality, but by the cynicism of a secularized culture that denies its own foundations."[71] But culturally and theologically, Islam belongs to a different sphere. It cannot mediate reason and offer humanity a liberating universality and a genuine modernity. By contrast, as an immanent and transcendent entity that is centered in the Mystery of Christ, the Church is open to all people. It speaks through reason that is supernaturally infused. In the person of Christ, *logos* becomes an existential reality.[72] It loves and redeems humanity and the *cosmos*: "Only that creative reason which has manifested itself as love in the crucified God can truly show us what life is."[73] It is very clear where Islam and Christianity part ways.

VI. Poetic Thomism

Though not an Islamicist himself, Maritain influenced Catholic scholarship on Islam. The doctrine of St. Thomas, he wrote in 1931, is "the uni-

70. Ibid., 144.

71. Ratzinger, *Christianity and the Crisis of Cultures*, 33.

72. On differences between Christian and Muslim anthropology, see Cornelia A. Tsakiridou, "Theophany and Humanity in St. Symeon the New Theologian and in Abū Hamid Al-Ghāzāli," *International Journal of Orthodox Theology* 2, no. 3 (2011): 167–87.

73. Ratzinger, *Christianity and the Crisis of Cultures*, 49.

versal Church's intellectual instrument," and the center of a new vision of Christian catholicity in which reason, love, and redemption converge.[74] Informed naturally and supernaturally with the truths of the faith and guided by its light, Thomism bears on all cultures and religions no matter what their temporal forms and peculiarities. A Thomist can go anywhere, in any religious tradition or culture, and find common ground. Maritain's friend and disciple, Louis Gardet (Brother André), remembered him greeting all conversations with "a rigor of thought and a liberty of spirit" that was always open to the world of the other ("*l'ouverture aux autres*").[75] Gardet credits Jacques and Raïssa for the "intellectual liberty" and the "philosophical instruments" that made his study of Islam possible.[76] Inspired by their friend's revival of Thomism, Gardet and Anawati undertook the study of Islamic theology and mysticism in the 1930s and 1940s while on mission in Algeria and Egypt.[77]

The presence of the Little Brothers of Jesus—the religious order inspired by de Foucauld that Maritain joined in the final years of his life—in Algeria was a constant reminded to Maritain of Christianity's encounter with Islam. So was his friendship with Thomas Merton, who became interested in Sufism through Massignon.[78] Merton considered Massignon and de Foucauld to have been converted to Christianity "through the Islamic revelation of a true God, living and one," suggesting an intensity of religious experience in the context of a different religion that was absent from French or European Christianity.[79] Raïssa describes in similar terms the conversion of Ernest Psichari (1883–1914), the French soldier and novelist who encountered Islam in colonial Africa. Psichari's fascination with Sufi mysticism only increased his fervor to restore France's Christian identity![80]

Writing in 1963 to the Pakistani Sufi Abdul Aziz, Merton contrasted

74. Jacques Maritain, *The Things That Are Not Caesar's*, translated by J. F. Scanlan (New York: Charles Scribner's Sons, 1931), 105.

75. Keryell, "Louis Massignon-Jacques Maritain et leur disciple, Louis Gardet," in *Louis Massignon et ses contemporains*, 115.

76. Ibid., 117, 119.

77. Dominique Avon, "Louis Gardet: A Catholic Thomist takes up Islamic Studies 1926," *Muslim World* 99, no. 2 (2009): 253–69.

78. *Louis Massignon au coeur de notre temps*, edited by Jacques Keryell (Paris: Karthala, 1999), 262, 265–66.

79. Ibid., 265.

80. Raïssa Maritain, *Adventures in* Grace, translated by Julie Kernan (New York: Longmans, Green and Company, 1945), 108.

"spiritual realities" with the "realm of words and ideas."[81] Whereas ideas differentiate, the spiritual life brings Islam and Christianity together: "But much more important is the sharing of the experience of divine light, and first of all of the light that God gives us even as the Creator and Ruler of the Universe. It is here that the area of fruitful dialogue exists between Christianity and Islam. I love the passages of the Quran which speak of the manifestations of the Creator in His Creation."[82]

Massignon's claim that Islamic monotheism with its emphasis on the oneness of God (*tawhid*), its prophetic spirit, and "simple worship" is essential to an understanding of Christian theology, resonated with Maritain's reflections about the centrality of unconditional love of God in religious experience.[83] But for Maritain this simplicity centered on Christ and found its intellectual expression in Thomism.[84] Thomism in his view is not a mere intellectual system. It is essentially a holy structure, the work of reason sanctified and therefore not strictly speaking a philosophy as such.[85] As the distinguished Thomist Étienne Gilson (1884–1978) has also argued, Thomism is an immersion in the reality of Christian revelation: reason "bathing in the light of theology," eclectic with regard to philosophical systems and drawing its unity from "a light higher than that of philosophy."[86]

In 1949, Maritain signed a Manifesto written by Olivier Lecombe which stated, among other things, that the philosophy of Thomas was "progressive and vitally open to all developments of truth in man."[87] An example of

81. Thomas Merton, *The Hidden Ground of Love: The Letters of Thomas Merton on Religious Experience and Social Concerns*, edited by William H. Shannon (New York: Farrar, Straus, Giroux, 1985), 54. See also Sidney H. Griffith, "'*Un entretien sur toutes choses, humaines et divines*': *La correspondence entre Louis Massignon et Thomas Merton*," in *Louis Massignon au coeur de notre temps*, 271.

82. Merton, *The Hidden Ground of Love*, 54.

83. Anthony O'Mahoney, "Louis Massignon, the Seven Sleepers of Ephesus and the Christian-Muslim Pilgrimage at Vieux-Marché, Brittany," in *Explorations in a Christian Theology of Pilgrimage*, edited by Craig Bartholomew and Fred Hughes (Burlington, Vermont: Ashgate, 2004), 127–28.

84. Griffith, "*Un entretien sur toutes choses, humaines et divines*': *La correspondence entre Louis Massignon et Thomas Merton*," in *Louis Massignon au coeur de notre temps*, 273.

85. "A whole rational organism with a universal value transcending place and time has so been constituted, which will endure forever. St. Thomas is entrusted with the task of maintaining its unity." Maritain, *The Things That Are Not Caesar's*, 105.

86. Étienne Gilson, *Christian Philosophy*, translated by Armand Maurer (Toronto: Pontifical Institute of Medieval Studies, 1993), 23; see also 21–22.

87. Ibid., 264.

this openness was the collaboration of Gardet and Gilson on the collection of Islamicist studies known as *Études Musulmanes*.[88] Like Gilson, Maritain saw in Thomism an inherent Christocentric sanctity that opens it to all reality and to all systems of thought. A Thomist will naturally explore Sufi mysticism.[89] Maritain could be equally fascinated with socialist thought, the theology of Luther, and the ideas of Voltaire. Like St. Thomas with Plato, Aristotle, or Avicenna, he sought to engage his philosophical others. Despite their errors, he wrote, "they exist in my universe of culture.... I converse with them there, and we battle mercilessly; they are still alive for me."[90]

In *The Degrees of Knowledge*, while discussing the limits of metaphysical knowledge, Maritain mentions al-Hallāj as an example of the desire for transcendent wisdom and spiritual union that metaphysical inquiry arouses in the human soul. Al-Hallāj receives from God, "far surpassing all human effort, a gift of deifying grace and free endowments of Uncreated Wisdom, [which] has as its beginning the *mad love* that Wisdom Itself has for each and all of us, and as its end, the union of spirit with it."[91] Maritain saw the Baghdad ascetic, who died dismembered and hanged (or crucified) on a gibbet for professing his union with God (Ana'l-Haqq, I am the Truth or My 'I' is God), as an *alter Christus*.[92] The ascetic's love of God and the proximity granted to him by God's grace (and mercy), generate mystical insights and utterances not available to ordinary theological discourse. Thus Al-Hallāj exclaims: "O people! When the Truth has taken hold of a heart, He empties it of all but Himself! When God attaches Himself to a man, He kills in him all else but Himself! When He loves one of His faithful, He incites the others to hate him, in order that His servant may draw near Him so as to ascent to Him!"[93]

Maritain wants to keep all voices speaking. The Christocentric humanism that he embraces is discursive, open, and integrative. Unlike the Marxist dialectic "whose only advance is over the dead," it does not silence alternative and dissenting voices.[94] His thought is open to spiritual traditions

88. Ibid.

89. Maritain, *Integral Humanism*, 288.

90. Ibid., 92.

91. Maritain, *The Degrees of Knowledge*, 7.

92. Ibid.

93. Louis Massignon, *The Passion of Al-Hallāj Mystic and Martyr of Islam*, abridged edition, Bollingen Series, vol. 98, translated and edited by Herbert Mason (Princeton: Princeton University Press, 1982), 143.

94. Ibid.

which emphasize the unity of the lovers of God and the ascetic's "way of constant purification and mental struggle."[95]

Benedict also sees Aquinas as a master of the spiritual life of reason. Thomas' view of theology as a secondary science rooted in "the light of faith" explains how revelation expands the range of reason.[96] "The science of God and the blesseds" is the foundation of theology.[97] It is the saint's intimate encounter with Christ, "the look of love that the Lord directs to man, this look that preserves the fullness of his truth and the ultimate guarantee of his dignity."[98] The difference between them perhaps is that Maritain had an intuitive grasp of this connection and the gift, as Yves Simon wrote some time ago, to bring to Scholastic philosophy a unique blend of "intuitive, poetic and thought-provoking expression."[99]

VII. Rationalist Pathologies

Benedict argues that when rationality is bereft of grace it gives rise to psychical and social pathologies.[100] Science loses its spiritual foundation and majesty.[101] Readily accessible technologies and a distorted sense of liberty create new forms of violence. Terrorist acts stem from the perpetrator's conviction that man can rely on his own imagination and will to author reality: "Even terrorism is ultimately based on this modality of man's 'self-authorization,' not on the teachings of the Qur'an."[102] Thus violence becomes instrumental to redemption and salvation.

Maritain explained the destructive ideologies of the twentieth century in the same terms. His views on this subject are essential in understanding Regensburg. In *Scholasticism and Politics,* he identified three major ruptures in European consciousness that gave rise to communism and fascism: Lutheranism (immanentism), Cartesianism (rationalism) and Rousseauism

95. Annemarie Schimmel, *Mystical Dimensions of Islam* (Chapel Hill, North Carolina: The University of North Carolina Press, 1975), 58. Schimmel refers specifically to one of the founding figures of Sufism in Baghdad, Abū'l Quāsim al-Junayd. See ibid., 830–910.

96. *Summa theologiae* I, q. 1, a. 1.

97. Ratzinger, *Christianity and the Crisis of Cultures,* 108, 110. See also ST I, q. 1, a. 2.

98. Ratzinger, *Christianity and the Crisis of Cultures,* 71.

99. John H. Griffin and Yves R. Simon, *Jacques Maritain: Homage in Words and Pictures* (Albany, New York: Magi Books, 1974), 5. Tsakiridou, "Redeeming Modernism: Jacques Maritain and the Catholic Vocation," in *The Vocation of the Catholic Philosopher,* 100.

100. Ratzinger, *Truth and Tolerance,* 158.

101. Ibid., 156–58.

102. Ratzinger, *Christianity and the Crisis of Cultures,* 42.

(individualism).[103] Communism dominated the Eastern Orthodox world; fascism the countries most affected by Protestantism—areas where the Church of Christ experienced its most lasting schisms.[104] European totalitarianisms (and perhaps all totalitarianisms) were perversions of the Christian spirit: secular versions of Christendom.

Samuel Huntington argued that as modern ideologies collapse, the quest for universality shifts from politics to religion.[105] Maritain would have objected. Religion that replaces ideology is ideology, not religion. True religion entails a supernatural, mystical love (*agape, caritas*); its ideological forms do not. This is why he insists that a "politics of Christian inspiration" cannot be a politics of oppression.[106] Where there is Christianity, there is "free Christian action" and "free Christian judgment on the things of the temporal order."[107] Ideologies resemble religions because they incorporate religious elements in their ethics and eschatology while relying on rationalist constructs to ordain persons to temporal institutions. These "most negative and destructive" ideas (e.g., materialism, atheism, etc.) were transplanted through colonialism to other nations.[108] This is why the Church must transcend "ethnical or cultural particularisms" and offer to the world "the natural catholicity (whatever may be its historical diversities) of reason and of the principles of natural law and the fundamental virtues of civilization."[109]

In *Scholasticism and Politics,* Maritain talks of the "tragic opposition between life and intelligence" in western civilization.[110] Where God is absent, a discarnate intellect assumes authority over all spheres of human life, merging abstraction with the crudest forms of utilitarianism. It creates all kinds of artificial worlds and constructs that promise justice, happiness and salvation.[111] It ignores evil and trivializes the good. Reason thus degrades and threatens human life.[112]

103. Maritain, *Scholasticism and Politics,* 190–92.

104. Ibid., 192.

105. Samuel P. Huntington, "The Clash of Civilizations," *Foreign Affairs* 72, no. 3 (1993): 22–49.

106. Maritain, *Integral Humanism,* 275.

107. Ibid., 284.

108. Maritain, *Scholasticism and Politics,* 186.

109. Ibid. "New cultural types" are needed but in principle, "Catholicism will always maintain the principles and the truths that govern every type of civilization." Jacques Maritain, *Freedom in the Modern World,* translated by Richard O'Sullivan (New York: Charles Scribner's Sons, 1936), 101–102.

110. Ibid., 3

111. Ibid., 13.

112. Ibid., 2–3

The perennial questions of human existence and morality are trivialized in the fleeting categories of cultural rhetoric. Ideas invoke virtues and ideals that never materialize. Subject to elusive and yet expedient moralities, human beings suffocate. Reason atrophies. The soul grows silent. Instinctual energies proliferate. The stagnancy of mediocrity and finitude in which ordinary lives are enveloped, the dominance of abstractions and empty forms of communion ("false wisdom which humiliates and deceives") in public and private life, generate an explosive discontent.[113] Now godless and "beheaded" pure reason recalibrates transcendence.[114] The era of human gods, mundane paradises, and human scapegoats begins. A tragic humanity sacrifices its freedom and life to ideologies that defer happiness to an ideal, eschatological time. Or, it descends into the solipsism of a "vegetative paradise"—addiction to drugs or phantasy. In communism (and capitalism) "the titanism of industry" promises salvation.[115] In National Socialism technology becomes a means of racial purification.

Today, cults of death and suicide take many forms. Their particular circumstances may differ, but the woman who takes her own life somewhere in America and the youth who commits himself to a suicide mission abandon a world that has lost substance, unity, and purpose. The causes may be alienation, poverty, authoritarianism, a de-humanized rationality, or an inflated sense of self and power that in reality speaks only of human impotence and desperation. No matter what the social, political, and psychical circumstances, Maritain's principle applies. Where the fundamental existential, moral, and spiritual questions of human life are exploited and manipulated (e.g., as commodities in capitalist societies) or suppressed by religious and state authorities (e.g., as blasphemy or sedition in Islamic theocracies), anything can be rationally justified. Reason and delusion converge.

Rationalist pathologies do not only affect secular systems of thought. They also affect a religion's conviction that it has a hold on rationality and a claim to total truth. This is why there should always be room in religion for taking reason out of its normative and "natural" forms and allowing it to sojourn, so to speak, with those who have made it their purpose to shed all things worldly and find God. Benedict alludes to this idea when he writes: "We need a new readiness to seek the truth and also the humility to let ourselves be found."[116]

113. Ibid., 13; see also ibid., 11–12.

114. Ibid., 16.

115. Ibid.

116. Ratzinger, *Truth and Tolerance*, 159.

VIII. Beyond Conversion

In the Paleologos dialogue, a Christian and a Muslim argue fervently for the superiority of their religion. No matter how confident one's arguments, dialogue kindles and expresses deeper uncertainties that reason, when placed in the service of doctrine, is called to silence. Thus certainty in the superiority of one's faith may be easier sought in the sphere of politics and in the seemingly tangible signs of history. Converting or destroying each other's holy places is one such sign. War is another. Transcendentalized and sacramentalized, war has provided a powerful amagalm of fantasy and reality for both religions. To those seduced by such fantasies, conquest and conversion have not lost their appeal. The more reason loses its subtlety and enters the domain of ideology, the more powerful it becomes. The more religion sheds the radical uncertainty that the encounter with God or a transcendent reality creates in the human mind, the less of a religion it becomes.

Maritain understood that religion can be made to serve power by being integrated in an ideological sphere where only its superficial forms remain active while its substance, the radical humanism of the saint, is either cynically dismissed or blatantly exploited. Yet, like Benedict and others who have tried to argue beyond their religion while still thinking (unavoidably) within it, he saw Islam through a Christian prism. There is nothing inherently wrong in this provided that one remains a marginal or radical Christian (or Muslim). To keep oneself on the margins and ever vigilant about ideological intrusions and absolute certainties in one's faith is not easy—and some would argue, not possible.

Charles de Foucauld described his encounter with Islam as "seductive beyond measure" because he, like Massignon, Gardet, and to a certain extent Maritain, was not immune to the ways in which his culture's fascination with the exotic (and dangerous)—the product indistinguishably of colonialist and Belle Époque sensibilities—had aestheticized Islam and Arabs.[117] In 1903 he vowed to work for "the conversion of Morocco," and "the war against Satan." "I have humbly offered Morocco to the Sacred Heart," he wrote, as if the country was a spiritual wasteland.[118]

117. De Foucauld wrote: "L'Islamisme est extrêmement séduisant. Il m'a seduit a l'excès," in *Louis Massignon et ses contemporains*, 102.

118. Charles de Foucauld, *Spiritual Autobiography of Charles de Foucauld*, translated by J. Holland Smith, edited by Jean-Francois Six (New York: P. J. Kennedy and Sons, 1964), 148–49.

Reflecting in 1965 on his own vocation with the Little Brothers of Jesus, Maritain described their work in Algeria as one of unconditional *caritas*, a sacrificial love that grafted the Muslims they served on the mystical Body of Christ. This union was both invisible (mystical) and real because they "loved them [and each other] in true brotherhood."[119] It was a form of conversion that made it possible for a Muslim to "live by the grace of Christ and die in Christ without ceasing to be a Muslim."[120] Could Maritain envision a similar conversion for a Christian?

For Maritain and Benedict, the saint is the living incarnation of *caritas* who keeps theology focused on the mystical reality of Christ. But this position comes with one condition. What is said of this reality must stem from those moments when the revealed word grows silent and incomprehensible and God is heard and seen in the flesh, in the recesses of one's being. When one then speaks, what is spoken has a divine carnality; it is God's language conceived in grace and in that sense truly a theology (the Word Divine). Christianity is not a religion of the book and perhaps not a religion at all. It is the encounter with Christ, the Living Word of the Father, and with the Holy Spirit that makes his voice heard. To this voice theology must yield if it is to be truly "theology." Love (*caritas, agape*), too, must be purified in asceticism so that one can love the other where she is. Where an authentic openness to the other is present, conversion is never an issue.

There is, finally, an interesting geographical shift in the Regensburg address. Benedict calls for the re-Hellenization of Christianity. The recovery of *logos* is a project that points to the shores of the Eastern Mediterranean, where Christianity and Islam were conceived and practiced for centuries. It is in this radically theological space that the ascetic, spiritual, and theological sources of both religions lie and where their encounter with Greek thought took shape. One need only think of the teachings of the Palestinian and Egyptian Fathers and Mothers with their terse locutions of Christian truth—never theorized or speculated—to hear the *logos* of the Stoic sage reverberate in Christian experience. Islam's early spiritual and philosophical ventures are indebted to the wisdom of the Christian ascetic and anchorite.[121]

Al-Hallāj, who like Socrates called himself "*namousi*" (Greek *nomos* or

119. Said Maritain: "*Ils aiment d'une façon veritablement FRATERNELLE*," in *Louis Massignon: Au coeur de notre temps*, 221.

120. "Vive de la grâce du Christ et meure dans le Christ sans cesser d'être musulman." Ibid.

121. Reynold A. Nicholson, "Sufis: The Mystics of Islam," in *Understanding Mysticism*, 183.

law), often sounds like a Desert Father. His servant's plea on the day of his martyrdom, "Master, bequeath me a maxim" is a verbatim translation of "Geronda eipe moi logo" with which since the third century ascetics and anchorites have asked for the counsel of Elders.[122] From this perspective, there are compelling reasons to direct Muslim-Christian dialogue to this distant heritage.[123]

122. Massignon, *The Passion of Al-Hallāj Mystic and Martyr of Islam*, 107, 108.

123. I wish to thank Professor Mahmoud Ayoub for discussing aspects of this paper with me.

JONATHAN J. SANFORD

Maritain, Anscombe, and Contemporary Virtue Ethics

Maritain declares the overarching theme of his rich and still timely book *Scholasticism and Politics* to be the recognition, explanation, and defense of the dignity of the human person. He recognizes the challenges facing this task within a cultural milieu he rightly regards to be at a point of crisis. Though World War II is long over, the totalitarianisms responsible for its instigation remain under different guises. Maritain argues that the task falls to philosophy, and particularly to realist and Thomistic philosophy, to reclaim its birthright and come to the defense of the dignity of the person within a culture trained to look only to science for its direction.

The work of G. E. M. Anscombe provides profound resources for advancing Maritain's goals, especially as they are announced in her provocative and groundbreaking 1958 article, "Modern Moral Philosophy."[1] Anscombe describes modern moral philosophy to be a set of techniques which employ a vocabulary devoid of its former intelligibility in support of the specious aims of consequentialism. As antidote, she points us in the direction of what she terms a "philosophical psychology" along the lines laid out in the Aristotelian tradition. Thus is born the contemporary virtue ethics movement in philosophy.

Does this movement, in its current dominant modes, measure up to the tasks of displacing the consequentialist aims of modern moral philosophy, developing an adequate philosophical psychology, and in doing so,

1. G. E. M. Anscombe, "Modern Moral Philosophy," *Philosophy* 33, no. 124 (1958): 1–19.

come to the defense of the dignity of the human person? I will argue that the answer, sadly, is "no." What we find instead in the dominant trends of contemporary virtue ethics is both a missed opportunity and an adherence to those very same afflictions which Anscombe finds definitive of modern moral philosophy. I will conclude with some considerations for Aristotelians, and particularly Thomists, regarding hoped-for alliances with the contemporary virtue ethics movement.

I. Anscombe's "Modern Moral Philosophy"

Despite the classical and medieval traditions of moral philosophy where considerations of virtue take center stage, and despite surface similarities with the work of Aristotelians and Thomists, *contemporary* virtue ethics is best understood as a very recent movement in moral philosophy. Its origins are easier to understand than its later permutations, since we can trace its initial inspiration to Anscombe's remarkable essay.

Her inspiration for contemporary virtue ethics notwithstanding, Ancombe cannot be blamed for the course of this movement's development. As Christopher Coope rightly notes, Anscombe never referred to what she was doing as "virtue ethics."[2] Her main focus was on practical rationality, seeking to revive a robust account of *phronesis*, and her work and that of other early thinkers in this movement are better described as contributing to what Coope contends is more aptly called "good sense ethics." The irony of modern virtue ethicists looking to Anscombe's essay as their inspiration is striking when one contrasts the radical nature of her views about modern moral philosophy against virtue ethical efforts to accommodate the virtues to modern moral philosophy.[3] Coope remarks:

> At first—way back in the late 1950s—a virtue ethicist would have been someone who found more of interest in 'Modern Moral Philosophy' than in modern moral philosophy. That article was disconcerting, and hence one expected to learn some-

2. Christopher Miles Coope, "Modern Virtue Ethics," in *Values and Virtues: Aristotelianism in Contemporary Ethics*, edited by Timothy Chappell (Oxford: Clarendon Press, 2006), 21.

3. Roger Crisp and Michael Slote, for instance, take note of the "huge effect" of Anscombe's article in the introduction to their anthology which begins with Anscombe's essay. See *Virtue Ethics*, edited by Roger Crisp and Michael Slote (Oxford: Oxford University Press, 1997), 1–2. Rosalind Hursthouse lists Anscombe as the first of those philosophers who has put virtue ethics on the map (see Rosalind Hursthouse, *On Virtue Ethics* [Oxford: Oxford University Press, 1993], 3), and dedicates *On Virtue Ethics* to both Anscombe and Phillipa Foot.

> thing from it. Turning to modern virtue ethics, what a contrast we find. It can be called concerting. Modern virtue ethics has become something soothing, edifying and familiar. It has grown up in the polluted atmosphere of contemporary expectations (assumptions, presuppositions, confusions, distractions) and naturally enough has quickly become tarnished by them.[4]

Coope seems on target here, and to appreciate his perspective on modern virtue ethics, we first have try to see Anscombe's remarkable essay with fresh eyes. Anscombe posits three theses:

> The first is that it is not profitable for us at present to do moral philosophy; that should be laid aside at any rate until we have an adequate philosophy of psychology, in which we are consciously lacking. The second is that the concepts of obligation, and duty—*moral* obligation and *moral* duty, that is to say—and what is *morally* right and wrong, and of the *moral* sense of 'ought', ought to be jettisoned if this is psychologically possible because they are survivals, or derivatives from survivals, from an earlier conception of ethics which no longer generally survives, and are only harmful without it. My third thesis is that the differences between the well-known English writers on moral philosophy from Sidgwick to the present day are of little importance.[5]

We see immediately the point of Coope's claim that the essay is disconcerting: if Anscombe is right, we need to cease and desist from engaging in moral philosophy in its current mode because we lack a coherent anthropology to support it, there is something profoundly amiss with our contemporary and prevalent use of "moral," and the great variety we find in contemporary Anglo-American ethics is of no consequence—and that because of its obsession with consequences.

II. To Ought or Not to Ought?

Of the three, it is the second thesis that has the greatest effect on the burgeoning contemporary virtue ethics movement as seen in the way that so much early virtue ethical literature seems primarily concerned to critique deontology.[6] Too often it has been overlooked, however, that Anscombe

4. Coope, "Modern Virtue Ethics," 31.

5. Anscombe, "Modern Moral Philosophy," 26; emphasis in original. This work has been anthologized several times, and the page numbers here are from the most easily accessible printing, chapter 1 of *Virtue Ethics*.

6. Kathleen Wilkes, "The Good Man and the Good for Man in Aristotle's Ethics," in *Essays on Aristotle's Ethics*, edited by Amélie Oksenberg Rorty (Berkeley: University of California Press,

does not seek to do away with every notion of "ought" or "obligation." This could not be clearer than in her use of a non-deontological "ought" in the very formulation of her thesis which claims that the use of "the *moral* sense of 'ought', ought to be jettisoned." What of course she means is that the special sense of "ought" which one meets everywhere in contemporary ethics, that which goes by the name of the "moral ought," needs to be rejected.

Nevertheless, "should," "ought," "needs" and related terms are needed to refer to ordinary senses of good and bad. For instance, for a lawnmower to be good—to cut well—you ought to sharpen its blades. Anscombe remarks that such terms as these are indispensable, and do not evoke any sort of "moral" connotations. The application of these terms in such a way as to harness connotations that indicate being bound by law is, she says, the result of history. It was Christianity's Torah-derived conception of divine law that gave "should" and its equivalents their obligatory bite. The modern world is no longer dominated by a Judeo-Christian worldview, and yet it is precisely a belief in God as law-giver that is required to make intelligible a conception of ethics that treats its prescription as dictates of law. Despite removing God from the equation, the *terminology* of our predecessor culture remains intact. Anscombe remarks:

> It is as if the notion 'criminal' were to remain when criminal law and criminal courts had been abolished and forgotten. A Hume discovering this situation might conclude that there was a special sentiment, expressed by 'criminal', which alone gave the word its sense. So Hume discovered the situation in which the notion 'obligation' survived, and the word 'ought' was invested with that peculiar force having which it is said to be used in a 'moral' sense, but in which the belief in divine law had long since been abandoned: for it was substantially given up among Protestants at the time of the Reformation. The situation, if I am right, was the interesting one of the survival of a concept outside the framework of thought that made it a really intelligible one.[7]

Where worldviews crumble, language remains—retaining the semblance of intelligibility but bereft of meaning. Hume exposes what Kant seeks to clothe—the vapidity of our language of obligation once stripped of its metaphysical underpinnings.

1980), 355; Bernard Williams, "Morality, the Peculiar Institution," in *Ethics and the Limits of Philosophy* (London: Penguin Books, 1985), 174–96; anthologized as chapter 2 in *Virtue Ethics*, 45–65.

7. Anscombe, "Modern Moral Philosophy," 31. It is precisely this "interesting situation" that MacIntyre elaborates on in the opening chapter of *After Virtue*, 3rd ed. (Notre Dame, Indiana: University of Notre Dame Press, 2007).

Anscombe concludes her thoughts on Hume's naturalistic fallacy in the following way: "I should judge that Hume and our present-day ethicists did a considerable service by showing that no content could be found in the notion 'morally ought', if it were not that the latter philosophers try to find an alternative (very fishy) content and to retain the psychological force of the term."[8] It is precisely the attempt to wiggle their way out from the implications of Hume's observation, the attempt to continue to employ an unintelligible concept which nevertheless retains its "mesmeric force," an attempt to clothe what in essence remains a naked imposter, that leads modern moral philosophy to run amok.

This is just the place, Anscombe protests, where the lesson of Aristotle ought to have been remembered—namely, that one can do ethics without the notion "morally wrong" through the employment of aretaic terminology, such as "untruthful," "intemperate," and "unjust." With varying degrees of successful avoidance of the notion "morally wrong," contemporary virtue ethics have striven to utilize elements of Aristotle's aretaic investigations.

III. Stop the Moral Presses!

Anscombe's first thesis, that regarding the need to desist from moral philosophizing in its current mode, has been largely ignored by contemporary virtue ethicists. Anscombe argues that following Aristotle's path requires far more than a well-heeled aretaic vocabularly. It requires an adequate and comprehensive account of human action: "In present-day philosophy an explanation is required how an unjust man is a bad man, or an unjust action a bad one; to give such an explanation belongs to ethics; but it cannot even be begun until we are equipped with a sound philosophy of psychology."[9] We cannot explain what injustice is without providing an account of what sort of characteristic a virtue is, and how it is related to the actions in which we find it. Anscombe contends that such an account is not a matter for ethics, but rather for a conceptual analysis that must be done before an ethics that highlights the virtues can be deployed, a task she undertakes in her work on intention and action theory.

Instead of painstaking conceptual analysis trained on action theory, what we find in the contemporary virtue ethics movement is the explosion

8. Anscombe, "Modern Moral Philosophy," 31.
9. Ibid., 30.

of descriptions of the virtues, the effect of which, as Coope observes, has been concerting. Coope again:

Goody virtues were soon being invoked (or invented or emphasized) by the dozen.... The new generation of virtue ethicists however all went for charity or benevolence.... Yet charity had inexplicably been left out by Aristotle.... Why this curious omission? How could Aristotle (to say nothing of Plato and the rest) have failed to notice what now seems to so many to be the most vivid and obvious of all the virtues? What have we learned since his day, and how did we learn it? There seems be to an enormous change—not to be characterized as a difference of emphasis! About all this there has arisen a not-to-worry complacency.[10]

Coope goes on to note that although Anscombe's fellow traveler, Peter Geach, emphasizes charity in his work on the virtues, the word for him names a supernaturally infused theological virtue, not the general benevolence celebrated by the standard bearers of contemporary virtue ethics, such as Rosalind Hursthouse and Michael Slote.[11] For this, and other reasons, Geach simply does not fit into the current virtue ethics circular hole—he is too square.

Like Anscombe's observations about the philosophical cum theological account that renders obligation intelligible, charity is an intelligible concept only if its theological core holds true. Charity in its secular context is groundless. It demands that we do good to others; but the all important question of "Why should we?" has received few, and most of them rather uninspiring, answers. Consider Michael Slote's reflection on secular charity, or as he terms it, a "generalized concern for other people":

The moral philosophies that today dominate the philosophical scene, (utilitarian) consequentialism and Kantianism, are both ready with answers as to why we must be concerned, at least to some extent, with all other human beings. And it has be-

10. Coope, "Modern Virtue Ethics," 33.

11. Rosalind Hursthouse elevates charity to a master virtue when she writes: "From the perspective of virtue ethics, one can say that it is 'absolutely required' that one does not 'pass by on the other side' when one sees a wounded stranger lying by the roadside, but the requirement comes from charity rather than justice" (*On Virtue Ethics* [Oxford: Oxford University Press, 1999], 6); and claims that every virtue ethicist recognizes this central role of charity: "Charity or benevolence, for example, is not an Aristotelian virtue, but all virtue ethicists assume it is on the list now." Ibid., 8. These claims beg the questions: Which justice? Which charity? Which benevolence? There seems to be a Kantian notion of justice competing with a secularized version of Christian charity in the first quotation. Michael Slote writes: "I hope to persuade you thereby that basing morality ultimately in a motive like caring or (universal) benevolence or even love makes a good deal of sense." *Morals from Motives* (Oxford: Oxford University Press, 2001), x.

come difficult to accept any overall moral philosophy, like Aristotle's, that offers no defense of generalized concern for (other) people. Such a moral philosophy now strikes most philosophers as retrograde, and, more particularly, it seems to be unhelpful in regard to one of the central moral issues of contemporary (or modern) life, namely: how *much* concern or help do we owe to those, half a world away, whose troubles or sufferings we hear about and can do something to relieve.[12]

The matter appears settled: Charity, benevolence, or its particularized "warm" agent-based "care" variety, as Slote will have it in this work,[13] is fundamental. Everyone knows this. Aristotle, if you hadn't noticed, is outdated. No moral philosophy that fails to make secular charity central is acceptable.

But, yet again, why should we exercise charity? Slote tells us we should because consequentialism and Kantianism are ready with answers for why we should. He also tells us that it is retrograde not to express this concern for others. Slote seems to offer little more than the popularity of this secularized virtue for the justification of its importance. The new question becomes not whether to care for distant and personally unknown persons, but rather how to determine how much to donate to them, and how to balance that universal benevolence with the particular care we should have for those we know and are responsible for. What Slote seeks is not an account that charity is required, but of how we are to be charitable, and he looks to our sentiments for an answer.

What would a Hume, or more pointedly a Nietzsche, make of Slote's efforts? They would point out that the reasons that charity or benevolence seem so central have to do with the force the word retains from its formerly Christian context. Absent that context, we find dressed up but empty platitudes.[14] The concerting, consoling effect of the sort of virtue ethics championed by Hursthouse and Slote uses to its advantage a notion of "charity" whose continued force is merely accidental to the religious and historical context that invest it with meaning. Like the "present-day ethicists" described by Anscombe, they seek to cloak themselves with, and to capitalize on, a notion bereft of its meaning but still retaining a lingering fragrance of nobility. Perhaps I should speak more plainly and say that they are party

12. Ibid., vii-viii; emphasis in original.

13. Ibid., 114–37.

14. "Clearly, a reasonable virtue ethic needs either be Geachean or Nietzschean. In the early days of its revival it was more or less so. But what a falling away there has been. Nietzsche would have talked of decadence: meaning here the replacement of good sense by goodyness." Coope, "Modern Virtue Ethics," 36.

to a truly great crime—that of having robbed God of his charity. If Anscombe and Coope, and Nietzsche too, are correct, the most successful of our contemporary virtue ethicists have perpetrated a fraud of enormous proportions and implications.

IV. Contemporary Virtue Ethics and Consequentialism

Anscombe's third thesis, that the differences between the many Anglo-American moral philosophies that can be observed today are negligible, has been for the most part ignored by Anglo-American moral philosophers, and successfully deflected by contemporary virtue ethicists. Is such maltreatment of Anscombe's thesis justified? To answer this question, we need first to look at her characterization of modern moral philosophy.

On Anscombe's view, what ties together the various dominant ethical theories in such a way as to justify calling them as a whole "modern moral philosophy" is their united anti-absolutist stand which is put to the service of ends which justify means. Consequentialism is the term Anscombe coins for this. She observes that in moral philosophy since Sidgwick, it is considered legitimate to conclude that there are circumstances wherein it can be "morally right" to do something that is simply and absolutely unjust, like punishing an innocent man when one knows he is innocent. Anscombe reflects on these attempts to legitimize what both the Bible and the Greeks consider nefariousness in these terms:

> [I]t is clear that a good man is a just man; and a just man is a man who habitually refuses to commit or participate in any unjust actions for fear of any consequences, or to obtain any advantage, for himself or anyone else. Perhaps no one will disagree. But, it will be said, what *is* unjust is sometimes determined by expected consequences; and certainly that is true. But there are cases where it is not: now if someone says, 'I agree, but all this wants a lot of explaining,' then he is right, and what is more, the situation at present is that we can't do the explaining; we lack the philosophic equipment. But if someone really thinks, *in advance*, that it is open to question whether such an action as procuring the judicial execution of the innocent should be quite excluded from consideration—I do not want to argue with him; he shows a corrupt mind.[15]

15. Anscombe, "Modern Moral Philosophy," 41–42; emphasis in original.

Anscombe is no Pollyanna. She readily admits we have yet to do the work, and even to develop the tools necessary to do the work, of explaining why it is the case that the good man is the just man. Nevertheless, like Aristotle remarking that philosophical ethics is only for those who have been properly educated about the basic facts of the ethical life,[16] there is no philosophizing with those who have thrown out the most basic of human insight into human action—namely, that there are some actions that are always wrong, and no circumstances can change that.

In a certain sense, consequentialists—those who are willing to consider the suspension of moral absolutes for the obtainment of so-called "good" results—are not doing moral philosophy at all. Instead, they are engaging in a variety of sophistry properly called rationalizing. This, I know, seems harsh, and philosophers are generally not fond of being called sophists, but it is not one of Anscombe's goals to avoid giving offence.[17] No opponents were more odious to Plato or Aristotle, and none fought against more fiercely, than those "wise ones" willing to give rhetorical cover to the corrupt. Anscombe is cut from this same cloth, and her essay is a contemporary assault on the sophistry of her day.

Exposing the sophistic doctrine of consequentialism is what, ultimately, seems to have prompted Anscombe to write "Modern Moral Philosophy." Her exhortation to cease and desist moral philosophy as it is currently practiced and to rebuild foundations for ethical philosophy through developing a "philosophical psychology" need to be understood as the response to the crisis Anscombe has discovered. Those other two theses are weapons meant to battle against the sophistical arms wielded by those she has grouped together and identified as her adversaries.

16. See Aristotle, *Nicomachean Ethics* (NE) 1.4, 1095a31–1095b12.

17. The charge of "a corrupt mind" indicates one is past the point of being persuaded. Aristotle reflects on such as these in the following: "Now if arguments were in themselves enough to make men good, they would justly, as Theognis says, have won very great rewards, and such rewards should have been provided; but as things are, while they seem to have power to encourage and stimulate the generous-minded among the young, and to make a character which is gently born, and true lover of what is noble, ready to be possessed by excellence, they are not able to encourage the many to nobility and goodness. For these do not by nature obey the sense of shame, but only fear, and do not abstain from bad acts because of their baseness but through fear of punishment; ... What argument would remould such people?" NE 10.9, 1179b4–16. All quotations from the *Nicomachean Ethics* are taken from W. D. Ross's translation in *The Complete Works of Aristotle*, vol. 2, edited by Jonathan Barnes (Princeton: Princeton University Press, 1984). It is for such as these that political institutions need to use force, not just the art of persuasion practiced on the few who are truly persuadable. Few things were more worrying to Plato or Aristotle than legislators who lack the requisite excellent character needed to govern well.

It is the case then that the third and most regularly dismissed of Anscombe's three theses is actually the true center of her project. This she accomplishes through peeling back the layers of some noble-sounding words in order to reveal the true nature of her enemy:

> It is left to modern moral philosophy—the moral philosophy of all the well-known English ethicists since Sidgwick—to construct systems according to which the man who says—'We need such-and-such, and will only get it this way' *may* be a virtuous character: that is to say, it is left open to debate whether such a procedure as the judicial punishment of the innocent may not in some circumstances be the 'right' one to adopt; and though the present Oxford moral philosophers would accord a man *permission* to 'make it his principle' not to do such a thing, they teach a philosophy according to which the particular consequences of such an action *could* 'morally' be taken into account by a man who was debating what to do; and if they were such as to accord with his ends, it might be a step in his moral education to frame a moral principle under which he 'managed' (to use Nowell-Smith's phrase) to bring the action; or it might be a new 'decision of principle', making which was an advance in the formation of his moral thinking (to adopt Mr. Hare's conception), to decide: in such-and-such circumstances one ought to procure the judicial condemnation of the innocent. And that is my complaint.[18]

Anscombe ought to be chiefly known as the champion of absolutism against barbaric consequentialism, for it is this which leads her to call for the recovery of elements of an Aristotelian approach to ethics.

Those deemed by Anscombe "consequentialists" are not, of course, generally thought of as barbaric. Academics who fall under this description are generally nice, thoughtful, and well-mannered. Like Gorgias, they enjoy good reputations, and are entrusted with the education of the youth of society's leaders. One finds those they have educated running universities, hospitals, cabinets, congresses, and countries. Yet they are nevertheless barbaric on Anscombe's telling, and her condemnation of the corruption at the heart of modern moral philosophy could hardly be clearer or more acerbic. Yet somehow, even though her essay continues to be read regularly, and even though consequentialism has become a regular classroom name, the barbs of Anscombe's probing critique have been removed. I wonder if Anscombe often felt like a Cassandra, and also what contemporary virtue ethics might have become if only it had heeded all three of Anscombe's theses.

But perhaps you are at this moment thinking, "Don't we find conse-

18. Anscombe, "Modern Moral Philosophy," 44; emphasis in original.

quentialism, and indeed all rule-based approaches, roundly criticized in most virtue ethical literature?" If so, I'd answer *sic et non*. Certainly criticisms of rule-based approaches to ethics abound, but the core of Anscombe's critique of consequentialism is not that it is rule-based, but that it is willing to suspend moral absolutes. And, on that score, one labors in vain to find prominent virtue ethicists who are unwilling to bend a few rules to achieve the so-called "right" results: it is not a matter of whether, but of in what circumstances it is required, for the "virtuous agent" to decide it is appropriate to kill the innocent or to lie. To wit, we find Michael Slote taking the side of Anscombe's opponents: "If killing an innocent person is necessary in order to avoid a large-scale human catastrophe, then one may and even should perform the killing. In such a case, we think a certain sort of moral shift occurs because large-scale humanitarian concerns enter the picture."[19] This vaguely described "certain sort of moral shift" is nothing other than the suspension of what everyone knows to be absolutely true: that it is always wrong intentionally to kill the innocent.

Providing further evidence of virtue ethical complicity with consequentialism, Slote goes on to argue that affecting such a "moral shift" is incumbent on those who have taken on a role of public service:

> For when a person has to decide whether to kill an innocent person in order to prevent a great human catastrophe, it is natural to think of her as having been effectively but unofficially *thrust into* a public or political role.... [P]olitical roles should override considerations of personal or family advantage in those who have a deep and genuine love of their own country.[20]

I do not see how else to read this passage other than that Slote is suggesting that caring for large numbers of people obligates you to lay aside your care and concern for your own good—even the good of maintaining a just character, as well as your care and concern for your family and friends—such as not sacrificing them on the consequentialist altar of the public good. The underlying presupposition is that care for one's country requires one to sacrifice care for what's in fact just. The good and the just have been put at opposite poles here, and Slote hardly seems to notice. Yet a contemporary Adeimantus cannot fail to note that Michael Slote has just given future leaders of America *carte blanche* for whatever heinous actions they deem necessary for the common good.

19. Slote, *Morals from Motives*, 96.

20. Ibid., 98; emphasis in original.

Rosalind Hursthouse, perhaps the most influential architect of contemporary virtue ethics, seems conflicted on this topic. Here is Coope's interpretation of the underlying meaning of Hursthouse's discussion of absolutism in the context of "Irresolvable and Tragic Dilemmas" in *On Virtue Ethics*:

> Rosalind Hursthouse thinks that one would be 'seriously lacking in virtue' if one has come to consider the world to be such that one is forced quite often—'not infrequently'—to lie or to kill ([*On Virtue Ethics*], 86). Again she maintains that 'a too great readiness to think that 'I can't do anything but this terrible thing, nothing else is open to me' is a mark of vice, of a flawed character' ([ibid.], 87). All this suggests a consequentialist attitude; for after one has checked, and double checked, to be quite sure one has not been 'too ready', one is presumably to go ahead. One is not to lie or to kill the innocent *too often*.[21]

Coope's description, despite its strident tones, is accurate.

Hursthouse, sensitive to claims that virtue ethicists are all too ready to throw moral principles to the wind, argues that virtue ethics is wrongly accused of doing away with absolutism in ethics, or at least doing easily away with them too quickly. Her protest, however, does not seem successfully to respond to the charge.[22] To see why this is so, it is worth recalling that a principle which one finds binding, say, 96% of the time, is not usually treated as an absolute. The whole point of an absolute, as the term is usually taken, is that it is always binding. The example offered by Hursthouse of one of her designated moral absolutes suggest that she may think that something close to an absolute can still be called an absolute. This example comes at the end of a dialogue she pursues over several pages, in which she concludes with modest support for the absolutist position with something less than full weight: "I am quite willing to stick my neck out and say that we find the world to be such that no genuinely virtuous person would ever sexually abuse children for pleasure."[23] But is this, in fact, an absolute? The "for pleasure" qualification is rather unsettling. It is clear enough that she thinks that sexually abusing children for pleasure is always wrong (or at least it is not what the virtuous agent *would* do). However, is this meant to leave open the possibility that doing so for the sake of saving lives, or

21. Coope, "Modern Virtue Ethics," 51; emphasis in original.

22. "The preceding discussion of tragic dilemmas ... should serve as a corrective to another misunderstanding of virtue ethics: the idea that it denies that there are any absolute prohibitions, some particular actions that one is categorically required not to do." Hursthouse, *On Virtue Ethics*, 83.

23. Ibid., 87.

educational purposes, or whatever, just *might* be the right thing to do in some circumstances? Hursthouse's standard way of dealing with dilemmas is to ask whether a particular choice is in accord with what a virtuous person would do, and it is of course hard to imagine any virtuous person ever sanctioning the torture of children for any reason whatsoever. Nevertheless, the qualification is troubling.[24] In any event, there are no examples of unqualified absolutes that I have discerned in Hursthouse's works, and approaching absolutes with some qualifications is consistent with the weak variety of consequentialism that Hursthouse endorses.[25] At the very least, we can conclude on the one hand that Hursthouse's defense of absolutism is unusual because it avoids both theistic and deontological principles, and because the absolutes she offers are not without qualification.[26]

Ironically, given the robustness of Anscombe's defense of absolutism, Hursthouse dedicates *On Virtue Ethics* to Anscombe, as well as to Philippa Foot, and her less than clear prohibition against the sexual abuse of children is directly preceded with what seems a note of approval of that quote from Anscombe regarding the consequentialist to be one who shows "a corrupt mind." Hursthouse puts stress on the corruption being due to thinking *in advance* that there can be conditions under which violating an

24. For a more recent reflection on dilemmas and moral absolutes, see Hursthouse, "Discussing Dilemmas," *Christian Bioethics* 14 (2008): 141–50. Her position in this article is, as far as I can tell, unchanged from her position in *On Virtue Ethics*. In remarking on an anecdote regarding a lecture by Anscombe that Hursthouse attended she writes: "One need not share her [Anscombe's] belief that lying is always a sin, nor her belief that God's Providence ensures that an agent will be confronted with a forced choice between forbidden acts only through previous wrongdoing of his own, to accept her point. I do not believe either." Hursthouse, "Discussing Dilemmas," 143. Lying is not always wrong, and neither is killing, as Hursthouse argues in her important work on abortion, in which she recognizes that abortion is the killing of a living being and that there is something fundamentally wrong with a callous approach to abortion, but also that there are a number of circumstances which can make abortion the right action to perform. See Rosalind Hursthouse, "Virtue Theory and Abortion," *Philosophy and Public Affairs* 20 (1991): 223–46; for a discussion of the circumstances in which abortion may be justified see ibid., 236–42.

25. This is taking consequentialism in broad terms to include varieties of moralities grounded on self-interest, to encompass Hursthouse's conclusion, "My conclusion, in this chapter, is that it offers a distinctively unfamiliar version of the view that morality is a form of enlightened self-interest, a version *so* unfamiliar that probably, as things are at the moment, that is a dangerously misleading way to describe it." Hursthouse, *On Virtue Ethics*, 190. What makes her position on self-interest, which she notes is similar to those of Hare, Gauthier, and Singer, different from theirs is that unlike defending enlightened self-interest from a neutral point of view she does so from the distinctive perspective of the work she sees *phronesis* performing. See ibid., 191.

26. The whole of chapter 3 of *On Virtue Ethics* deserves careful reading on this topic, especially pp. 83–87.

absolute is right, and she also seems to endorse Anscombe's claim that the mark of a "modern moral philosopher" is one who considers that "in such-and-such circumstances one is to procure the judicial condemnation of the innocent," or the killing of defective children, or the telling of lies, or the sexual abusing of children. Nevertheless, Hursthouse's modest defense of absolutism seems to leave open the possibility that there are conditions in which a virtuous person may have to violate an absolute, and that seems to be a matter of envisioning such possibilities *in advance.*

V. Some Lessons for Admirers of Maritain

It is hard to imagine a doctrine more inimical to the Christian humanism Maritain so ably promotes in *Scholasticism and Politics,* or the dignity of the human person that such genuine humanism nurtures, than consequentialism. Clearly, Anscombe is a champion of those same aims. Sadly, the dominant voices in the movement she birthed seem not to be.

My impression is that the relationship between Thomists and virtue ethicists has been a one-way street. Thomists are happy to hear of a movement that uses much of their vocabulary and generally professes an admiration for the The Philosopher, and have tried to build some bridges with virtue ethicists. Some even think that Alasdair MacIntyre serves as an example of a Thomistic virtue ethicist. Though MacIntyre is a Thomist, he is no virtue ethicist. For that matter, neither are Aristotle or Aquinas. MacIntyre, like Anscombe, points back to Aristotle and shows us how a common vocabulary can mask a lurking moral nihilism, but those are no distinguishing marks of a contemporary virtue ethicist.

Many Thomists have tried to be friends to virtue ethicists. If you are one of them, please do not mistake the common courtesy of those in the mainstream of the contemporary virtue ethics movement for friendship. Know that most secular virtue ethicists do not necessarily endorse your teleology, your natural law, your ethical absolutism, or your faith. Be on your guard.

ANNE M. WILES

Habit, Natural Law, and Natural Rights

In chapter three of *The Degrees of Knowledge*, preparing the ground for his treatment of Thomistic realism, Maritain gives a devastating critique of both Cartesian and Kantian idealism. Regarding Thomistic realism, Maritain remarks, "Realism is lived by the intellect before being recognized by it."[1] This sentence bears reflection. It naturally leads to the question of what, if any, role habit plays in the Thomistic approach to truth and being. Is there a natural habit that underlies and gives rise to realism such that this habit is always present unless corrupted by faulty teaching or ill-founded philosophy? Since Maritain's account of natural law and natural rights is based on realism and would not be possible on the basis of either idealism or materialism, does the role habit plays in realism also have implications for natural law and natural rights?

In this essay, I address some of these interconnections. I first consider Aquinas' analysis of habit. Then, on the basis of this analysis, I show that certain intellectual habits are a pre-condition of realism, and that intellectual and moral habits are integral to the articulation of natural law, and to the exercise of natural rights.

Before considering the role of habit, it will be useful to have as a frame of reference the main points of Maritain's exposition of the Thomistic doctrine on the nature of knowledge.[2] On this view, the relation of knowing

1. Jacques Maritain, *Distinguish to Unite or The Degrees of Knowledge*, translated by Gerald B. Phelan (Notre Dame, Indiana: University of Notre Dame Press, 1995), 83.

2. Ibid., 119–25.

is between a knowing being and the object known. The relation is not a material union; rather, it is a relation in which the knower becomes, immaterially and intentionally, the object known. The act of knowing does not produce anything, but is an immanent action that perfects the knower. The kind of existence the known has in the knower is *esse intentionale* (intentional being) to be distinguished from *esse naturae* (the being a thing possesses in its own nature). The intentional presence of the object in the soul and the intentional transformation of the soul into the object are functions of the immateriality of the cognitive faculties. The operation of the intellect has its origin in the senses, but the intellect knows many things the senses cannot perceive. Material things are sensible in act, but intelligible only in potency. There is in the intellect an active 'light' that, by leaving aside individual characteristics of the sensible, apprehends the intelligible. The concept is the means whereby intellection takes place. Maritain concludes the account by saying that what we know by means of the concept (or mental word) is the "very nature or intelligible determination of an actually or possibly existing thing."[3]

I. The Thomistic Understanding of Habit

The word "habit" is derived from the Latin (*habitus* from *habere* [to have]) and has a wide range of meaning. For the purposes of this essay, the discussion of habits is limited to those habits distinctive of humans, specifically the intellectual and moral habits. The treatment by Aquinas of habits is based in large part on the definition that Aristotle in the *Metaphysics* gives of habit, namely, "a disposition whereby that which is disposed is disposed well, or ill, and this either in regard to itself or in regard to another."[4]

Aquinas notes that while habit may be considered a species of disposition, it specifically differs from disposition in that "habit" implies a certain lastingness or difficulty in changing, whereas "disposition" does not.[5] Since

3. Ibid., 127.

4. Aristotle, *Metaphysics* 5.20, 1022b10–12. All English quotations of Aristotle are from *The Complete Works of Aristotle: The Revised Oxford Translation*, 2 vols., edited by Jonathan Barnes, Bolligen series, vol. 71, no. 2 (Princeton, New Jersey: Princeton University Press, 1995).

5. St. Thomas Aquinas, *Summa theologiae* (ST) I-II, q. 49, a. 2, ad 3. All English quotations of the *Summa* are from Thomas Aquinas, *The Summa Theologica of St. Thomas Aquinas*, translated by the Fathers of the English Dominican Province, rev. ed., 3 vols. (New York: Benziger Brothers, 1948).

the *telos* (nature or end) of a thing is that by which the disposition of that thing is determined to be well or ill disposed, disposition implies a certain order.[6] Habit implies both a relation to a thing's nature and to the operation whereby the habit is conducive to achieving the end of its nature.[7] The same *habit* cannot be related to both good and evil, but the same *power* can be so related, therefore habits are necessary so that the powers can be determined to good.[8] The human soul is not determined to one operation only, and since the soul is the principle of operation through its powers, habits are in the soul in respect of its powers.[9]

The habits of the soul are related to the apprehensive power and to the appetitive power. Good habits related to the apprehensive power are sciences; good habits related to the appetitive power are virtues.[10] The sensitive appetite has an inborn aptitude to be moved by the rational appetite, thus habits may exist in the sensitive powers only if they are acting at the command of reason.[11] The proper act of the intellect is to understand and to consider, so the habit by which one considers is an intellectual habit.[12]

There are habits in the will, because the will is a rational power that may be variously directed to act. The power in the will is inclined to the good identified by reason; since this good is varied in many ways, the will needs a habit to incline it to a fixed good identified by reason so that action follows more promptly.[13]

No human intellectual habits are entirely from nature, but some are called "natural" because they are partly due to nature; the understanding of first principles is called a "natural habit." For example, from the very nature of the intellectual soul when one understands what is a whole and what is a part, one immediately grasps that every whole is larger than its part.[14] All the first principles of the apprehensive powers are in this sense "natural," but the apprehension of first principles cannot occur without sense experience. Thus Aristotle at the end of the *Posterior Analytics* shows that the knowledge of first principles comes to us from the senses[15]; from or through the senses, but the first principles are not, of course, what Hume would call "matters of fact." On Aristotle's account, the mode of knowing

6. ST I-II, q. 49, a. 3.
7. ST I-II, q. 49, a. 3, ad 3.
8. ST I-II, q. 49, a. 4, ad 3.
9. ST I-II, q. 50, a. 2.
10. ST I-II, q. 50, a. 3, ad 3.
11. Ibid.
12. ST I-II, q. 50, a. 4.
13. ST I-II, q. 50, a. 5.
14. ST I-II, q. 51, a. 1.
15. Ibid.

first principles would be that of "rational intuition." Because one needs the sensitive powers for the operation of the intellect and the disposition of the organs of sense differs from person to person, one person may be more apt than another to understand well.

Habits are classified according to the faculty they determine or perfect, so there are intellectual habits of thinking and knowing as well as appetitive habits that involve the will and emotions.

The habits of the appetitive powers are directed by the reason and may be corrupted when reason, through ignorance, passion, or deliberate choice, moves contrary to the habit.[16] The habits of moral *virtue* are caused by reason moving the appetitive powers toward their objective good; the habits of moral *vice* are caused by reason moving the appetitive powers towards a good that is only *apparent*, but is mistaken for their objective good. The habit of virtue is more lasting than learning because the use of virtue continues throughout the whole of life, while the use of learning does not.[17]

With respect to the habits of science when the intellect is moved by first principles, one act may overcome the power of the passive principle, for example, one self-evident principle convinces the intellect so it firmly assents to the conclusion.[18] The habit of opinion makes use of probable propositions rather than necessary or self-evident ones and since a merely probable proposition must be supported by argument using examples and reference to experience, many acts of reason are needed to cause a habit of opinion.[19] At the lowest level of apprehension, the same acts need to be repeated many times for anything to be firmly impressed on the memory.[20]

The habit of understanding first principles of both speculative and practical reason cannot be corrupted by forgetfulness or deception.[21] The habit of science caused in the possible intellect by reason (Aquinas calls it the "habit of conclusions") can be corrupted in two ways. It can be corrupted by a faulty position being taken as the starting point, for example, if the proposition, "Good is good" is replaced by the assertion, "Good is not good." It can also be corrupted if the reasoning is faulty, for example, if a sophistical syllogism is taken to be a dialectical or demonstrative syllogism.[22]

16. ST I-II, q. 53, a. 1.
17. ST I-II, q. 53, a. 1, ad 3.
18. ST I-II, q. 51, a. 3.
19. Ibid.
20. Ibid.
21. ST I-II, q. 53, a. 1.
22. Ibid.

A demonstrative syllogism must be valid and have true premises, else it does not demonstrate. If an argument has a syllogistic form with premises that are opinions (a dialectical syllogism) or premises that are false, ambiguous, or misleading (a sophistical syllogism) and the premises are taken to be true as if it were a demonstrative syllogism, the reasoning is faulty. The habit of true opinion may similarly be corrupted.[23]

A good habit is one that disposes to an act suitable to the agent's nature; an evil habit disposes to an act unsuitable to nature. The acts of virtue are suitable to human nature because they are according to reason; acts of vice are discordant from human nature because they are against reason.[24] A habit is engendered little by little because the subject does not acquire all at once a firm and difficult-to-change disposition.[25] A habit begins by being imperfectly in the subject and then gradually perfected.[26] Like acts cause like habits. If the intensity of the act corresponds to the intensity of the habit or surpasses it, the act either increases the habit or disposes it to increase. If the act falls short of the intensity of the habit, it lessens the habit or disposes it to lessen. Acts contrary to the habit diminish the habit.[27]

In habits of both science and virtue, cessation from the acts whereby the habit was developed weakens or destroys that habit.[28] The habit of moral virtue disposes one to choose the mean in actions and feeling, and when one does not use this habit to moderate one's feelings and actions, the habit is weakened from the inclination of the senses and other external factors. The same holds true of intellectual habits that enable one to judge rightly of what the imagination presents. Strange fancies may arise in the imagination and if they are not kept in check by frequent use of good intellectual habits, one becomes less fit to judge rightly. Thus the intellectual habit is also diminished, or even destroyed, by ceasing to act.[29]

Given the foregoing account of habit, we now return to the question whether realism is a habit, perhaps even a natural habit. In the first sentence of the *Metaphysics*, Aristotle says that all men *by nature* desire to know, and that "this is evident from the delight we take in our senses."[30] The natural end of the human intellect is truth, so is there a corresponding general habit by which the intellect is well disposed to this end?

23. Ibid.
24. ST I-II, q. 54, a. 3.
25. ST I-II, q. 54, a. 4, ad 1.
26. ST I-II, q. 50, a. 3.
27. ST I-II, q. 52, a. 3.
28. ST I-II, q. 53, a. 3.
29. Ibid.
30. *Metaphysics* 1.1, 980a1–2.

According to Maritain, a critique of knowledge, showing that realism is the only way to achieve truth, presupposes a long experience of various kinds of knowing, including spontaneous, scientific, philosophical, and psychological knowing. While recognizing that common sense is not homogenous and that certain instances of modern scientific progress might seem to be in opposition to common sense, he holds that there is a complete solidarity between common sense, properly understood, and philosophy.[31] An adequate critique of knowledge can only properly begin with reflection on the experience about which one would have to say, "*I am aware of knowing at least one thing, that what is, is.*"[32] Common sense recognizes the being of sensible things and this basic apprehension implicitly depends on three factors: the irrefutable evidence of the principle of identity, the general veracity of our powers of knowing, and the notion of truth.

Before one is corrupted by bad philosophy, one does not doubt that one can know some things, and that what is known is distinct from the intellect that knows it. This is a natural habit, a way of approaching reality that has a certain constancy and is not easy to change, arising from a disposition toward the natural desire of knowing, a desire distinctive of a human being. But as Aquinas noted, a natural habit can be strengthened by deliberate, rational reflection, and by repeated acts that reinforce the habit. Thus, reflection on a critique of knowledge, such as Maritain gives in *The Degrees of Knowledge*, or as found in the writings of Aristotle and Aquinas, can reinforce the habit of knowing, of attaining truth. Realism may be practiced before it is articulated, but a reasoned account can also be given of it.

Thomistic realism—perhaps we should say "classical realism," for it is a continuation and elaboration of the realism espoused by both Plato and Aristotle—underlies the account that Maritain gives of natural law and natural rights. Unless it is understood through sense-perception, not empirically, but by rational intuition, that the nature of a human being is unique and distinct from the nature of all other living beings, there is no adequate foundation for natural law, or for the claim that there are natural rights based on the natural law.

31. Maritain, *The Degrees of Knowledge*, 87.

32. Ibid., 80; emphasis in original.

II. Natural Law

Maritain distinguishes two elements in natural law—the ontological element and the gnoseological (or epistemological) element. A human being, *like* every other natural being, has its own ontological structure or essence from which necessarily arises its own natural law, i.e., the normal way of functioning for the type of being it is.[33] A human being, *unlike* all other natural beings, is intelligent and has the capacity to choose whether to follow the ends necessarily determined by human nature. Natural law for humans is a moral law because one is free to obey or disobey it. Beginning with the unchangeable structure of human nature, it is possible to trace out the intelligible necessities required by this structure and identify a *formal* standard for the development of persons. It goes without saying that a *formal* standard does not specify *precisely* the actions that one must take in a particular situation, and every situation is particular. Maritain says, "there is an order or a disposition which human reason can discover and according to which the human will must act in order to attune itself to the essential and necessary ends of the human being. The (unwritten) natural law is nothing more than that."[34]

Natural law is *ontological* because human nature exists in each human being and thus natural law "dwells as an ideal order in the very being"[35] of all existing human persons. However, since human situations are existential, there is nothing in the nature or essence of man from which one can deduce *a priori* the correct moral regulation for each possible human situation. While practical reasoning must take into account the existential situation, it cannot violate the precepts of natural law; natural law thus acts as a constraint on practical reasoning. The role of natural law in respect to the practical reason is analogous to the role of the first principles of demonstration in respect to speculative reason; nothing is strictly deduced from the principle of non-contradiction, but no argument can stand if it violates the principle. It is for this reason that Aquinas (correctly) claims that "the precepts of the natural law are related to practical reason, as the first principles of demonstration are related to the speculative reason, for, both are self-evident principles."[36]

33. Jacques Maritain, *The Rights of Man and Natural Law*, translated by Doris C. Anson (New York: Charles Scribner's Sons, 1943), 86–87.

34. Ibid., 86.

35. Ibid., 89.

36. ST I-II, q. 94, a. 2.

Maritain distinguishes between natural law and knowledge of natural law. The first principle of natural law: "Do good and avoid evil" is self-evident; Aquinas will say that it is known by a natural intellectual habit. Everyone knows and accepts the directive to do good and avoid evil. Parenthetically, the first principle of practical reason is essentially the imperative form of the ancient principle formulated by Socrates, and in the early writings of Plato, that "no one does wrong willingly." One may mistake an apparent good for a real good, but each person sees the action he deliberatively chooses as good under *some* aspect. Natural law is not written law and is not merely this first principle, but rather, "the ensemble of things to do and not to do which follow therefrom in *necessary* fashion."[37] Natural law is known through inclination, a type of knowing Maritain characterizes as "a vital knowledge by connaturality."[38] While both kinds of knowing issue in judgments, knowing by inclination or connaturality differs from knowing through discursive reasoning. Connatural knowledge is obtained from attention to and sympathy with the subject rather than by a process of reasoning.

Knowledge of the natural law is at the same time both ancient and contemporary. Maritain writes that the knowledge of natural law is "embodied in the most general and most ancient heritage of humanity."[39] As examples of this heritage, he mentions both ancient literature and the data of anthropology that shows a history of dynamic schemes of moral regulation in societies. While natural law does not change, knowledge and articulation of the natural law are continuously developing, and will so continue as long as human history endures.[40]

The natural law requires that what it leaves undetermined be ultimately determined by human reason. Human reason does not create natural law since its precepts are universal and invariable, but it may play a role in the articulation and reasoned support of these precepts. [41] Both natural law and *jus gentium* are concerned with rights and duties connected with the first principle in a necessary manner while positive law, since it is the cus-

37. Jacques Maritain, *Man and the State* (Washington, D.C.: The Catholic University of America Press, 1998), 90.

38. Ibid.

39. Jacques Maritain, *Natural Law: Reflections On Theory and Practice*, edited by William Sweet (South Bend, Indiana: St. Augustine's Press, 2001), 36.

40. Ibid., 37.

41. Ibid.

tomary law or statute law that is made for a particular group or society, has only a contingent relation to the first principle of natural law.[42] Parenthetically, both Maritain and Aquinas hold that an unjust law is not a law at all, and is not morally obligatory. Maritain, following Aquinas, holds that "The just law binds in conscience because it binds by virtue of the Natural Law. If we forget the one, we forget the other."[43]

Maritain distinguishes between natural law and the *jus gentium* (the law of nations) not on the basis of their *content*, which in some cases is the same, but according to the way in which they are known. Natural law is known through inclination or connaturality whereas the law of nations (Maritain prefers the expression, "law of civilization") "is known through the conceptual exercise of human reason or through rational knowledge."[44]

Although Aristotle, in his account of the nature of the moral virtues and vices, does not specifically distinguish connaturality as a mode of knowing, such knowledge is implied in the importance he places on his own "customary" procedure of considering not only the opinions of the many and of the wise, but also literature, especially Homer and the tragic poets, as well as the views of earlier philosophers.

Maritain would agree with Aristotle that an accurate knowledge of human nature, of what constitutes the common good, and especially the possession of good moral habits formed with a view to the common good, enables one in particular circumstances to construct positive law, or to act according to natural law.

III. Natural Law and Natural Rights

The philosophical foundation of natural rights is natural law. The concept of human rights is "only valid and rationally tenable if each existing individual has a nature or essence which is the locus of intelligible necessities and truths."[45] There are no human rights unless a certain order "is inviolably required by what things are in their intelligible type or their essence, or by what the nature of man is, and is cut out for, an order by virtue of which

42. Ibid., 52. Maritain claims that if a positive law obliges by virtue of the natural law, it is one's moral duty to follow it. He gives as an example of a morally obligatory positive law, the law that requires motorists to stop at the red light and to go when the light is green, since this law conforms with a principle of natural law that forbids harming one's fellow man.

43. Ibid., 53.

44. Ibid., 48.

45. Maritain, *Man and the State*, 96.

certain things like life, work, freedom are due to the human person, an existent who is endowed with a spiritual soul and free will."[46]

Maritain argues that human (or natural) rights,[47] like natural law, have an intrinsic and necessary relation to the common good.[48] He distinguishes between rights that are absolutely inalienable and those that are inalienable only substantially. Absolutely inalienable rights are those rights, the possession of which cannot be restricted without endangering the common good, such as the right to existence and to the pursuit of happiness.[49] Rights that are inalienable only substantially are those rights, such as the rights of association or free speech, which the body politic must be able to restrict in some measure if it is to preserve the common good.[50]

One always possesses inalienable rights, but under certain circumstances, the exercise of some of these rights may be limited. Generally, a right can be justifiably limited if it can only be realized by ruining the social body. Maritain offers the interesting observation that the transformation of societies is fostered by people trying to change existing social conditions that deprive them of the *exercise* of rights which they *possess* as inalienable rights.[51]

The purpose of the state is to promote the temporal good of its citizens, which is, in fact, the common good of society. How is "the common good" to be understood? Beginning from the basic truth that a society which pursues the common good is a whole, comprised of parts that are themselves autonomous wholes, "an organism composed of liberties, not just of vegetative cells,"[52] Maritain identifies three essential features of what is properly identified as "the common good."

First, the common good is not a mere collection of private goods, not the good of a whole that sacrifices the part to itself. Rather, it is the good human life of a multitude of persons and is common to the whole and to the parts. The good that flows from fully autonomous persons enriches both the individual person and the society as a whole. Secondly, the common good is the foundation for authority. In complex societies, some individuals have to lead and need to be obeyed. Leading others toward their

46. Ibid., 97.

47. Maritain here uses the phrase "human rights" for what in this paper I have referred to as "natural rights." The name is different, but the concept is the same.

48. Maritain, *Man and the State*, 101.

49. Ibid.

50. Ibid.

51. Ibid., 102.

52. Maritain, *Rights of Man*, 7.

own and the common good, rather than towards the good of a master, is the authority appropriately exercised over free persons.[53] Finally, the common good is intrinsically moral and not just a set of advantages and conveniences. It depends upon the integrity of the persons comprising the society; therefore, justice and moral rectitude are essential.[54]

Given that persons can only find the communion of civic friendship in an object, or a task, what is the appropriate object for which people work together in setting up a political society? The task is not narrow or limited to one human activity, but is principally to help each person to his most fundamental aspiration, the freedom of expansion and personhood, "which consists above all in the flowering of moral and rational life, and of those ('immanent') interior activities which are the intellectual and moral virtues."[55] The political task is essentially that of civilization and culture, a task that depends on the adequate habituation of citizens in both the intellectual and moral virtues along the lines suggested by Aquinas' treatment of habit.

While this is not the place for a full critique of contemporary culture, a few observations about habit and education may be in order. At the conclusion of the *Nicomachean Ethics,* Aristotle notes that the first duty of legislators is to make laws such that the citizens will come to love what they ought to love. Legislation is thereby treated as a *moral* duty of the legislators. Requiring citizens to follow just positive laws is one means to instill good habits in the citizens. Habits also result from what one sees and hears, and from observing and copying the behavior of persons one admires. In the *Republic,* Plato urges that only certain kinds of stories and music should be heard by young children, also noting that there cannot be a change in the modes of music without that change affecting the fundamental laws of the state.[56]

The education of Thomas Jefferson included, among other positive influences, early studies in Latin, Greek, and French, and six years of liberal studies at the College of William and Mary, all of which formed his character and education. In writing the *Declaration of Independence,* the first two paragraphs of which emphasize inalienable natural rights belong-

53. Ibid.

54. Ibid., 10.

55. Ibid., 44.

56. Plato, *Republic* 4, 442c. For a contemporary critique of the relation between music and morals, see Roger Scruton, "Music and Morals," *American Spectator* 41, no. 1 (2010): 42–45. The article can be accessed online at http://spectator.org/archives/2010/02/11/music-and-morality/.

ing to all human persons, he drew upon these experiences and studies. In 1779, Jefferson authored the *Bill for the General Diffusion of Education*, a bill that proposed specific means of ensuring that young Virginians be educated according to their ability to receive education and to contribute to the common good. Of the need and value of such education for the commonwealth, he writes, "it is generally true that the people will be happiest whose laws are best, and are best administered, and that laws will be wisely formed, and honestly administered, in proportion as those who form and administer them are wise and honest; whence it becomes expedient for promoting the publick happiness that those persons, whom nature hath endowed with genius and virtue, should be rendered by liberal education worthy to receive, and able to guard the sacred deposit of the rights and liberties of their fellow citizens."[57] Good habits and education lead to good habits and education.

While habits are essential to human life and to the continuation of social structures, some habits are more adequate than others for what Aristotle would call "human flourishing." As Aquinas showed, it is from the *telos* (nature or end) of a thing that the disposition of that thing is said to be well or ill disposed. It is from an understanding of the nature of a human being, a political animal possessed of a speculative, practical, and productive intellect, and "a spiritual soul and free will,"[58] that the natural law can be articulated along with the correlative "natural rights." Only on this basis is it possible to give an adequate account of the common good, and only on this basis are legislators and educators in a position to understand which habits should be inculcated and why.

Realism is a natural habit; "natural," since it arises from the common human trait of the desire to know. Realism enables one to know certain truths about human nature and to develop certain social constructions. But how does one come to participate in and value these constructions? The short answer is by the development of habits conducive to the common good. For the way our lives turn out, Aristotle says, "it makes no small difference to be habituated this way or that straight from childhood, but an enormous difference, or rather *all* the difference."[59]

57. Thomas Jefferson, "Preamble to a Bill for the General Diffusion of Knowledge," in *The Founders' Constitution* (Chicago: The University of Chicago Press, 1987), vol. 1, chap. 18, doc. 11, p. 672.

58. Maritain, *Man and the State*, 97.

59. *Nicomachean Ethics* 2.1, 1103b23–25; emphasis in original.

ERIC MANCHESTER

Beatitude as the Foundation of Freedom

Re-Reading the First Amendment in Light of Maritain

I. Introduction

In *Scholasticism and Politics*, Jacques Maritain warns of the risks of injustice and oppression that arise when democracies mistakenly conceive of themselves as preserving the freedoms of "individuals" rather than "persons."[1] While these terms nowadays are often used interchangeably, the conceptual distinction between "individual" and "person" is critical for Maritain in properly understanding the nature of freedom itself, and thus in discerning which political systems are adequately suited to recognize and protect the rights and freedoms of their citizens.

For Maritain, authentic democracy is possible only where citizens are understood as "persons" whose freedom is rooted in a determination toward God as the infinite eternal good Who transcends all particular goods.[2] By comparison, the concept of the "individual" is rooted in matter, thereby reducing "freedom" to what today philosophers would call so-called compatibilistic freedom. On this view, "freedom" and "determinism" are taken to be compatible concepts, with "freedom" referring simply to the ability to act without impediment on one's prevailing desire, even though this desire

1. See Jacques Maritain, *Scholasticism and Politics*, translated and edited by Mortimer J. Adler (Garden City, New York: Image Books, 1960), 61–70.

2. Ibid.; cf. 99–102 and 132–38.

is determined extrinsically or intrinsically by various genetic, neurological, psychological, cultural, and/or sociopolitical conditions.[3] While Maritain does not speak of "compatibilism" himself, such freedom is comparable in certain respects to certain levels of Maritain's freedom of spontaneity as the absence of constraint,[4] as the mere fulfillment of desires which themselves are intrinsically or extrinsically determined within the individual.[5] As Maritain notes, such freedom "is a precarious unity" which can quickly "decompose" as a "fragment" which is "subject to the determinations of the physical world" that exist as an "immense network" of "cosmic, ethnic, historic" and, one might add, economic forces.[6]

In developing these distinctions in Maritain, I contend that a fundamental task of government is to recognize that the freedom it aims to protect is rooted in each citizen's relation to God, and ultimately in the prospect of eternal beatitude. Accordingly, it is the government's responsibility to realize that this end is served by citizens' participation in ecclesial life in a way that surpasses the temporal goods that can be provided primarily by the state. In this case, states are to avoid assuming a status that rightfully belongs to religious institutions or ecclesial communities. In particular, I will examine how Maritain's insights elucidate favorable implications of the First Amendment of the United States Constitution regarding the role of religion and ecclesial participation within society. In addition, I will explore how these insights shed light on the manner in which this understanding of religious belief and ecclesial life provides critical conceptual support for the notions of personal liberty presumed by American democracy.

3. For a fairly detailed overview of "classical compatibilism," see the Stanford Encyclopedia of Philosophy at http://plato.stanford.edu/entries/compatibilism/. While there is not space here to explore whether or not St. Thomas's account of free choice can be interpreted compatibilistically, in any case Maritain's assessment clearly seems to preclude such interpretation. At the same time, St. Thomas's account might also not conform completely to standard "libertarian" conceptions of free will. For libertarianism, see http://plato.stanford.edu/entries/ incompatibilism-theories/, as well as Kevin M. Staley, "Aquinas: Compatiblist or Libertarian?" in *The Saint Anselm Journal* 2, no. 2 (2005), available in part online at http://www.anselm.edu/Documents/ Institute%20for%20 Saint% 20Anselm%20Studies/ Abstracts/ 4.5.3.2h_22Staley.pdf.

4. For Maritain, spontaneous freedom is defined relative to the manner in which each kind of being is able to act according to its nature. Hence, the levels of such freedom for inanimate objects, plants, and animals are compatible with various kinds of determinism, whereas spontaneous freedom for rational agents, both created and divine, requires the ability to act apart from particular determinations. Rational creaturely freedom, however, is still inferior to God's in that God alone is not directed toward anything beyond Himself. See Maritain, *Scholasticism and Politics*, 128–32.

5. Ibid., 117ff.

6. Ibid., 66.

In certain respects, my "Maritainian" assessment of the First Amendment resembles John Courtney Murray's analysis of this Amendment in relation to natural law,[7] which Maritain himself praises.[8] At the same time, I recognize the poignancy of certain critiques, such as those raised by *Communio* theologian David. L. Schindler, which accuse Murray (and perhaps, by implication, Maritain) of underestimating the extent to which the First Amendment presupposes conceptions of freedom and religion fundamentally at odds with those embodied by the liturgical, creedal, and dogmatic tradition of the Catholic Church.[9]

Briefly stated, Schindler finds Murray's defense of the Amendment as being merely theologically neutral, purely formal-juridical "articles of peace" to overlook the implicitly negative conception of liberty as "freedom from" oppression (religious imposition) rather than a "freedom for" religion as a positive good.[10] This, in turn, is taken both to derive from, and further to undergird, a distinctly Protestant and eventually secular conception of theology and, by extension, anthropology and ecclesiology. Even so, I am hopeful that Maritain's insistence that authentic democratic freedom requires a distinction between persons and individuals enables a reading of the First Amendment that at least softens the skeptical assessment of writers like Schindler.

It is not possible here to touch upon Fr. Murray's and Schindler's views in more than a cursory fashion. Nevertheless, even cursory attention to each is useful insofar as their examinations help one to discern both the promise and limitations of applying Maritain's analysis of freedom to a generally religious, and specifically Catholic-friendly, reading of the First Amendment.

II: Eternal Beatitude as the Necessary Foundation for Authentic Democracy

If democracy is regarded as the form of government which most values the freedom of its citizens, then presumably it characterizes the capac-

7. See John Courtney Murray, *We Hold These Truths: Catholic Reflections on an American Proposition* (Kansas City, Missouri: Sheed and Ward, 1988), 109–23 and 295–336.

8. See Maritain, *Man and the State* (Chicago: University of Chicago Press, 1951), 171–72.

9. David L. Schindler, *Heart of the World, Center of the Church: "Communio" Ecclesiology, Liberalism, and Liberation* (Grand Rapids, Michigan: Eerdmans, 1996), 44–88.

10. Ibid., 45–46, and esp. 63.

ity for freedom as constituting the most significant feature of human existence, at least in this life. Likewise, this very presumption of the primary significance of freedom indicates a conception of freedom which clearly distinguishes and elevates human beings above other creatures.

With this in mind, it is important to delineate the difference between freedom as the mere ability to pursue one's desires apart from external constraints, which even animals may enjoy to an extent, and freedom as the authentic capacity for choosing among alternatives, apart from any extrinsic *or* intrinsic determination. One may ennoble the former by framing it in terms of "choice," thereby implying a greater intellectual capacity for simultaneously comparing various desires than attributed to non-human creatures. Even so, this conception ultimately places human action within a deterministic framework essentially on par with animals, insofar as particular choices are conceived to follow inevitably from whatever considered option is associated with the strongest desire.

This compatibilistic conception of choice differs starkly from Maritain's explication of "freedom of choice." For Maritain, true choice necessitates freedom from a determination to any particular good, with authentically free agents being determined only toward universal, infinite, absolute goodness (God).[11] Humorously, Maritain comments that only philosophers worry about whether human beings possess freedom of choice, which non-philosophers correctly believe they have through the evidence of their own immediate experience.[12] For them, the concern with freedom is not a theoretical one, but a practical one; namely, a concern that they will be able to act, free from external constraint, on those desires to which they assent.

Next, we will see that for Maritain it is freedom of choice as a higher manifestation of a freedom of spontaneity which defines us as *persons* whose definition and significance transcend, and hence cannot be reduced to a part of, the social whole. This is contrasted to their *individuality* which is defined in terms of material participation within the body politic. Moreover, Maritain's conviction (addressed in greater detail shortly) that freedom of choice is possible only where there is an infinite and universal good (God) Who transcends all particular goods suggests that persons are aware, at least implicitly, that their authentically human freedom is rooted in their relation to God. Indeed, because non-philosophers take it for

11. Maritain, *Scholasticism and Politics*, 118–28.
12. Ibid., 118.

granted that their actions are not utterly determined, they may almost instinctively grasp this relation of freedom to God much more readily than certain philosophers who have come to embrace various forms of determinism. Accordingly, the practical concern for freedom of choice signifies a tacit awareness that one's political circumstances should accommodate his or her ontological condition.

To elaborate on the above point, the reality of an infinite and universal good, as the foundation of all particular goods, precludes determinism among particular goods precisely because it alone is, as universal, desired absolutely.[13] As universal and infinite, it transcends all particular goods, rather than being one good among others. As transcendent, particular goods cannot compete with it, but rather necessarily participate in, through the derivation of their very being, in its universal goodness.[14] In short, creatures desire what they judge to be conducive to their well-being, which they deem "good,"[15] and this in turn requires there to be a first cause of all being, both of their being as well as that of those things which support their being.[16] Hence, all particular desires express only a limited, and therefore undetermined, desire for being-in-general, which alone in being infinite is desired absolutely.

Similarly, because rational creatures are capable of understanding the transcendence of this universal good over and above all particular goods, they are necessarily determined to desire only this foundation of goodness (whether or not they are explicitly aware of this), and cannot be determined toward anything finite. This awareness also reveals why coercion and suppression of freedom as the natural ability to pursue various paths to personal well-being are rightfully resisted. They are repugnant precisely because they attempt to determine persons in a particular way contrary to their God-given nature as creatures determined to no particular good, but only to God Himself.

The above explication, of course, is in line with standard Thomistic accounts of voluntary action in respect to goodness and particular choice.[17]

13. This notion in Maritain essentially follows St. Thomas in *Summa theologiae* (ST) I-II, q. 2, a. 8 and q. 9, a. 6.

14. E.g., St. Thomas Aquinas, *Summa Contra Gentiles* (SCG) III, chap. 20, and ST, I, q. 6, aa.1–2, 4, and I-II, q. 9, a. 6.

15. E.g., SCG III, chap. 3.

16. E.g., SCG III, chap. 17.

17. Cf. ST I-II, q. 13, a. 6 on freedom of choice in relation to the necessity of desiring happiness, and q. 3, a. 8 on happiness as perfected in the contemplation of the divine essence.

At the same time, while the desire for particular goods constitutes a participation in (or, perhaps better, is "directed toward") God as the universal infinite good, particular goods, by virtue of their very finitude, can never satisfy this desire for universal infinite goodness.

Beyond this, satisfactory participation in infinite goodness requires eternal existence. This is true in that no temporal succession of particular enjoyments can ever extend to infinity. Even more profoundly, however, this desire for infinite goodness requires that we desire something beyond even the fulfillment of our own finite nature. Obviously, though, we must exist to attain what we desire. Hence, our own finitude must somehow be conjoined to the Being of that which is universal and infinite. This, of course, points to St. Thomas's teaching of the Beatific Vision.[18] Consequently, this desire to attain an eternal goodness beyond our own existence reveals that we are persons, and not merely individuals. We transcend individuality in that our desire for universal goodness exceeds all finite boundaries, including the restrictions of our own bodily existence.[19]

In reflecting on the eternal nature of goodness in respect to political concerns, the above analysis illustrates that a society can recognize authentically human freedom as a supreme value, as in the case of democracy, only if it presumes the existence of a universal good which suggests that citizens are persons whose lives are directed toward an eternal existence beyond the finite goods provided or protected by the state. Indeed, as the state merely represents finite earthly institutions, customs, and laws designed to defend the dignity of persons, its significance is surpassed not only by God as the eternal ground of goodness and being, but by each and every person whose participation in this universal eternal good elevates him or her above the finite value of the state. As Maritain expresses in *The Person and the Common Good*: "For in the person there are some things—and they are the most important and sacred ones—which transcend political society and draw man in his entirety above political society—the very same man who, by reason of another category of things, is a part of political society."[20] This is asserted even more poignantly in *Scholasticism and Politics,* when he declares that because human persons have a "destination to the absolute"

18. E.g. ST I-II, q. 3, a. 8 and q. 5, a. 5.

19. See Maritain, *Scholasticism and Politics,* 120 and 130.

20. Jacques Maritain, *The Person and the Common Good,* translated by John G. Fitzgerald (New York: Charles Scribner's Sons, 1947; Notre Dame, Indiana: University of Notre Dame Press, 1966), 73.

by which they are "called to fulfill a destiny superior to time ... the human person, as a transcendent Whole, *surpasses* all temporal societies and is superior to them."[21]

Simply put, the approach highlighted here realizes that the state exists for the good of the person, rather than the person for the good of the state. We may, though still speak of persons existing both for their own good and the good of other persons. Along these lines, there is not only a danger of the state assuming an importance belonging only to God, but also of the state replacing the authentic personhood of citizens with a conception of itself as the supreme social person. These risks are envisioned in *Scholasticism and Politics* where Maritain speaks of the reduction of citizens to the status of mere individuals whose personal wills are to be displaced by the "General Will," as though society itself is an agent with a will.[22] One thinks also of Hobbes, mentioned by Maritain in *Man and the State*, who discusses how individuals, as the sum of purely determined mechanistic desires defined foremost by the desire for continued motion (survival), assent with compatibilistic "liberty" to merge their will with the will of the state as *Leviathan*.[23] In the process, Hobbes shifts from comparing the civil society to a "building" or a "bridge"[24] to conceiving of it as a "person" in its own right,[25] and later to even a quasi-divine being.[26] Such examples, of course, are precursors to even more explicit deifications of the State, such as found in the pantheism of Hegel.[27]

To apply Maritain's insights, government's awareness that its ends are excelled by those of authentically religious institutions safeguards the state from the similarly motivated temptations toward fascism, on the one

21. Ibid.,75; emphasis in original. See also ST I-II, q. 21, a. 4.

22. E.g. Maritain, *Scholasticism and Politics*, 80 and 95.

23. Maritain, *Man and the State*, 36–39.

24. See Hobbes, *Leviathan*, part 1, chap. 16.

25. Ibid., part 1, chap. 16 and part 2, chap. 17

26. Ibid., part 2, chaps. 18 and 30. It should be mentioned that Hobbes ostensibly speaks of God as a transcendent Being not explicitly identified with government. Nevertheless, the equation between government and the divine is practically accomplished by his insistence that "the State and Church are the same men" (*Leviathan*, part 3, chap. 42, §79) in reserving ultimate ecclesiastical power for the civil authority (see all of chap. 42, "Of Power Ecclesiastical"), such that "there can be no contradiction" between the laws of God and those of the commonwealth (part 4, chap. 43, end of §22), whether the civil authority is Christian or infidel (beginning of §22).

27. See for example Maritain, *Man and the State*, 13 and 192, and Jacques Maritain, *Christianity and Democracy*, translated by Doris C. Anson (London: Geoffrey Bles: The Centenary Press, 1945), 15. For a similar discussion of Rousseau's "political pantheism," see Jacques Maritain, *The Things that are Not Caesar's* (New York: Charles Scribner's Sons, 1931), 132.

hand, and communism, on the other.[28] In fascism, the "State" comes to be viewed as the embodiment of nationalistic or ethnic identity, and thus as something which transcends persons. Similarly, communism aims to avert this perversion only by equally perniciously replacing the supremacy of particular nationhood or ethnicity with an even more abstract valuation of "the people" or "the collective" whose supposed embodiment of radically egalitarian economic aspirations necessarily downplays, if not denigrates, the uniqueness of each person.

Given that a democracy which authentically champions truly *personal* freedom must recognize humanity's eternal end that transcends the state, proper democratic government humbly recognizes that ecclesial institutions are equipped to facilitate the pursuit of humanity's greatest end in a way that the state cannot. Accordingly, a properly democratic state committed to protecting truly personal freedoms should place limits on itself which prevent it from encroaching on or obstructing the rightful operations of ecclesial institutions in accommodating this pursuit. Likewise, the government should recognize and defend religious liberty in understanding that one of its foremost tasks is to protect the capacity for citizens to pursue their highest eternal end.

Simply put, while the task of ecclesial institutions transcends the activities of the state, the state itself can cooperate with this end which exceeds it by facilitating the material and political conditions needed for persons and ecclesial institutions to perform realistically their proper tasks. As Maritain develops in detail in his chapter "Catholic Action and Political Action"[29] as well as elsewhere,[30] it is perfectly appropriate for government to cooperate with religious institutions in, say, the performance of charitable work, or for it to welcome input from ecclesial institutions on matters touching upon the physical security and material well-being of human persons. Thus, because they are in the position to perfect the life sustained by the temporal concerns of civic government, ecclesial institutions should not be construed as operating antithetically or with indifference toward civil government, or *vice versa*.

28. On fascism and communism, see esp. Maritain, *Scholasticism and Politics*, 19–20 and 227–30. See also the section entitled "The Communist Problem" in *Christianity and Democracy*, 53–58, as well as "Three Forms of Nationalism" (on fascism) and "On China" (regarding communism) in *The Things that are Not Caesar's*, 153–55 and 156–61, respectively.

29. Chapter eight in *Scholasticism and Politics*, 185–211.

30. See for example the section on church-state "cooperation" in Maritain, *Man and the State*, 171–79, esp. 178.

On the view expounded here, because government and ecclesial institutions serve distinct (though related) ends, cooperation between the two should be legally permitted. This does not require, however, that certain ecclesial communities be legally granted a privileged status over others. Consequently, while naturally I would agree with Maritain that the fully sacramental and properly dogmatic character of the Catholic Church provides her with the most efficacious means of preparing persons for their eternal perfection, it is important to remember that the Church herself values efforts outside her formal purview which retain features of this perfecting character.[31] Maritain himself explicitly recognizes this, proclaiming that despite their serious theological errors, the secular rationalists of eighteenth-century French insistence on human rights, the Puritan condemnation of slavery, and even the Russian communist atheist denunciation of reducing human beings to mere means for profit, all evidence vestiges of "Christianity as leaven in social and political life."[32] Hence, the extension of religious liberty to other Christian and non-Christian religious traditions insofar as they support the dignity of persons is entirely appropriate.[33]

With these concerns in mind, we may next identify some of the strengths and possible limitations of the First Amendment in accommodating this Maritain-inspired vision of what might be called the mutually interested cooperative independence of church and state. As addressed in this essay's introduction, John Courtney Murray and David L. Schindler will receive mention here as representatives of more and less favorable assessments of the possibility of this accommodation, though their views can be given only a perfunctory introduction.

III. Strengths and Limitations of the First Amendment in Respect to Beatitude

Space does not allow us to go into extensive historical assessments of the original purpose and subsequent applications and interpretations of the First Amendment. Nevertheless, a few words of historical context are useful in setting the stage for considering the extent to which the Amend-

31. See for example *Dominus Iesus: On the Unity and Salvific Universality of Jesus Christ and the Church,"* issued by The Congregation for the Doctrine of the Faith, esp. §8, 17, and 19–21.

32. Maritain, *Christianity and Democracy*, 25.

33. For a developed discussion by Maritain on the benefits and limits of religious liberty in respect to the precepts of natural law, see *Man and the State*, 168–71.

ment is amenable to the understanding of the relationship between persons and state, and hence between state and church, elucidated in the previous section. We will accomplish this by briefly surveying Maritain's insights in comparison to Murray and Schindler.

To begin, one can point out with Murray that the writers of the Constitution consciously conceived of natural rights as being something God-given, wholly consistent with the notion of providence.[34] As Murray notes, this marks an intentional departure from the explicitly secular, rationalistic and largely anti-religious Jacobin democratic philosophy favored in much of Europe.[35] In light of this, Murray understands the First Amendment to reflect an understanding of religion as a positive good, rather than something to be merely tolerated. He is aware that the Amendment historically reflects a range of predominantly Protestant ecclesiological understandings,[36] a point of grave concern for Schindler. Even so, Murray sees the Catholic Church's longstanding emphasis on natural law as being accessible, whether consciously or unconsciously, to those of virtually all or even no religious affiliation, as demonstrating that she best embodies religious ideals, in part precisely because this emphasis allows her to commend much that is found in other traditions. Maritain raises a similar point, going beyond general natural law to consider explicitly "the grace of Christ" found even in those "not visibly belonging to His Church."[37]

Murray's underscoring of natural law further evidences, consistent with Maritain, that religious institutions are to be respected as excelling government not because of their religious character *simpliciter*, but insofar as religious activities alone possess the capacity to provide coherence to notions of authentically personal dignity and freedom. Put differently, what is implied here is that "religion" only possesses the character of authentic religion insofar as it recognizes the inviolable dignity of persons, particularly if it accurately understands them to be rooted in an eternal end.[38] Given this,

34. See, for example, Murray's mention of Lincoln and of the Declaration of Independence in *We Hold These Truths*, 29–30 and 37, respectively.

35. Ibid., 28.

36. Ibid., 48ff.

37. Maritain, *Scholasticism and Politics*, 170.

38. I say "particularly" so as to recognize a number of Eastern religions (e.g. certain forms of Buddhism) which commendably engender compassion for persons, even if they consciously avoid construing these practices in relation to a personal divine Being or to a personal afterlife, or even eschew the metaphysical category of "personhood" altogether.

the standard question of how one determines which exercises of religion are to be respected can be more or less satisfactorily addressed.

Admittedly, the above response by itself does not entirely avert disputes between many traditional religions and more secular liberal (in the technical sense of the word) perspectives as to whether or not certain alleged rights, perhaps especially in matters in areas related to so-called "life issues" and "family values," can be coherently grounded in notions of natural law and personal dignity. This difficulty perhaps justifies the lower levels of confidence in appeals to natural law within the context of American political life, as will be considered shortly in respect to Schindler. At the very least, this may accentuate the importance of protecting the right of religious institutions to express publically an unpopular prophetic witness by pointing out the significance of linking freedom of speech and press to the free exercise of religion. This signifies that their mutual inclusion in the very same amendment should not be overlooked as mere coincidence. More acutely, there is the need to point out that where personhood is linked by God in the very act of creation to a particular biological nature, freedom expresses the good of manifold actions that consort with, but are never contrary to, this nature.

Having reviewed Murray's, along with my own Maritain-based, basically positive assessment of the First Amendment with an eye toward the notions of natural law and eternal beatitude, a balanced treatment requires acknowledging at least some potential shortcomings with this approach. As mentioned previously, David L. Schindler is particularly helpful in diagnosing the oversights of this interpretation. Only a few of these can be addressed here.

First, Schindler surmises that the Amendment's phrasing of religious exercise as something to be protected but not promoted essentially advances a decidedly un-Catholic (and one may even say un-natural law-like) negative "freedom from coercion" rather than positive "freedom for" good.[39] Similarly, Schindler contends that where there is formal silence about God, a positive relation to God can be at best only inadequately implied.[40] Accordingly, he regards the First Amendment's posture of religious neutrality as masking a "practical" or "covert" and "passive" "a-theism" in

39. See esp. Schindler, *Heart of the World,* 45, 63–4, and 68.
40. Ibid., 63.

contrast with Europe's "more overt" and "aggressive" atheistic response to the Church.[41] Secondly, beyond this Schindler indicates that its acknowledgement of an entirely generic conception of religion advances an implicit theology which presumes, in classically liberal fashion, the essence of religion to be something properly left to be defined by individuals. In this case, the more specific the liturgical, creedal, and dogmatic content of a religious tradition (in effect, the more traditional it is!), the more "improperly" religious, and thus suspect, it is taken to be.

The above assessment, of course, explicitly counters Murray's claim that the principles of the First Amendment are in no way religious or secular "dogma" or "articles of faith" but only "articles of peace" and "good law."[42] Schindler avers that where a non-specific conception of religion is positioned as something to be permitted but not conspicuously recognized as a positive good, the more specific religious content will be regarded as a mere conceptual appendage extraneously "added on" to what is "essential" to liberty and even religion itself.[43] In this case, rather than according religious institutions a status which excels the interests of the state as claimed previously, the state is prone to regard its own aspirations as being more relevant to our civic existence than the merely private or individualistic convictions of religious faith. Indeed, despite being ostensibly protected by the First Amendment, one wonders to what extent prophetic challenges to state activities may in time lead to the increased marginalization, and eventually outright suppression, of the institutions which raise these challenges. Presumably, such reactions would stem from the government's conviction that what is actually a proper understanding of the relationship between religious institutions and government is unduly subversive in denouncing the state's efforts to exceed its rightful limits.

IV. Contexts for Salvaging a "Maritainian" Defense of the First Amendment

I grant that the First Amendment does not offer the most secure foundation for recognizing the priority, with proper qualifications, of ecclesial over civil life in a way that robustly safeguards the Catholic faith from social mar-

41. Ibid., 69.
42. Murray, *We Hold These Truths*, 56.
43. See, for example, Schindler, *Heart of the World*, 69.

ginalization and even governmental opposition to important aspects of her mission. This is likely to be particularly true in respect to policies pertaining to so-called life and family issues.

On the other hand, there may be more room for counterbalancing these tendencies than the brief, admittedly perfunctory, above indictment of the First Amendment acknowledges. For example, it is worth noting that religious liberty is acknowledged in the very first clause of the very first amendment. Admittedly, it uses the negative language of prohibiting religious establishment ahead of positive language acknowledging religious exercise. Nevertheless, one must ask what the conceptual implications are of granting religious liberty such foremost attention. Of course, one might prefer that it was not "relegated" to an "amendment" at all. Even so, in practical fact, the Bill of Rights carries more weight in public consciousness than the more technical explication of governmental procedures enumerated in the main text of the Constitution.

In any case, it does not seem sufficient to say that religion receives attention simply because it is important to people. Such an explanation merely begs the question of *why* religion is important enough to mention when other practices some people might value are not. More reasonably, it seems that the importance of religion is acknowledged as a tacit realization that God might very well exist, and if He does exist, that His relation to people would be of utmost importance. While this answer does not preclude Schindler's concern that Protestant ecclesial notions are tacitly advanced over a Catholic one, it at least mitigates against the slide from "Protestantization" to outright secularization, or to regarding religious concerns as mere "appendages" to be tolerated.

One might counter this appeal to context by noting that freedom of speech and press, as well as of assembly and of petitioning government, are mentioned in the same amendment. In this case, the fact that religion is mentioned first might be downplayed by a suggestion that it is ultimately taken to be simply on par with these other concerns. There is no need, however, to interpret the mutual attention of these various clauses to those dealing with religion as necessarily undermining religion's importance. To the contrary, one can just as reasonably read these to suggest that these are included together precisely because religious institutions are recognized to have a noteworthy role in expressing "grievance" (to use the Amendment's own term) against government actions.

Likewise, while the mutual reference to assembly can be read as reducing ecclesial life to the status of a mere "voluntary association," to the extent that such association is taken to be the basis of society itself (even if this conception of society is more classically liberal and contractarian than Catholic), it may well indicate that one's ecclesial affiliations are at least on par with, rather than subordinated to, other civil allegiances. In fact, if one allows for coupling this interpretation with the Declaration of Independence's assertion that civic association itself results from "Creator-endowed" rights, this would resonate with Maritain's point that the relationship of the citizen, as a person, to the state cannot be conceptualized apart from his or her relationship to God.

Finally, where Schindler defensibly exposes the First Amendment as manifesting a "stripped down" and thus subtly un-incarnational conception of religion (without explicitly using these adjectives), Maritain offers assistance in recognizing this purported detriment as also at least a mixed blessing. As the latter speculates, it may well be that the "diffuse and diluted forms" of Christianity in America actually serve to downplay the "divorce between the democratic principle and the Christian principle" compared to Europe, where "minds are divided between a Christianity, which is irreducibly formed in its structure and doctrine, but separated for too many years from the life of the people."[44]

Maritain echoes this appraisal in *Man and the State,* commenting on the different connotations of "separation of Church and state" in Europe compared to the United States. According to him, whereas Europeans are more prone to expect this to mean "complete isolation" between the two, the American understanding remains more open in principle to a *practical* "good feeling" of "actual cooperation" despite making a *theoretically* sharp distinction.[45] In other words, the same liberal principles which engender an impoverished ecclesiology also temper the inclination to extirpate the social witness of the Church altogether. Though this final point cannot be developed here, one can hope that a diminished basis for anti-ecclesiastical reaction leaves open at least the theoretical possibility that the Church can freely exercise its call to evangelically transform the culture. If this is possible, then one can further hope that citizens and their elected representatives may increasingly form public policy with the mind of the Church,

44. Maritain, *Christianity and Democracy,* 21.
45. Ibid., 182–83.

such as to guide *voluntarily* public life by her witness, free from the coercion of law.[46]

V. Conclusion

By insisting upon the distinction between "person" and "individual," Maritain demonstrates that the robust (i.e. incompatibilist) conception of freedom recognized and protected by authentic democracies are rendered coherent only if they acknowledge a relation of citizens to God as universal transcendent good above the state. This realization is reinforced by the awareness that this relation further points to the highest end of human existence in eternal beatitude, which by its very nature surpasses the operations of the state. In recognizing these points, states should also acknowledge that insofar as the religious institutions explicitly focus on humanity's relation to the divine, these communities are in certain respects of greater importance than the state. Accordingly, government is obliged to protect their right to exist, as well as to evaluate morally the actions of the state. Likewise, voluntary cooperation between state and religious institutions is appropriate in addressing temporal concerns of human beings which constitute the proper ends of the state. Given this, the First Amendment admittedly suggests a rather generic conception of religion and may tacitly support a decidedly un-Catholic ecclesiology and negative conception of freedom. Even so, the prominent attention it gives to religion indicates a realization that humanity bears a relation to God, and hence religious institutions, which is of fundamental importance. Moreover, the coupling of the rights of free exercise with speech and assembly are amenable to welcoming the Church's prophetic witness and moral evaluation of the actions of government.

46. For a discussion of Maritain's own vision of Church-state cooperation, see *Man and the State*, 172–79.

III

CONTEMPLATION AND HUMAN PERFECTION

HEATHER M. ERB

The Mountain and the Valley

Medieval Orderings of Contemplation and Action

I. Introduction

Aquinas's commentary on Psalm 23,[1] "Who may go up to God's holy mountain," contains a poetic analogue of the uneasy peace between contemplation and action that permeated the Greek and Patristic minds and crystallized in various controversies in the twelfth and thirteenth centuries. In the Psalm commentary, God's universal dominion is described as extending to the center of the earth and through the Church, which proceeds towards rivers of consolation through troubled seas and tribulation. As in his commentary on Isaiah 2, the mountain is a symbol of contemplation and spiritual ascent that signifies the perfection of Christ, towards which humanity is drawn. In the Prologue to the *Commentary on the Psalms,* Aquinas states that the end or goal of the Psalter (which itself contains the whole of

1. Psalm 24 in modern Bibles. Modern Bibles (such as the *New Revised Standard Version,* and the *Jerusalem Bible*) adopt the numbering of the Hebrew Bible, which, from Psalm 10 to Psalm 148 is one figure ahead of the Greek (*Septuagint*) and Vulgate (these two latter join certain Psalms, and divide others into two). Aquinas's *Commentary on the Psalms* follows the distribution of St. Jerome's Vulgate Bible. In his Prologue to the *Commentary on the Psalms,* Aquinas notes three translations of the work into Latin, all by Jerome. The first version (a corrected version from 383 of an old Latin translation that had become "vitiated by scribes") became known as the "Roman Psalter," used in Italy. The second version (from 392), more faithful to the Greek *Septuagint,* became known as the "Gallican Psalter," ordered by Pope Damasus for use in France. Yet a third version was most faithful to the Hebrew, Aquinas states. Comparison of Psalters reveals that Aquinas used the widespread, standard Vulgate text (the Gallican Psalter) for his own commentary. On Aquinas's use of the Vulgate see, for example, James A. Weisheipl, *Friar Thomas d'Aquino: His Life, Thought, and Works* (Washington, D.C.: Catholic University of America Press, 1983), 302–304.

Scripture) is prayer, or the raising of the mind to God. This goal is accomplished through a fourfold elevation or spiritual ascent: the admiration of the loftiness of divine power, the lifting of the mind towards the excellence of eternal happiness, the conformity to divine goodness and holiness, and the imitation of divine justice through works. Aquinas's Christocentric interpretation of the Psalms (the subject matter, he states, is Christ and His members) supports his view that our spiritual "elevation" occurs through conforming our souls and actions to the life of Christ. In the *Commentary on the Gospel of John,* the Exemplar of the perfect blend of action and contemplation is introduced, as Christ's sacrifice, teaching, and example radiate the superabundance of Trinitarian love.

In a chapter entitled "Action and Contemplation" in *Scholasticism and Politics,* Maritain indicates that the "debate" between action, associated with the West, and contemplation, often associated with the East, ignores the influence of philosophical and supernatural contemplative traditions in the West.[2] Christian wisdom overcomes the false antithesis of contemplation and action on the deeper philosophical and theological levels, such that the highest operation of the human spirit is both action and *passio,* and contemplation is divinely measured, "walking towards those that are without, redeeming the time."[3] Despite a perfect unity of contemplation and action exemplified in the life of Christ and treated by Aquinas in his biblical commentaries, paradoxes abound in the vocabulary of contemplation. Believers worship a transcendent God Who is immanent in all creation, while the descent of God in the Incarnation pulls humanity beyond creatures to the Father. The combination of action and contemplation in the soul's path to God is anticipated by the Psalmist in his question: "*Who shall ascend so greatly that he comes to Christ and God?*" and the answer resounds, "*Holy men, those who command ascents in their heart, will ascend.*"[4]

2. "The debate between action and contemplation not only concerns each of us personally, but is also of vital importance to human culture and to the destiny of civilization.... The West ... had once a habit of contemplation in harmony with the deepest postulations of spiritual reality." Jacques Maritain, "Action and Contemplation," in *Scholasticism and Politics,* 2nd ed., translated and edited by Mortimer Adler (London: Geoffrey Bles—The Centenary Press, 1945), 135.

3. Maritain, "Action and Contemplation," 145.

4. "Quis ergo ascendet tantum quod deveniat ad Christum et Deum? Sancti viri qui disponunt ascensiones in corde suo ascendant, ut dicit Psalmista." Aquinas, *In psalmis Davidis expositio* (Parma ed. 1863). Aquinas notes in the prologue to his *Commentary on the Psalms* that the fullness of Christian grace is contained therein, for the Psalms' contents bear on the Incarnation, such that one might believe oneself to be face-to-face with the Gospel, not prophecy: "Omnia

Aquinas presents our ascent to God as an interplay between action and contemplation in his reflections on the virtues, the states of life, stages within the call to holiness, and the perfection of Christ. His solution to the theoretical and pastoral tensions involved in reconciling the two domains has several facets. In responses to objections from both seculars and Franciscans, he defends the Dominican charisms of teaching, study, and preaching, and an instrumentalist view of the counsel of poverty. He also affirms the perfect unity of action and contemplation played out in the two natures of Christ through His ministry and Passion. Finally, he Christianizes the intellectualist version of happiness he derived from Aristotle, whose scientific and perfectionist ideals guided the medieval concept of theology as a science and a profession.

A surprising amount of twentieth-century philosophy still bears the marks of a contemplative drive towards the transcendent, although some contemporary thinkers such as Martha Nussbaum and Pierre Hadot either critique this drive as inauthentic, or deride medievals for impinging on philosophy's domain. For Hadot, medieval philosophy was a step along the way towards the predicament in which we find philosophy today—the demotion of philosophy from its earlier status as a set of spiritual exercises to a wooden, discarnate discourse reduced to the status of handmaiden for the queen of the sciences. Without the medieval syntheses, the professionalization of philosophy would not have occurred, according to Hadot, and a crisis would not have arisen by divorcing the discipline from the purposes for which it was created.[5]

Scholasticism, in short, had transformed the philosophical life into a

enim quae ad fidem incarnationis pertinent, sic dilucide traduntur in hoc opere, ut fere videatur Evangelium, et non Prophetia." Parma ed. He further notes in the prologue that the works of God treated in the Psalms are those of creation, governance, reparation, and glorification.

5. See Pierre Hadot, *What is Ancient Philosophy?* translated by Michael Chase (Cambridge, Massachusetts: Harvard University Press, 2002), 258–61. Here, Hadot distinguishes the Scholastic tradition in general (from its inception) from ancient Greek philosophy by the former's overly intellectualist approach, which is said to have cut the practice of philosophy off from its "vital, existential dimension." In another book (*The Present Alone is our Happiness: Conversations with Jeannie Carlier and Arnold I. Davidson*, translated by Mark Djaballah and Michael Chase [Stanford, California: Stanford University Press, 2009]), Hadot develops his preference for Plotinian mysticism as an alternative, precipitated by an "oceanic sentiment" from his childhood. Upon analysis, Hadot's view (ibid., 114) contains an interesting paradox: the medieval synthesis of philosophy and Christian theology forged an inexorable link between philosophy and a Christian mode of life, yet one that hindered the autonomy of philosophy, annulled its status as a spiritual exercise, and reduced its power and ultimate relevance.

system. For Nussbaum, any Greek- inspired *theoria* is a variety of Platonic "escapism" that seeks an invulnerable distance from the fragility of human life through a conscious bracketing of the "intelligence" of the emotions.[6] Her attempt to de-Platonize Aristotle's ethics stems from her rejection of an elitist dualism that portrays us as mired in original sin, in the messy particulars of ordinary human life. Her target is Augustinian Christianity, which she views through a critical Nietzschean lens, accusing speculative thinkers of self-hating patterns of life rooted in the illusory dream of redemption[7]—a view which, in fact, has no bearing on the Christian understanding of this world, the body, or active and contemplative lives. Both Nussbaum's and Hadot's views miss the rich complexity of the monastic and mendicant charisms and overlook the genius of medieval contemplation. But in fact, it is contemplation that salvages philosophy from the perils of an individualist and monistic mysticism, and re-vitalizes it by annexing it to sacred doctrine and the service of God in the ecclesial community.

Before detailing the problem of contemplation and action in Aquinas, a few distinctions are in order. First, we should distinguish contemplative and active *lives*, on the one hand, from either transitive actions stemming purely from practical reason, or immanent actions involving either speculative reason or infused contemplation, on the other. No properly human life is reducible to a series of non-reflective external actions. The term "life" refers not to bare existence, but to the specific act of a living substance that is characterized by its mode of being—in our case, our cognitive and volitional acts.[8] Thus, all properly human life involves a measure of interior contemplation.

6. The close link Nussbaum perceives between cognition and the passions is seen in the title of her work, *Upheavals of Thought: The Intelligence of the Emotions* (Cambridge: Cambridge University Press, 2001). Nussbaum draws on Stoic thought to develop her thesis that emotions involve thought, judgment, and evaluation. See Diana Fritz Cates, "Conceiving Emotions: Martha Nussbaum's 'Upheavals of Thought,'" *Journal of Religious Ethics* 31, no. 2 (2003): 325–41.

7. Nussbaum states that for Lucretius and Nietzsche, the religious worldview "had deeply poisoned human desires … constructing deformed patterns of fear and longing." Martha Nussbaum, *Love's Knowledge: Essays on Philosophy and Literature* (Oxford: Oxford University Press, 1990), 306. For Nussbaum, the Augustinian view of original sin besets Christian doctrine and literature (such as Beckett's *Molloy* trilogy) alike, promoting ideals that involve disdain for everyday life and a view of the flesh that is permeated by false guilt.

8. See *In IX Ethicorum*, lect. 1, nos. 1901–902; *In XIV Ioannem* lect. 2, no. 1869. Three meanings of "life" in Aquinas are: (1) the being of a substance which possesses self-motion, as in Aristotle's definition, "vivere viventibus esse est" (Aristotle, *De anima* 2.7, as quoted by Aquinas in *Summa theologiae* (ST) I, q. 18, a. 2, and Aquinas's commentary on Aristotle, *In II De Anima*, lect.

It is important to note that by the thirteenth century, the terms "action" and "contemplation" had become fluid and ambiguous, and that Aquinas was more interested in the vocabulary of prayer than in unraveling the "action/contemplation" distinction.[9] By the thirteenth century, the terms "contemplation" and "contemplative" referred either to intellectual study or to specific activities associated with the interior life, such as reading, meditation, or prayer. The phrase "contemplative life" also carried a dual meaning: either a philosophical connotation ("the life of reason"—Aquinas preferred this sense in his later work on the topic[10]) or Gregory's affective, religious meaning, as a life of prayer separate from practical action, in which one clings solely to one's desire for God. While the latter sense is mirrored in Aquinas's early treatment of the link between contemplation and the Gifts of wisdom and understanding, by his later career, Aquinas demoted the "contemplative life" of any supernatural status, in his effort to broaden the Gifts' practical as well as speculative role.[11] Finally, by the same time, the term "active life" had both an Aristotelian interpretation as the cultivation of the moral virtues, or the sense established by Gregory, as the practice of fraternal charity.[12]

In its first and simplest sense, the contemplative life is one which demonstrates a tendency or direction towards the search for truth for its own sake; the active life is one which focuses more on the ends of practical reason. Aquinas states:

7, no. 319—the soul gives life to the body as its form); (2) the specific act of a living substance that is its mode of being—in the case of man, his volitional and cognitive acts (*Nicomachean Ethics* (NE) 9.11 [1170a16], and Aquinas's commentary, *In IX Ethicorum*, lectio 11, no. 1902; cf. *In XIV Joannem*, lectio 2, no. 1869); and (3) the chief direction of a human being (a type of life, referring to the sensual life, the honorable life, the contemplative life, and so on (NE 1.5 [1095b14–19], and Aquinas's commentary, *In I Ethicorum*, lectio 5, no. 58). These three meanings are outlined in Carlo Leget, "The Concept of 'Life' in the *Commentary on John*," in *Reading John with St. Thomas Aquinas*, edited by Michael Dauphinais and Matthew Levering (Washington, D.C.: The Catholic University of America Press, 2005), 154–55.

9. On this point, see *Albert and Thomas: Selected Writings*, translated and edited by Simon Tugwell (New York: Paulist Press, 1988), 279–81. As Tugwell notes: "there had not yet developed the technical usage which later prevailed, with its systematic distinction between 'contemplation' and 'meditation.'" Ibid. 281.

10. ST II-II, q. 180, a. 2, ad 3.

11. On this topic, see Tugwell, *Albert and Thomas*, 286.

12. See *In 3 Sent.*, d. 35, q. 1, a. 2. Cf. ST II-II, q. 180, a. 2, ad 1. Cf. Tugwell, *Albert and Thomas* 280. The matter becomes even more complex when considering the fact that Aquinas viewed prayer as an exercise of practical reason in focusing on prayer's petitionary function; see ST II-II, q. 83, a. 1; q. 180, a. 3, ad 4.

> There are two human lives: one which centers around the operation which is proper to the intellect taken by itself; and this is the contemplative life; and another which centers around the operation of the intellect and of reason insofar as it orders and rules and commands inferior parts, and this is the active life.[13]

Both lives are properly human and thus rational, but one attends more carefully to goals of the practical intellect, the other, more to the goals of *theoria*. Both lives involve knowledge and love, and a persevering exercise towards a properly human end.

There is a second distinction, that between natural and supernatural contemplation. Due to a variety of factors, not least among which is the defense of the mendicant mixed apostolate of teaching and preaching by way of Aristotle's intellectualist ethics, Aquinas moved away from the earlier dichotomy of *sancti* and *philosophi*, towards a view of continuity between modes of contemplation. The *Summa theologiae*'s treatise on the two lives uses book ten of the *Nicomachean Ethics* as the scaffolding for the traditional thesis of the superiority of contemplation, while the Prologue to the *Commentary on John* introduces the nature of Christ's contemplation through a discussion of ancient philosophers' ascent to God. John's perfect supernatural contemplation, which adheres to God by affection and understanding, is bolstered, not threatened, by a natural wisdom unable to surpass its limits.

Participation in God's life through supernatural spiritual understanding also engages intellect and will and sets the tone for one's general direction as active or contemplative, or as partaking in both equally. So, while natural reason involves life choices and a variety of temperaments, infused contemplation surpasses philosophy by attaining the fullness and perfection of the cause of order and beauty in the world, and by giving a Christian account of the effects of this cause.

In this light, the Prologue to the *Commentary on John* glosses the vision text of Isaiah 6: "I saw the Lord seated on a high and lofty throne, and the whole universe was full of his majesty and the things that were under him filled the temple." Aquinas says it is through the sacraments of Christ's humanity, which fill up the faithful (the temple), that God shares His divine, eternal life, which then bears abundant fruit in the world of action through ecclesial witness. In the language of the Gospel of John, we might say that while philosophy prepares the way for spiritual life, and gives conceptual

13. *In III Sententiarum*, d. 35, q. 1, a. 1, n. 14.

intimations of its height, depth, perfection, and fullness, it is the Mystical Body alone that gives testimony about our final destination. Through charity, we anoint our Lord's feet by serving his faithful, and by faith we come to know the "most excellent of teachers," the Shepherd, the Way or the Gate, Who is also our truth and our home.[14]

There is no conflict or tension between contemplation and action in God, Christ, the angels, or Adam in the state of innocence. The errors of Gnosticism and activism, and the debates on states of life, however, highlighted the tension on the human level for Aquinas. I will elucidate Aquinas's theory on the relation of contemplation to action from the vantage point of three perspectives. First, there is the relation of action to contemplation in his Greek and Patristic predecessors, and its impact on his own theory. Second, Aquinas' metaphysics of order is seen to navigate between, and balance, the Greek perfectionist ideal and a Christian union of contemplation and action in the imitation of Christ. Third, there is a contrast of Aquinas's and Henry of Ghent's views on the intellect and will in relation to contemplation, action, and the debate about religion and the states of life.

II. Greek and Patristic Precedents

The patrimony of the concepts of action and contemplation is deeply rooted in the Greek, Neoplatonic, and Patristic traditions. The two terms are opposed as practical to speculative; as labor or affliction to rest; as time to eternity; as this life to the next; as slavery to freedom; as wife to husband; and as humanity to divinity. In addition to a host of biblical figures and pairs, including Jacob, Mary and Martha, and Rachel and Leah, there is the monastic well of terms that describes contemplation as *otium, vacare, quies, sabbatum,* and *visio,* as Jean Leclercq has shown.[15]

Aquinas's treatment of the distinction between contemplation and action[16] is faithful to the vocabulary of *vacatio* and *quies* developed by Gregory the Great, and presupposes the twelfth-century inventory of considerations, such as whether action and contemplation are two hierarchical aspects or stages of a single life, or two separate ways of life (more common

14. Cf.: "Christ is the way to arrive at the knowledge of the truth, while still being the truth itself." *In XIV Joannem,* lectio 2, no. 1868.

15. See his many articles and his book on the topic, especially *Otia Monastica: Études sur la vocabulaire de la Contemplation au Moyen Âge* (Rome: Herder, 1963).

16. See ST II-II, q. 182.

in the later Middle Ages), or whether two activities which taken together constitute a fusion or mixed life.[17] The shift in the notion of action from purification or *acsesis* to external works of teaching and preaching was one way in which personal austerity and interiority was balanced with the demands of service to neighbor.

In the Greek and Neoplatonic worlds, there was a gradual simplification of three lives to two, and an interiorization of action to fit a contemplative scheme. In Plato's cave allegory, there is both an ascent and a descent or move towards action in the world as a result of contemplation. As in Diotima's discourse on love in the *Symposium*,[18] the fecundity of the spiritual overwhelms the value of the bodily and particular.

Aristotle's list of the two states of life, namely, the theoretical or contemplative and the political or practical (with the life of pleasure being discounted as slavish and beastly, and not properly human), appears in *Nicomachean Ethics* 1.4. The contrast between true and false leisure (*otium* vs. *otiositas*) was to come with Benedict's *Rule.* Although Aristotle's life of contemplation is superior to the active, as that which is divine and self-sufficient exceeds the merely human (cf. NE 10.7), *theoria* is constituted by three forms of science or *episteme*, and corresponds to a staple use of the human mind in its drive for truth.

The pair "action/contemplation" as *praxis/theoria* thus refers to both ways of life and uses of the intellect. The mind can search for truth as an end in itself, or it can seek the good which conforms to right desire, which guides the achievement of virtue (*praxis* as an act of the intellect). The contemplative way of life based on *theoria* (NE 10.7) is an intellectual achievement flowing from moral virtue into a godlike self-sufficiency—the philosophical life, in which we act "from what is highest in us," to achieve a sort of personal immortality. Acting "like a man" is not acting from our animal nature, but rather involves maintaining a precarious balance between practical (human) and theoretical (more divine) activities in the political life.

17. On this summary of possibilities, see Caroline Walker Bynum, *"Docere Verbo et Exemplo": An Aspect of Twelfth Century Spirituality* [Harvard Theological Studies, vol. 31] (Missoula, Montana: Scholars Press, 1979). The concept of the "mixed life" was more prevalent in the thirteenth century than in the twelfth.

18. See, for example, *Symposium* 210d1–8: "[B]y scanning beauty's wide horizon, ... turning his eyes toward the open sea of beauty, he will find in such contemplation the seed of the most fruitful discourse and the loftiest thought, and reap a golden harvest of philosophy." Translated by Michael Joyce, in *The Collected Dialogues of Plato*, edited by Edith Hamilton and Huntington Cairns [Bollingen Series, vol. 71] (Princeton, New Jersey: Princeton University Press, 1961).

Here, the contemplative life is not the *vita contemplativa* of the medievals, for its object is not God but the manifestation of the divine in the visible world, in the movement of the heavenly bodies.[19]

Plato and Aristotle are ambivalent towards action taken as an end of life. In rejecting the life of pleasure (*apolaustikos*) as beastly, Aristotle limits the human life to the political and the search for honor, and relegates the contemplative to self-perfection through self-transcendence (to "that which is divine in us"):

> We must not follow those who advise us, being human, to think of human things, and being mortal, of mortal things; but must, so far as we can, must make ourselves immortal, and strain every nerve to live in accordance with the best thing in us; for even if it be small in bulk, much more does it in power and worth surpass everything.[20]

The practical or active life is happy in a secondary degree, as the merely human work of prudence and the moral virtues, while the contemplative life, reserved for the leisured and proficient is more fruitful and self-sufficient. The notion of a mixed life appears with the Stoic search for a life in conformity to the cosmic logos, a rational and "royal" (Plutarch's term) life of self-governance in harmony with nature that eschews contemplation in favor of a *praxis* that attunes us to fate. For Seneca, contemplation is the "thinking" characteristic of a cultured and virtuous man.[21] Plotinus reduces *episteme* to an indirect preparatory means, subordinate to nondiscursive union with the One.[22] The active life is either the profane political life of the many, or an ascetic prelude to mystic withdrawal. Monastic union with the Absolute precluded civic engagement as a viable goal.

Augustine's and Gregory's perspectives on charity initiated the rehabilitation of the notion of action. Augustine depicts the active life as a work of perfection necessitated by love and the limitations of earthly existence. External

19. Aristotle, *Metaphysics* 5.1, 1026a18; *Physics* 2.4, 196a33. The three areas of inquiry constituting theoretical contemplation for Aristotle are (1) natural philosophy (the universal features of matter in motion), (2) mathematics (closely connected to astronomy for him, and (3) first philosophy, or the study of ultimate causes. Wonder gives rise to contemplation as scientific inquiry, and the possession of this knowledge sets us beyond mortal bounds into the divine, in some way. See *Metaphysics*, 1.2, 982b17–983a7.

20. Aristotle, *Nicomachean Ethics*, translated by W. D. Ross, in *The Basic Works of Aristotle*, edited by Richard McKeon (New York: Random House, 1941), 10.7, 1177b32–1178a1.

21. Seneca, *De otio* VII.

22. Plotinus, *Enneads* VI, 9.4. Here, contemplation is a "touching," "vision," or "presence" that transcends discursive *episteme* or theoretical knowledge, which is only a "knowing *about*."

action, the unleisured *vita negotiosa*,[23] is an integral part of Christian perfection, and is not merely a "stirrup to contemplation" to use Origen's term,[24] yet it is subordinate to the "holy leisure" by which one seeks and delights in truth.[25] Martha's service will disappear, he says (*Serm.* 179.4) with the burdens of necessity itself, whereas Mary's contemplation, not a *vita negotiosa* but a *negotiosum otium*, is a busy, fruitful leisure[26] which has its model in God Himself, in an eternal identity of action and contemplation. One exceeds the other as eternity exceeds time (*Serm.* 104.4) and as the destination fulfills the journey.

Augustine places contemplation above action when referring to the stages of spiritual progress in an individual,[27] but subordinates both to charity in speaking of them as genera in *The City of God* 19.2.[28] All three lives, the contemplative, the active, and the mixed, are possible routes to perfection. As in Augustine's monastic *Rule*,[29] the motive of charity is central, demanding a balance of both dimensions, creating a unity of hearts and a common life. It is the turning away from the common truth to our *private good* and not to the service to *others*, which makes us lose contact with wisdom and happiness. In *On Free Choice of the Will* 2.9.26–27, the issue of contemplation and action is discussed in light of the unity of wisdom, which contains them

23. Augustine, *The City of God* 19.2.

24. Origen, *In Lucam fragmenta*, edited by M. Bauer, in *Origenes Werke* (Leipzig: Hinrichs 1905) [Die Griechischen Christlichen Schriftsteller der Ersten Drei Jahrhunderte] vol. 19, 26ff., as cited in Nicholas Lobkowicz, *Theory and Practice: History of a Concept from Aristotle to Marx* (Notre Dame, Indiana: Notre Dame Press, 1967), 60.

25. *The City of God* 19.19.

26. Jean Leclercq sums up the dimensions of this *negotiosum otium*: "This sort of leisure lies halfway between inertia and undue haste; it is a fruitful leisure consisting in a certain relaxation of the mind as it refuses to be entirely taken up with immediate worries, with business; it is an open, disinterested time that leaves scope for an interest in truth, for ideas, and for humankind." Jean Leclercq, "Action and Contemplation: Two Ways Toward the Ultimate Reality," in E. Glenn Hinson, *Spirituality in Ecumenical Perspective* (Louisville, Kentucky: Westminster/John Knox Press, 1993), 64.

27. "[O]ne division of philosophy may be called active; the other part, contemplative. The former deals with the conduct of life; that is to say, with the cultivation of morals. Contemplative philosophy considers natural causality and truth as such." Augustine, *The City of God*, translated by Gerald Walsh, Demetrius Zema, Grace Monahan, and Daniel Honan, edited by Vernon Bourke (Garden City, New York: Doubleday, 1958), 8.4.

28. Here, Augustine speaks of the threefold division of lives: the *genus vitae negotiosum*, *genus otiosum*, and *genus compositum* or *modificatum*. See Robert Bonnell, "An Early Humanistic View of the Active and Contemplative Life," *Italica* 43, no. 3 (1966): 226.

29. On Augustine's monastic *Rule*, see George Lawless, *Augustine of Hippo and His Monastic Rule* (Oxford: Clarendon Press, 1987). Cf. Carol Harrison, *Augustine: Christian Truth and Fractured Humanity* (Oxford: Oxford University Press, 2000), 182ff.

both. Even though some may prefer gazing upon a high mountain, while others prefer a plain or valley, it is the one sun that illumines both, and one light of wisdom in which things are seen and possessed.

The palm of victory goes to neither alone, but to contemplation of truth which condescends to action when charity demands. The "one wisdom common to all," however, forms the substance of our eschatological hope. Cultural works (art, institutions, sciences, leisure) are pressed into the service of the Church, as citizens of the heavenly city make use of the goods of the earthly city, these goods falling under the direction of the corporeal and spiritual works of mercy.

Origen's interpretation of the pagan culture as the "spoils of the Egyptians" was adopted in some measure by Augustine, yet rejected by Ambrose and Jerome. For Ambrose, the saved will leave this world (Egypt) and return with the precious gifts of the virtues to clothe their souls, above all, with the treasure which is the chastity of the passions.[30] In the East, Gregory of Nyssa adopts Origen's interpretation, while Augustine is the sole heir of his view in the West. In the last chapters of the second book of *On Christian Doctrine*, Augustine draws the parallel between the pagan liberal arts and the treasures of Egypt, defending the Christian use of pagan culture, including select aspects of Platonic doctrine (concerning the soul and God), the liberal arts, human institutions, and some moral precepts.[31]

30. Ambrose, *On Abraham* 2.9.66.

31. "Any statements by those who are called philosophers, especially the Platonists, which happen to be true and consistent with our faith should not cause alarm, but be claimed for our own use, as it were from owners who have no right to them. Like the treasures of the ancient Egyptians, who possessed not only idols and heavy burdens, which the people of Israel hated and shunned, but also vessels and ornaments of silver and gold, and clothes, which on leaving Egypt the people of Israel, in order to make better use of them, surreptitiously claimed for themselves ... [S]imilarly all the branches of pagan learning contain not only false and superstitious fantasies ... which each one of us must loathe and avoid as under Christ's guidance we abandon the company of pagans, but also studies for liberated minds which are more appropriate to the service of the truth, and some very useful moral instruction, as well as the various truths about monotheism.... These treasures—like the silver and gold, which they did not create but dug, as it were, from the mines of providence, which is everywhere—which were used wickedly and harmfully in the service of demons must be removed by Christians, as they separate themselves in spirit from the wretched company of pagans, and applied to their true function, that of preaching the gospel. As for their clothing—which corresponds to the human institutions, but those appropriate to human society, which in this life we cannot do without—this may be accepted and kept for conversion to Christian purposes." *On Christian Teaching*, in St. Augustine, *On Christian Teaching*, translated by R. P. H. Green (Oxford: Oxford University Press, 1997), bk. 2, chaps. 144–45, pp. 64–65. Cf. Pier Franco Beatrice, "The Treasures of the Egyptians: A Chapter in the History of Patristic Exegesis and Late Antique Culture," in F. Young et al., *Historica, Biblica, Ascetica et Hagiographica*, Studia Patristica, vol. 39 (Leuven: Peeters, 2006), 160–83.

This view balances action as purification with a public life concerned with justice and the welfare of others. Further, the "sweets of contemplation" tasted in holy leisure are not to be relinquished in service to others, since they nourish active work taken on for love's sake.[32]

Augustine's distinction between *scientia* and *sapientia* in *On the Trinity* XV.10 also helps to clarify his views on contemplation. Wisdom is distinct from science on four counts. First, wisdom is conditioned by purity of heart, which permits us to perceive the divine. Sin, he says, blurs the image of God in us, and darkens our vision.[33] He introduces an analogy of a mirror to emphasize the link between moral dispositions, faith, and wisdom. The wise man, one who knows the limitations of his human knowledge, is like one who recognizes that images in a mirror are reflections of something *beyond* the glass. A clever but unwise man, on the other hand, lacks the purity of heart to admit the limitations of his intellect (somewhat like Socrates' doubly ignorant interlocutors). Instead of recognizing the mirror's reflections for the limited traces that they are, he mistakes the image for the original. He confuses science with wisdom, or mistakes the product of his perception with truth itself. Augustine warns that only a wise person will benefit from the arguments of *On the Trinity*, for only such a man possesses a purified heart and seeks union with the Trinitarian Origin of the image.

The second way in which wisdom exceeds science is through its personal and universal character, which is not shared in by the individual sciences and which transcends human minds and gives us true liberty.[34] Wisdom is personal in that in seeking truth, the soul seeks to attain unfading beauty securely, and wisdom draws souls by degrees to participate in its light. It is universal as shared, without itself being diminished, by all who seek it.[35] In its connection to the Word, wisdom is the source of all truths,

32. *The City of God* 19.19.

33. *On the Trinity* 15.10.

34. "Herein is our liberty, when we are subject to truth.... Here is something which we can all enjoy equally and in common.... [Wisdom] receives all her lovers, being grudging to none, shared by all in common but chaste to each." St. Augustine, *On Free Choice of the Will*, in *Augustine: Earlier Writings*, translated by John Burleigh (Philadelphia: The Westminster Press, 1953), 2.13.37. All English quotations of *On Free Choice of the Will* are from this edition.

35. "All cleave to the same wisdom. All are brought into contact with it. Nothing is consumed as in the case of food, and you cannot drink so as to prevent me from drinking too. From that common store you can convert nothing into your private possession.... [T]he beauty of truth and wisdom, so long as there is a persevering will to enjoy it, does not exclude those who come by any packed crowd of hearers." Ibid., 2.14.37–38.

transcending all sciences and human minds; seeking it lends freedom and joy to all pursuits.[36]

Thirdly, wisdom is a disinterested discovery of transcendent truth. Elsewhere, he argues that that which is beyond use has great use, whereas science searches out what is useful to man. Wisdom opens into the community of love through our participation in a transcendent and perfect good; but the lover of science, through pride and curiosity, can idolize the good of his mind by confusing the means for the goal itself.[37] Finally, wisdom is a deeper union with reality through attaining the highest causes, whereas science deduces conclusions from these principles.[38]

Contemplation in the Augustinian sense has ethical connotations and transcends Aristotelian *theoria*—it stands in relation to science as love does to knowledge, and as rest and unity do to labor. Further, holy action is the fruit of supernatural contemplation. Augustine notes in his sermon on the Transfiguration that this action is that of Peter, commanded to go down from the mountain with Christ, whose action culminated in His passion:

> Life came down, that it might be slain; the Bread, that It might hunger. The Way came down, that It might be wearied on the journey, the Fountain, that It might thirst: and you refuse to labor? Seek not your own.[39]

What Leclercq has called the astonishing reconciliation of contemplation and action in monastic culture[40] began with Benedict's *Rule* and Gregory's synthesis of the two types of life in the same motive of charity. Action was not divorced from contemplation but incorporated in its works of purification, spiritual exercises (reading, meditation, study) and in a monastic economy of pure, disinterested work, impervious to greed. St Bernard, that self-described chimera of his age, favored the contemplative side of the monastic hybrid, but stressed the theme of "unity" in his *Consideration.*[41]

Echoing the Franciscan tradition bearing out its Dionysian debt, love is

36. "A strong and vigorous mental vision may behold many true and changeless things ... but directs its regard to the truth itself whereby all things are made clear, and cleaving to the truth and forgetting, as it were, all other things, it enjoys them all together in the truth." Ibid., 2.14.36–37.

37. See, e.g., *On the Trinity* 12.12.

38. For Aquinas, wisdom also assesses science's conclusions, which fall below it in the order of perfection. But Aquinas's natural contemplation is clearly the intellectual virtue that sets an order in things and judges the principles of the sciences. See ST I-II, q. 57, a. 2.

39. Augustine, "Sermon on the Transfiguration," in *Sunday Sermons of the Great Fathers*, vol. 2, translated by M. F. Toal (Chicago: Regnery, 1958), 65.

40. Leclercq, "Action and Contemplation," 70.

41. Ibid., 72.

the unitive force binding creation and the soul to God, and regulating the dialectic of will and intellect. The narrative of self-emptying and self-transcendence is the mystical stream that would soon lend itself to the voluntarist emphasis on action and on *praxis* that was showcased by Henry of Ghent and Giles of Rome, in contrast to the more intellectualist view of Aquinas.

III. Thirteenth Century Metaphysics of Action and Contemplation: Thomas Aquinas and Henry of Ghent

In the Secunda Secundae of the *Summa theologiae* (qq. 179–88), Aquinas defends a view that combines the superiority of contemplation to action with the mendicant mixed apostolate of study, teaching, and preaching. The Dominican ideal of *contemplata aliis tradere* ("passing on the fruits of one's contemplation") is developed alongside the claim that the active life precedes contemplation as a stage in life. When considered as aspects of one life, they coexist in dynamic tension, both being required by charity until their resolution in the beatific vision. Aristotle's notion of transitive action captures well the imperfect nature of the active life, which involves, according to Maritain, a mendicant quality of neediness: action needs a recipient for one's acts of virtue.[42]

Aquinas adopts an Augustinian outlook on the necessity of the active life for human beings. Unlike angels, who, according to Gregory, "do not wander abroad from the Divine vision, so as to be deprived of the joys of inward contemplation,"[43] we are shackled to the demands of the active life by the "weight of the body.[44] This theme recurs in the question on the kinds of religious life (q. 188) where the contemplative's desire to dedicate himself to God alone appears. "*Soli Deo vacare desiderat*" points to the exclusivity of the goal, to the preference of the means as monastic, and to the eschatological status of love as a state of desire and hope (q. 188, a. 2). Aquinas's notion of perfect contemplation incorporates Augustine's holy leisure (q. 187, a. 3), the freedom of eternal life (q. 181, a. 1, ad 2; q. 181, a. 4), and Gregory's affective "taste of God" and "inchoate beatitude."[45]

42. Jacques Maritain, *Scholasticism and Politics*, 136.

43. St. Thomas Aquinas, *Summa Theologica*, translated by the Fathers of the English Dominican Province (New York: Benzinger Brothers, 1947), II-II, q. 181, a. 4, ad 2. All English quotations of the *Summa* are from this translation.

44. ST II-II, q. 181, a. 4, ad 3.

45. "The contemplative life has something to do with our appetitive power." ST II-II, q. 182, a. 1.

Aquinas uses the notion of intent (*intentio*) or study (*studium*) to refer to a deliberate, persevering application of the mind toward obtaining a particular end (ST II-II, q. 166, a. 1). The division established in ST II-II, q. 179, a. 2 stems from the two functions of the intellect—the sheer knowledge of truth (contemplation), or practical understanding of an appetible good leading to action. While every life contains both elements (cf. q. 181, a. 1), one predominates (q. 179, a. 2, ad 2). With Aristotle, he discounts the life of pleasure and rejects Augustine's addition of a third life, the mixed, deeming the predominance of one or the other sufficient. Since *intentio* or "aiming at something" signifies an act of will,[46] contemplation involves love, not just knowledge. Citing Gregory (an equal influence to Aristotle in his theory of the two lives), Aquinas says that the influence of the will in contemplation is threefold, as the motive to begin to know, as the enjoyment of the act of knowing, and as the delight in obtaining what we love (God).[47]

Unlike the *Commentary on the Sentences*, the two modes of contemplation, that of the *philosophi* and *sancti*, are not now opposed. As he says in ST II-II, q. 180, a. 4, ad 4, "all kinds of truth fulfill the human intellect, so the contemplative life consists in *all sorts* of contemplation of truth."[48] The intellectualist version of contemplation is tempered by a wide sweep of spiritual insights, culminating in Augustine's insight of the best existence as an eternal life which joins wisdom and happiness.

What about the relative priorities of the two lives? In ST II-II, q. 182, a. 1, Aristotelian reasons, grafted onto a biblical scaffolding, show the intrinsic superiority of contemplation ("the simple gaze of the mind upon truth": q. 180, a. 3, ad 1) to action. In contrast to external action, its object ("intelligible reality") is more immaterial and lofty. Further, the act which attains it is more continuous, long-lasting, intrinsic, focused, more free and properly our own,[49] and more self-sufficient. Aquinas treats the issue of nobility in distinguishing the state of perfection and its concrete example. An ecclesiastically assigned order culminates in an episcopal state of perfection, but some individuals surpass their canonical superiors in perfection through greater charity. Abraham, for instance, had both wives and property, but excelled in faith.

46. See ST I-II, q. 12, a. 1; II-II, q. 180, a. 1.

47. ST II-II, q. 180, a. 1.

48. Emphasis added.

49. Cf. ST II-II, q. 182, a. 1, ad 2, where Aquinas quotes Gregory: "the active life is bondage, whereas the contemplative life is freedom."

Aristotle's self-sufficient ideal recurs in the treatment of types of religious life (q. 188), where the solitude of monastics (q. 188, a. 8) is said to be better than the activity of communal life. The order of perfection dictated by this schema begins with hermits, and descends down to monastics, clerics, and laity. Christ's charity, Aquinas says, lives more in solitaries than in social persons, and their utility to the Church is through example and prayer. The tension between the ecclesiastical and the natural orders of perfection is implied here, where contemplation's primacy holds a nuanced place. But in itself, and all things being equal, contemplation is more perfect than action.

Action is a temporally prior preparatory stage as well as being the fruit of contemplation's superabundance (ST III, q. 40, a. 1, ad 2). As less perfect, action is not naturally prior and images God less than the inchoate beatitude of contemplation. Despite the perfectionist cast of his view, Aquinas defends the dignity of action as a component of an apostolic life and as a stage leading to contemplation. Aquinas shows this in four ways. First, proper moral dispositions and the Victorine exercises of reading and meditation (ST II-II, q. 180, a. 3, ad 1) precede contemplation temporally (q. 180, a. 7, ad 2; q. 182, aa. 3–4). Second, taking up an active life when directed by charity to do so must occur by way of addition (q. 182, a. 1, ad 3), not subtraction. Here, Aquinas quotes Augustine's view (*The City of God* 9.19) that if the demands of charity call one from the life of "holy leisure" to the active life, the delights of truth must not be relinquished, or the burden of toil would be too great. Third, he laconically states that the proper motive for the contemplative life is "the love of God and neighbor."[50] Prayer, he says, is as much a part of the contemplative life as contemplation is (q. 181, a. 3, ad 3). So, we cannot simply distinguish contemplation as God-centered from action as being neighbor-centered. And fourth, he takes Christ as the example of the Dominican ideal, whereby the life of preaching and teaching flow from a "superabundance" of contemplation (ST III, q. 40, a. 1, ad 2).

The rise of the mendicants paralleled the renewed stress on the humanity and suffering of Christ, and helped close the gap between a monastic rural contemplative elite and an urban lay emphasis on *praxis* and devotion. Both Franciscans and Dominicans pointed to Christ as the moral example through Whom we participate in God's life. The Incarnation as moral

50. ST II-II, q. 180, a. 2, ad 1; cf. a. 1, ad 3. An interesting question to consider is how Aquinas views the love of neighbor as a necessary disposition for the contemplative life.

ideal is featured in questions on the nature of humility, on obedience, and on the Lord's circumcision, for example.[51] Not only His birth and Passion, but even Christ's glorified body, which retains the wounds of the crucifixion, point to humility as a path of virtue.[52] The mixed apostolate of prayer, study, teaching, and preaching favored by Dominicans also mirrors the life of Christ to the extent that service to others flows from a superabundance of contemplation. The mixed life imitates and shares in the creative act—a movement of descent[53] from the superabundance of contemplation to the ministry to others in preaching and teaching (*contemplata aliis tradere*) exemplified by the life of Christ.[54]

Shortly after Aquinas's death, Henry of Ghent spearheaded the secular clergy's reaction to mendicant professionalism and to the perceived detachment of contemplation from the theological enterprise. He became the spokesperson for the life of action and the primacy of the will and the laity through his various *Quodlibets*,[55] opting for the primacy of the active to the contemplative life.[56] Henry's approach to the question of the priority of love to knowledge, to the primacy of action, and to mendicant disputes over matters of power and privilege,[57] is colored by his refusal to make abstractions of moral realities.

When considered *in se*, or abstractly, Henry agrees with Aquinas that

51. ST II-II, q. 161, a. 5; q. 186, a. 5; III, q. 37, a. 1, ad 2; q. 39, a. 3, ad 3. On this topic, cf. Giles Constable, *Three Studies in Medieval Religious and Social Thought* (Cambridge: Cambridge University Press, 1995).

52. See ST III, q. 54, a. 4, ad 1 on whether the wounds of the crucifixion are signs of corruption or defect.

53. Hans Urs von Balthasar develops the diachronic movement of ascent and descent in contemplation and action entitled "Action and Contemplation," in his *Explorations in Theology*, vol.1 (San Francisco: Ignatius Press, 1989), 227–40.

54. ST III, q. 40, a. 1, ad 2. As Thomas Hibbs puts it: "The mixed life not only contemplates the source of beauty, but also imitates and participates in the creative act whereby that beauty is communicated to creatures." Thomas Hibbs, *Virtue's Splendor: Wisdom, Prudence, and the Human Good* (New York: Fordham University Press, 2001), 200.

55. As, for example, in his *Quodlibet* XII 1.28. See Henry of Ghent, *Quodlibet* XII, edited by Jos Decorte, in *Henrici de Gandavo Opera Omnia*, coordinated by Raymond Macken, Gordon Wilson (Leuven: Leuven University Press, 1979–).

56. On this *quodlibet*, see Stephen Marrone, "Speculative Theology in the Late Thirteenth Century and the Way to Beatitude," in *Les philosophies morales et politiques au Moyen Âge, Moral and Political Philosophies in the Middle Ages, Actes du IXe Congrès international de philosophie mediévale*, edited by B. Carlos Bazán, Eduardo Andújar, and Léonard G. Sbrocchi, vol. 2 (New York: Legas, 1995), 1067–80.

57. Contested privileges included the prerogative to preach in parishes, the ability to own communal and private property, and the right to substitute study for manual labor.

contemplation is superior to action. But in this life of sin, and in reference to sinful practitioners of these activities, there is "nothing for itself alone" (and thus, it is a theoretical detour to consider things "in themselves" alone).[58] Rather, we should evaluate acts in relation to the demands of charity, here and now. For the *viator*, action and love join us to God and neighbor more closely than do knowledge and contemplation. Aquinas's view of the superiority of contemplation to action embodies the classical ideal, in terms of the nature and superabundant power of contemplation.[59] His view of the ultimate superiority of contemplation to action is based on a consideration of "all things being equal," and on the simpler, more abstract qualities of the intellect's object in contrast to the will's (ST I, q. 82, a. 3). But for Henry, all things are certainly *not* equal, in this life of sin.

Parts of the *Glossa Ordinaria* are in agreement with Henry's emphasis on the active life, in stressing sedulous attention to preaching for a church in peril. The *Glossa* on the *Song of Songs* reverses the traditional monastic priority of contemplation to action, stressing the time of "pruning" in which preaching's salvific role is a corrective to the individualistic character of contemplation, which cannot properly attain its lofty goal.[60] Henry's *Quodlibet* VII (qq. 29–30) of 1282 likewise defends the active life, neces-

58. The rise of ambitious professionalism and the scientific model of theology in the thirteenth century created a reaction of fear to what was perceived as Dominican "rationalism." The high value put on contemplation, supported by its association with learning in the Neoplatonic tradition, led Henry (among others) to attempt to sever the tie between scholastic learning and true contemplation, and to denigrate the contemplative ideal itself. Duns Scotus retrieved theology's prestige, but in a way that was neither contemplative nor supernatural. On this entire topic, see Stephen Marrone, "Speculative Theology in the Late Thirteenth Century and the Way to Beatitude."

59. Aquinas justifies the "mixed" life of the Dominican apostolate as a superabundance of contemplation (ST III, q. 40, a. 1, ad 2), defending contemplation's preeminence by way of Aristotle's "eight reasons" of NE 10.7 (cf. ST II-II, q. 182, a. 1). Contemplation is not only a goal and summit, but moves and directs the active life, and is superior by nature (ST II-II, q. 182, a. 1; q. 188, a. 6). For Plotinus, the superiority of contemplation became associated with mystical union with the One. At *Enneads* VI.9.4 he argues for the elevation of mystical union in contrast to *theoria*. In Aquinas's work, the intellectualist Greek heritage is balanced by charity and the role of public revelation, as well as concerns regarding the role of love in the beatific vision. Aquinas does not approve of a life of pure contemplation for humans (ST I-II, q. 3, a. 6, ad 2). On the complexity of Aquinas's position, see Thomas Hibbs, *Virtue's Splendor*, 163–92.

60. See *Glossa ordinaria in Canticum canticorum*, edited by Mary Dove (Kalamazoo, Michigan: Western Michigan University Press, 2004), 170. Cf. Suzanne LaVere, "From Contemplation to Action: The Role of the Active Life in the *Glossa Ordinaria* on the Song of Songs," *Speculum* 82 (2007): 54–69.

sitated by the demands of preaching.[61] Action also takes precedence over contemplation, in part because charity or love is an interrelational virtue, not defined in relation to its possessor alone, as in the case of knowledge.[62]

Henry's ordering of action and contemplation also stems from his rejection of Aquinas's intellectualist theory of the will. He agrees with Aquinas that in this life it is better to love than to attempt to know a lofty reality such as God,[63] and Aquinas admits that concretely, there are situations where charity dictates sacrificing oneself to action. Henry, on the other hand, extols the virtues of the active life and the role of the secular clergy and its right to property. He also highlights the role of the laity and the practical character of theology as conduits to love of God, and resists what he calls the "accidental" character of will assigned by Aquinas.[64]

Instead of determining the hierarchy of intellect and will on the basis of their objects as Aquinas does, he turns, in his first *Quodlibet*,[65] to the actions of these powers. Even though the intellect's object is more abstract and simple than the will's object (the appetible good thing), the will's act transforms the self by transferring it to the desired thing.[66] Unlike Aquinas, who assigns the power of self-motion to intelligence, Henry assigns it to the will. While the intellect assimilates something to its own mode, the will's action adapts to the beloved, and so transcends the self, carrying it over to something greater, namely, God. Here, Henry draws on Dionysius' sense of the ecstatic and unitive nature of love. One could say, in Aristote-

61. On Henry's *Quodlibet* VII, see Stephen Marrone, "Henry of Ghent and the Debate over Ways of Life and the Role of the Clergy," in *Henry of Ghent and the Transformation of Scholastic Thought: Studies in Memory of Jos de Corte*, Ancient and Medieval Philosophy Series I, edited by Guy Guldentops and Carlos Steel (Leuven: Leuven University Press, 2003), 241–59.

62. Henry of Ghent, *Quodlibet* VII, q. 27. See Marrone, "Henry of Ghent," 256.

63. ST I, q. 82, a. 3.

64. The accidental nature of the will refers to the dependence of its acts (specifically inclination, love, and delight) on prior and concomitant apprehension. At ST I, q. 83, a. 2, Aquinas argues for the superiority of the intellect over the will from the perspective of their respective objects. Intellect is a higher (*altior*) power absolutely (*in se*), since its object is simpler and more abstract than that of the will (the desirable thing). In addition, the will relies on the intellect for its determination (ST I, q. 83, a. 2, ad 2). In relation to something else (*secundum quid*), however, the will can be more eminent than the intellect, in the case of things higher than the *viator's* mind (namely, God). The intellect's unqualified eminence reappears in the intellectualist cast of Aquinas's portrait of the beatific vision, where true happiness involves the highest power in the soul (ST I-II, q. 3, a. 4).

65. On Henry's first *Quodlibet*, see P. S. Eardley, "Conceptions of Happiness and Human Destiny in the Late Thirteenth Century," *Vivarium* 44, nos. 2–3 (2006): 276–304.

66. The language of *extasis* is used in the sense of propelling the will beyond itself to the object of desire.

lian terms, that the prior act is one which draws us closer to our principle, for "prior" means what is nearer to some particular principle.[67] In addition, the nature of will is to perfect the entire agent, and the universal good includes truth as a particular object. These reasons also establish, for Henry, the greater nobility of will.

Henry's account of the primacy of action involves a sweep of issues, from the dignity of secular clergy and their rights to property, to an ecstatic theory of the will which echoes Dionysian mysticism and its view of the cosmic power of love. To the extent that a divine ecstatic love[68] or Dionysian deification[69] constitutes our blessedness, and is not just a general inclination to good or a delight accruing to knowing,[70] the will and its action are more perfect than the intellect for Henry. The will impresses itself on the end by means of its own action, whereas the intellect is more receptive.[71] The self-transcendence of ecstatic love is the straightest route to deification, rather than the focus on self-perfection through passive assimilation.

Henry conceives the Dionysian *extasis* or the will's self-transcendence as a corrective to Aquinas's intellectualist view of beatitude. One advantage of Henry's view is its distance from the Aristotelian identification of happiness with a human act of rationality, a view which Aquinas was also at pains to correct[72] by adapting the soul to God as a purely transcendent and uncreated end. Henry achieves his voluntarist notion of beatitude by shifting the analysis from the objects of the powers of intellect and will to their respective acts insofar as they perfect their subjects, and by applying Aristotle's dictum that whatever moves is nobler than that which undergoes

67. See Aquinas, *In 5 Meta.*, lectio 13, no. 936.

68. On "extaticus divinus amor," see Henry of Ghent, *Summa (Quaestiones ordinariae)* (SQO), aa. 41–56, edited by Ludwig Hödl, vol. 29 of *Opera omnia* (Leuven: Leuven University Press, 1998), a. 46, q. 4.

69. SQO, a. 49, q. 6. Only by ecstatic or self-transcending love can the lover "become" the beloved, he states. Aquinas's view of beatitude is conceived as self-perfective, while Henry speaks of the "transference" of the soul into God, occurring by a "conversion" of the will. SQO, a. 48, q. 2. Cf. Eardley, "Conceptions of Happiness and Human Destiny in the Late Thirteenth Century," 294.

70. On the "accidental" character of the will in beatitude in Aquinas, see ST I-II, q. 3, a. 4; q. 4, a. 2.

71. SQO, a. 49, q. 5.

72. In ST I-II, q. 1, Aquinas argues against Aristotle's view that the final end is a human act, however noble and self-sufficient. He states that all human action is in relation to an end, even when one does that action in which the last end consists; see ST I-II, q. 1, a. 1, ad 2.

motion.[73] In Henry's view, the will is this commanding power, as the first mover in the "whole kingdom of the soul."[74]

In Henry's view, the beatific vision cannot be steered or engineered by the intellect's adaptation of its object to its own mode. Such imperfect and self-redounding assimilation ends in a failure of self-transcendence and of self-perfection, and thus, of beatitude. But in Aquinas's defense, his own description of the role of the will as inclination towards an apprehended end, and as an attendant delight in its attainment, equally avoids the Aristotelian idolization of human acts of reason as our destiny, without the vagueness of Henry's Dionysian *extasis* explanation.

For Aquinas, the will is an inclination towards a perceived good, or a concomitant delight in its possession.[75] The will is directed to its end either as absent (inclination, desire), and as present (delight, as resting in its possession).[76] The perfect repose of the will that is delight is "on account of the goodness of that thing in which it reposes", such that the end is not an operation itself (cf. Aristotle's error), but accompanies an operation which is its good.[77] Happiness involves the end being *made present* to him who desires and enjoys it.[78]

If it is argued that since (the beatific) vision terminates in delight, and thus it is the will which attains perfection in the beatific vision (an argument which Henry used, distinguishing temporal from natural priority), Aquinas argues that repose requires an operation, and that good itself, not delight is the end.[79] Only when rational creatures know God's essence will their intellects be perfected and their wills be lulled to rest. Aquinas's account of beatitude as Augustinian "joy in truth"[80] balances intellect and will, for creatures are loved in the beatific vision through the common notion of good (which is *known*), which fulfills right desire. Contemplation

73. Henry of Ghent, *Quodlibet* I, q. 14, in "Heinrich von Gent im Gesprach mit seinen Zeitgemossen uber die menschliche Freiheit, " edited by Macken, *Franziskanische studien* 59 (1977): 125–82. Cf. Aristotle, *De anima* 3.5, 430a18–19.

74. Cf. Eardley, "Conceptions of Happiness and Human Destiny in the Late Thirteenth Century," 282.

75. See Aquinas, ST I-II, q. 4, a. 2. In ST I-II, q. 3, a. 4, he calls delight the "proper accident" of the essence of happiness.

76. ST I-II, q. 3, a. 4.

77. ST I-II, q. 4, a. 2.

78. ST I-II, q. 3, a. 4.

79. ST I-II, q. 4, a. 2, c. and ad 2: "The intellect apprehends the universal good, the attainment of which results in delight: wherefore its purpose is directed to good rather than to delight."

80. ST I-II, q. 3, a. 4, referring to *Confessions* 10.23.

involves the will in that beatitude involves due order to the end, both in tending towards it and in final enjoyment. Attaining happiness depends on the rectitude of will, in its first movement of love, its hope which causes the search, and in delight resulting from perfect union.[81]

IV. Conclusion

Contemplation and action (like Burke's laws or houses[82]) lean on each other, and their operation is delicate. Had Hadot or Nussbaum delved more deeply into the seas of medieval theology, they would have retrieved the rich treasure prepared by Augustine and Aquinas, and would not have so quickly dismissed contemplation as a false transcendence, divorced from life.

This essay began by tracking the path of action and contemplation from their Greek roots as *theoria* and *praxis*—acts of intellect and ways of life—to Augustine's holy leisure made fruitful in the corporal and spiritual works of mercy. Contemplation's primacy was seen to stem from its imaging of God, the substance of our eschatological hope. Augustine's sermon on the Transfiguration pointed to the necessity of the active life as an effect of contemplation in the divine condescension made known in Christ, Who is the incarnate identity of action, passion, and contemplation.

Aquinas argued for the nobility of both lives in his defense of the mendicant ideal, but subordinated action to a broadly construed contemplation that toggled between a beatified intellectualism and the communion of the active life. Propelled in part by the desire to carve out spiritual territory that had been annexed by the ingenuity of the mendicant mixed apostolate, Henry of Ghent argued for the primacy of action, the will, and the role of the laity, against Aquinas's more Aristotelian beatitude. For Aquinas, beatified contemplation weds vision with acts of love and delight in a synthesis both self-perfective and participative of the divine essence, whereas Henry's *theosis* stresses Dionysian *extasis* to the extent of asserting love's primacy to knowledge in all orders.

81. ST I-II, q. 4, aa. 3–4. The differences and lesser known commonalities between Aquinas (representing the Western tradition) and Gregory Palamas (representing the East) on the doctrine of deification are examined in A. N. Williams, *The Ground of Union: Deification in Aquinas and Palamas* (Oxford: Oxford University Press, 1999).

82. Edmund Burke, *Tracts Relative to the Laws against Popery in Ireland*, vol. 5 of *Works of the Right Honorable Edmund Burke* (Boston: Wells and Lilly, 1826), chap. 3, part 1.

In the end, the fruitfulness of both lives stems from charity alone, which stokes the active life of service to others with the abundant fires of contemplation and draws the fragmentary sparks of light back to immanent repose. Contemplation, freedom, generosity, and rest are mutually dependent dimensions of human life. As Maritain notes, contemplation overflows into the sphere of action "in virtue of the abundance of love, which consists in giving oneself."[83]

83. Maritain, *Scholasticism and Politics*, 144.

MICHAEL KROM

Contemplation in America?

Maritainian Reflections on Life in the New World

In July of 1859, Israel Joseph Benjamin (an itinerant Jewish preacher) took upon himself the task of visiting and strengthening the lost tribes of Israel and set sail for the New World. For the next three years he traveled throughout this expansive country, studying the phenomenon of a new American way of life. A Jewish Tocqueville of sorts, Benjamin provides us with "the only coherent account by a Jewish traveler of American life in the period prior to 1870."[1] His account does not reflect the erudition of a Tocqueville, yet his travels from New York to California and back again afforded him an opportunity to survey the many and varied lands united under the banner of republican government, and thus to reflect on the general characteristics of the American soul. While no man of letters, his religious training provided him with an appreciation for the contemplative and spiritual longings of the human spirit, and a keen interest in a way of life that would satisfy the deepest of man's desires. In his view, on American soil the seeds of such speculative inquiries could find no purchase.

According to Benjamin, America's cultural climate at the time did not support contemplative inquiry, for it was materialistic and did not value knowledge for its own sake. He saw in America a world in which even the dearest of all goods, knowledge, "is only the slave and the handmaiden of the passions that can only be goaded on by the pursuit of money. We have

1. Israel Benjamin, *Three Years in America, 1859–1862*, edited by Oscar Handlin (New York: Arno Press, 1975), 5.

no love for knowledge for its own sake; ... but look on it as merchandise."[2] Similarly, Tocqueville commented that "in no country in the civilized world is less attention paid to philosophy than in the United States"[3] and found as a general principle that democratic peoples are unsuited to theoretical pursuits.[4] In the spirit of these keen observers, and out of a common concern for the flourishing of contemplative life in America, this essay (1) presents Maritain's account of the role and value of contemplation in public life in *Scholasticism and Politics*, prefacing this with Aristotle's understanding in order to indicate how Maritain builds upon ancient thought; (2) discusses American educational theory in order to assess how the US fares on the criterion of supporting the contemplative life; and (3) analyzes Maritain's relatively optimistic assessment of Americans' openness to Truth in his *Reflections on America*.

I. Contemplation and the Common Good in Aristotle[5]

"Philosophers exhibit a *telos* for human activity, without which there would be nothing for humans to want but more of the same.... This is their 'practical' contribution, however indirect, to the well-being of the city."[6]

Most ancient political philosophers presuppose that humans are directed towards a natural *telos*, which is to say that they act with some final aim in mind; political philosophy is an attempt to determine the constituents of this *telos* and the circumstances in which the individuals within political societies can fulfill this end. Only by performing activities in accordance with that *telos* can humans secure happiness, and social and political relations are ordered towards allowing each member of a given society to perform those actions most uniquely human. As such, politics aims at a teleological common good.

The notion of a common good is central to such an account of political

2. Ibid., 98.

3. Alexis de Tocqueville, *Democracy in America*, edited by Richard D. Heffner (New York: Penguin Books, 1984), II.I.16, p. 143.

4. See esp. ibid., II.I.20, "Why Americans Are More Addicted to Practical Than to Theoretical Science."

5. This section is a modification of passages from Michael P. Krom, "The Relevance of Contemplation: Aristotle on the Philosopher and the Common Good," *Philosophy in the Contemporary World* 14, no. 2 (2007): 30–38.

6. David Roochnik, "Aristotle's Defense of the Theoretical Life: Comments on *Politics* 7," *The Review of Metaphysics* 61, no. 4 (2008): 737.

philosophy in that humans are understood to have an end given to them by nature the satisfaction of which brings happiness. To suggest that there is a common good is to say that politics considers a rightly-ordered community as the locus of the human good, for it is only when humans are organized in certain kinds of communities that they are able to perform those activities towards which nature directs them. The political community is necessary for human fulfillment because it allows for leisure, and hence a concern with activities that are uniquely human.

When Aristotle considers the development of the city out of the household and village, he claims that the city is essential to human happiness because it is self-sufficient: the city is an arrangement of individuals, non-political relationships, and political institutions that, unlike the village and household, is sufficient for satisfying man's nature as a rational, social, and political animal. Whereas non-political relationships between individuals such as obtain in economic endeavors are only concerned with procuring the instrumental good of their members, the political community affords humans an opportunity to engage in those activities towards which they are directed by nature *as humans*. Only in civil society are humans able to engage in activities for their own sake rather than for the sake of a utilitarian end. To put this in ethical terms, the relationships that obtain in non-political arrangements are for the sake of external goods, whereas in the political the purpose is to cultivate good habits and thus make virtuous action possible. And, since virtuous action alone is properly speaking human, only in the political can the rational creature live in accordance with its nature. As Aristotle puts it, the political community "was formed for the sake of living, but exists for the sake of living well."[7] While the intention of humans as they form the political community is utilitarian, the political arises as a result of the leisure made possible in this association.

The political community allows for leisure and thus the possibility of engaging in truly human activities done for their own sake.[8] Positing a teleological common good necessitates viewing leisure as of central importance to civic life.[9] As Josef Pieper says, "leisure is possible only on the

7. Aristotle, *Politics*, translated by Hippocrates G. Apostle and Lloyd P. Gerson (Grinnell, Iowa: The Peripatetic Press, 1986), 1252b30–1.

8. See Richard Mulgan, "Aristotle and the Value of Political Participation," *Political Theory: An International Journal of Political Philosophy* 18, no. 2 (1990): 195–215, esp. 208ff.

9. For an interpretation of Aristotle's account of leisure, see Joseph Owens, "Aristotle on Leisure," *Canadian Journal of Philosophy* 16, no. 4 (1981): 713–24.

premise that man consents to his own true nature and abides in concord with the meaning of the universe."[10] Without leisure, humans are incapable of being happy, for they are unable to engage in those activities that are unique to them as rational, social, and political animals. They are too concerned with living as such to be able to live well.

Aristotle explains in book seven of the *Politics* that the aim of the lawgiver is to teach the citizens how to be leisurely in the proper sense of the word. If the aim of politics is the good of the individual (in that those who rule seek the common good understood as the good of each of the citizens), and the good of the individual is happiness (which is secured when one performs activities for their own sake), and it is in leisure that this is the case, then the primary concern of the lawmaker is the right use of leisure. Leisure is important, then, not only to prevent a political community at peace from perishing like unused steel,[11] but because it is in leisure that citizens are so-called in the fullest sense of the word, for citizens are distinguished from non-citizens in that they are free: "as the proverb says, 'leisurely activity is not a mark of slaves.'"[12] The right exercise of leisure is the true aim of the lawmaker, and this right exercise is virtuous activity.

According to Aristotle, there are two types of individuals who exemplify leisurely action in distinct ways: the magnanimous man and the philosopher. The magnanimous man performs the noblest of actions with respect to the moral virtues; the philosopher is concerned with the divine life of contemplation. Since the *telos* of humans and therefore of society is to engage in such activities, these two embody distinct public goods in the political community: whereas the magnanimous man is of practical benefit to society through his morally virtuous activity, the philosopher is of benefit precisely in that he lives a life that transcends the practical. Since the beneficial role of the moral virtues is well-understood, the following focuses on the role of contemplative activities in the political community.

Thales of Miletus once cornered the olive market by renting all the olive presses in Miletus and Chios just before a bumper crop. His philosophical investigations, then, proved useful in providing him with material gain. However, as Aristotle sees it, the point Thales was trying to make was that

10. Josef Pieper, *Leisure, The Basis of Culture*, translated by Alexander Dru (New York: Random House, 1963), 42.

11. See *Politics* 7.15, 1334a5–9.

12. *Politics* 7.15, 1334a20–1.

philosophers can be useful if they want, but "wealth is not their main pursuit in life."[13] The philosopher is concerned with leisure, or the condition of performing activities for their own sake.

Unlike practically oriented actions, philosophy is a *useless* activity, for it is a leisurely activity engaged in for its own sake; there is no aim to the philosophical act of contemplation beyond the act itself, and this is the mark of a supremely human activity. In addition, philosophy is a *divine* activity that elevates the philosopher to the universal, eternal, and necessary; those who engage in it do so "not insofar as [they] are human, but because there is a divine element in [them]."[14] Philosophy is an activity in the political community that reveals the natural human desire for self-transcendence. Therefore, philosophy is the best life and of the utmost importance for a political community concerned with the good for humans.

Since the common good is secured when there are citizens engaging in those activities most uniquely human, philosophy is essential to the political community. When discussing the types of activities the citizens should engage in while at peace, Aristotle has an explicit recommendation as to the best activity for citizens: "bravery and fortitude are needed for instrumental activities, philosophy for leisurely activities."[15] He even goes on to say that the more leisure a political community has, the more such activities it will require; philosophy is the most leisurely activity, and thus the more leisure a political community has the greater the place of philosophy. Since it is when they are at leisure that the citizens devote themselves to uniquely human activities, and philosophy is the most leisurely activity, philosophy is the activity in the political community most essential to the common good. The philosopher turns out to be essential to civil life as one who is devoted to contemplation.

According to Aristotle, rulers should not consider philosophy as essential to the common good because it is capable of producing any end, but should recognize that that for the sake of which they rule is the proper activity of leisure. Since the truest leisurely activity is philosophy, the rulers are concerned that it flourish in the community. Philosophy, then, does not rule in the Aristotelian political community, for philosophy does not exist in order to serve politics, but to transcend it. The philosopher is essential

13. *Politics* 1.11, 1259a7ff.

14. *Nicomachean Ethics* 10.7, 1177b27.

15. *Politics* 7.15, 1334a22.

to the political community because he is engaged in the highest activity possible for humans, and because a healthy respect for philosophy and encouragement of it by rulers is necessary for the common good.

Leisure is the space of the uniquely human. Only when humans are allowed the ability to perform activities for their own sake are they able to fulfill their *telos*, and thus the common good requires securing those conditions that make leisure possible for the citizens. Since leisure must be rooted in an affirmation of one's own nature and existence, those who engage in uniquely human activities are afforded a unique public role in the political community insofar as their activities are essential to the common good. Both the magnanimous man and the philosopher are such models of human excellence.

Since the aim of the political community is to allow for those activities conducive to the attainment of the human *telos*, there is a natural limit placed on law and politics; only by acknowledging the limitations of politics can there be happiness in a civil society, for humanity's end transcends politics. The philosopher, while ultimately directed beyond the political community towards the eternal, finds him- or herself at home in civil society as the seat of the goods and activities towards which natural reason is directed. At the same time, the presence of the philosopher is a reminder to those engaged in political rule that the common good of the political community requires allowing space for the transcendent. Thus the philosopher helps remind the community that, while man does in some sense exist as a part of the body politic, more importantly he exists for Truth. As Aquinas puts it, "Man is not ordained to the body politic, according to all that he is and has.... But all that man is, and can [do], and has, must be referred to God."[16]

II. Contemplation and the Common Good: Maritain's Christian Development

"One of the striking things about Christianity, in contrast to the Greek notion of contemplation, something Maritain often notes, is that it is, without ceasing to be contemplative, action oriented."[17]

16. St. Thomas Aquinas, *Summa Theologica*, translated by the Fathers of the English Dominican Province (New York: Benzinger Brothers, 1948), I-II, q. 21, a. 4, ad 3.

17. James V. Schall, "On the Prospect of Paradise on Earth: Maritain on Action and Contemplation," in *Truth Matters: Essays in Honor of Jacques Maritain*, edited by John G. Trapani Jr. (Washington, D.C.: The Catholic University of America Press, 2004), 13.

Maritain certainly agrees with Aristotle that contemplation is the highest human activity, and as such the aim of human life. And yet, as a Catholic philosopher he also recognized that the Christian introduction of the supernatural virtues of faith, hope, and charity modifies and reshapes the Aristotelian schema. Thus, without losing sight of the primacy of truth as the object man desires, Maritain sought to develop an account of Christian contemplation faithful to the twofold love of God and man to which the believer is called. After noting Maritain's agreement with Aristotle on the relationship between contemplation and the common good, this section addresses the "Christian difference" and Maritain's account thereof.

In "The Human Person and Society," Maritain distinguishes between two "poles" of the human being, the material and the spiritual. Our material pole is the source of individuality and is "a narrowness of being."[18] While individuality is not bad per se, it needs to be complimented by the spiritual pole, or personality. Maritain describes personality as the ability to envelop oneself "by intelligence and freedom, and of super-existing in knowledge and free love."[19] Self-development or education takes place by allowing one's individuality to "diminish" and one's personality to "increase." This duality of the human person provides a framework for examining political life.

In terms of individuality, man is a part of a temporal society that can make claims on him and even demand that he subordinate himself to the common good. Were one to stop there, however, the body politic would be a "mortal god," and the path to totalitarianism would be rather short. Like Aristotle, Maritain is able to account for man as a political animal and yet as one who, by the very rationality that makes political life possible, simultaneously transcends the body politic: "the person as such is a *totality*, ... through his ordination to the transcendent whole, he even surpasses the temporal society."[20] As a being whose fulfillment is found through contemplation as an act of self-transcendence, man can never be sacrificed to politics; and yet, as a being situated in a political community, his transcendence must somehow serve the common good. It is interesting to note that the example Maritain uses to illustrate his meaning refers to intellectual

18. Jacques Maritain, "The Human Person and Society," chapter 3 in *Scholasticism and Politics*, translated and edited by Mortimer J. Adler (New York: Macmillan, 1940), 61.

19. Ibid., 63.

20. Ibid., 73; emphasis in original.

life: a mathematician has an obligation to return the favor of being educated to the body politic (owing to his individuality), and yet the body politic cannot demand that he hold as true mathematical propositions society finds useful (owing to his personality).[21]

When discussing Aristotle's account of the role of philosophy in promoting the common good, the non-utilitarian aspect of philosophy is stressed: the act of contemplation itself turns out to be good for the body politic despite the fact that it transcends political action. While Maritain speaks often of the need for transcendent activities, he broadens the category of people engaged in them; Christianity opens the door to contemplation by inviting all to its delights. Yet understanding how all can take part in this highest of activities requires understanding how Christianity transforms it. Aquinas' account of the priority of sacred doctrine among the sciences and of charity among the virtues illustrates this Christian "transfiguration" of philosophy.

In the first question, fourth, and fifth articles of the *Summa theologiae,* Aquinas explains that the highest science, namely, sacred doctrine, is unique among sciences because it is both practical and speculative. Since it contains the knowledge of both God and of how man can achieve union with God, it transcends all other sciences and is identifiable with wisdom itself. The culmination of the study of this science is found in charity, for charity is the form of the virtues by which one achieves union with God. Finally, this union with God includes within itself union with other men, who are to be loved in God. In this way, all are called to contemplation, and by being drawn into God's presence, are given to actions directed toward bringing others into this mystical union.

As Maritain explains in "Action and Contemplation," the Greeks were aware that contemplation is superior to action but mistakenly concluded from this "that mankind lives for the sake of a few intellectuals."[22] Christianity's innovation with regard to the Greek conception of contemplation is four-fold: (1) "love is better than intelligence"[23]; (2) the transfiguration of the notion of contemplation to be oriented toward love of the one contemplated, namely, God; (3) work as a dignified activity inasmuch as it is a participation in God's creation *ex nihilo*; and (4) contemplation, or, better, "*entrance into the very states of God, of God Incarnate*"[24] is for everyone. The

21. See ibid., 75–76.

22. Ibid., 172.

23. Ibid., 173.

24. Ibid., 175; emphasis in original.

universality of love makes possible, even for those called to an active life, a participation in contemplative life. And, on the part of those committed to contemplation in the fullest sense, generosity will abound as they seek to share the Good News. As Thomas Merton notes when discussing Aquinas' preference for the "mixed" life of contemplation and action, "Saint Thomas is here teaching us that the so-called mixed vocation can only be superior to the contemplative vocation if it is itself *more contemplative*."[25]

In political terms, everybody is called to the fullness of personality found in acts of love, and by doing so act as a leaven in the body politic. As Maritain explains in *Scholasticism and Politics*, it is essential that even those engaged in political life maintain a contemplative foundation, for all political action must flow from prayer, from love seeking to inform justice. Following Aquinas, Maritain asserts that politics needs "the contemplation of the saints and their love, because it causes the gifts of divine life and of substantial Love to abound on the earth."[26]

III. Contemplation in America

How does one begin assessing whether or not a culture values contemplative activity? This is a daunting task and would require a wealth of research for which this essay could only serve as a preliminary. In general, St. Augustine's explanation of a republic as a people held together by agreement as to what is lovable[27] would be a guiding principle: what do Americans love? How do they order the wealth of goods available to them? The following will examine early American views on education, for the aim of education is to provide the citizenry with the means to attain the goods it loves. While the general thesis offered here would suggest that Americans' utilitarian/political conception of education reveals a lack of appreciation for contemplative activities, the concluding remarks will suggest a more optimistic conclusion.

The centrality of leisure, or activities performed for their own sake, in Aristotle's conception of the highest good led him to conceive of education for citizens as an education for freedom. Rather than devote themselves to

25. Thomas Merton, *The Seven Story Mountain* (New York: Harcourt, Brace and Company, 1948), 416; emphasis in original.

26. Maritain, *Scholasticism and Politics*, 231.

27. See Augustine, *City of God*, bk. 29, chap. 21.

studies that are exhausted in a particular trade, citizens are to be trained in the art of living well. This is the essence of a liberal arts education, and a good measure of how much a society respects contemplative activity is its understanding of the ends of education. In the American case, while it would be narrow and unfair to assert that education was seen as an entirely vocational affair, it would also be fanciful to look back to the early days of the Republic as being filled with Chaucerian scholars who could be said to be "gladly to learn and gladly to teach."

The educational institutions founded during the colonial era were generally established with an eye toward ministry. While this necessitated reading of the classics and theological studies, the aim was clearly vocational rather than liberal. V. T. Thayer boldly asserts that "to the Puritans are we indebted for establishing early the practical role of education in American history and the subordinate position assigned to scholarship for the sake of scholarship."[28] To be sure, the vocational aim of education at such institutions did not prevent them from asking of their students, in the words of Cotton Mather, "the Grand Question, Why they live; and what is the End of their Actions that they fill with their lives"[29]; yet a trajectory was set that would not be changed with the birth of common schools and, more generally, when government took control over the educational process.

On the eve of the ratification of the US Constitution, the founders of this new nation showed a concern for education to be central to the destiny of the republic. Most prominently, the *Northwest Ordinance* of 1787 included the following provision: "Religion, morality, and knowledge, being necessary to good government and the happiness of mankind, schools and the means of education shall forever be encouraged."[30] Of interest to twenty-first-century Americans is the fact that the members of congress who ratified this proposal did not consider it problematic that under this provision the government would support religious-based schools; but, for our purposes what stands out is that education here serves the purpose of the

28. V. T. Thayer, *Formative Ideas in American Education: From the Colonial Period to the Present* (New York: Dodd, Mead and Company, 1965), 12; see also 19–20, where he contends that, "At no time have Americans established schools and colleges or organized curricula within these institutions purely out of respect for learning or scholarship."

29. Cotton Mather, *Bonifacius,* quoted in *Colonial Times to 1860*, vol. 1 of *Social History of American Education,* edited by Rena L. Vassar (Chicago: Rand McNally and Company, 1965), 20.

30. *Northwest Ordinance of 1787*, Art. 3, *The Avalon Project* (Yale Law School, Lillian Golman Law Library).

public good. More specifically, good government is seen to depend upon an educated citizenry. While the US Constitution is mute on this theme,[31] the generation of the founders would see a firm commitment to education for civic life.

To some extent, the vocational gearing of the colonial schools continued in the common school movement, though ministerial training was replaced as an end with civic training. While early educational reformers in the Republican movement such as Benjamin Rush shared Cotton Mather's concern with education for character, the aim was no longer to form the Christian soul but the industrious patriot; in Rush's own words: "Above all ... [the educated man] must love life, and endeavour to acquire as many of its conveniences as possible by industry and economy, but he must be taught that this life 'is not his own,' when the safety of his country requires it."[32] While it could be argued that neither Mather nor Rush possess a full appreciation for an education in freedom, at least Mather directed his efforts toward a transcendent end. If the essential role of the contemplative is to model an activity that is higher than politics and to which the knee of politics must bend, the move toward government control over education thwarted this end, as the aim was "to convert men into republican machines ... [so that they can] perform their parts properly, in the great machine of the government of the state."[33] As such language suggests, education for civic freedom is insufficient for freedom *simpliciter*.

Admittedly the sketch of education in America here provided focuses on the Republican era, and ignores the developments that, especially in the twentieth century, proved that liberal education has a home in this more mature nation. It would only be expected that a young nation first seek what is useful, and only after what is liberal. Yet it is not clear that liberal education is thriving, much less that it will continue to do so. Further, it must be said that the Chicago movement was relatively insignificant in comparison to the progressive movement's insistence that education serve democratic ends. As Mortimer J. Adler stated in 1939: the progressive educators "are so

31. A concern with the flourishing of the arts and sciences is found in Article 1, Section 8: "The Congress shall have Power ... To promote the Progress of Science and useful Arts, by securing for limited Times to Authors and Inventors the exclusive Right to their respective Writings and Discoveries." This is the only article that even indirectly addresses education, and it is clearly with an eye toward utilitarian purposes.

32. Benjamin Rush, "Of the Mode of Education Proper in a Republic," in *Social History*, 124.

33. Ibid., 126.

anxious to save democracy that they are willing to make the educational process serve no other end than the perpetuation of a form of government."[34] Finally, the liberal educational establishments that pride themselves as vanguards in this movement tend to emphasize their utilitarian or activist spirit via such terms as "critical thinking skills" or "creating future leaders". Liberal education may remain part of the American landscape, but it may do so despite rather than because of our national character.

In *Education at the Crossroads,* Maritain puts forth a model of liberal education while simultaneously exposing various errors that plague contemporary pedagogy. While he does not direct his remarks specifically at American educational institutions, the general features outlined in the previous section are precisely what concerns him. In his day the instrumental model of education had been taken up, pushed to further extremes, and wedded to the reigning Pragmatist-Progressive ideology. After outlining Maritain's general views on education, this section looks at the errors he finds in modern pedagogy.

The language of whole and part, personality and individuality, covered in section II will be helpful here. The primary goal of education is the development of personality, of assisting the student achieve the supernatural end for which he was created. In this sense the student is a whole, and not simply a part of some collective body. And yet, due to his individuality, the student is also a part, for he is situated within a particular culture and must contribute to the common good peculiar to his society. As Maritain puts it, the aim of education "is to guide man in the evolving dynamism through which he shapes himself as a human person—armed with knowledge, strength of judgment, and moral virtues—while at the same time conveying to him the spiritual heritage of the nation and the civilization in which he is involved, and preserving in this way the century-old achievements of generations."[35] Thus in the primary sense education is a liberation from ignorance and from being controlled by external force; education is an attempt to foster the spiritual freedom that can only come from the truth. Secondarily and consequent to this internal formation is a

34. Mortimer J. Adler, "Liberalism and Liberal Education," in *Reforming Education: The Opening of the American Mind,* edited by Geraldine van Doren (New York: Macmillan Publishing Company, 1988), 45.

35. Jacques Maritain, *Education at the Crossroads* (Clinton, Massachusetts: The Colonial Press, 1961), 10.

social good, namely, integration into the common good of one's society.[36] While educators would be remiss to overlook the need for vocational training, "this practical aim is best provided by the general human capacities developed."[37]

Maritain's philosophical anthropology is at the root of his conception of education, for it is only by knowing the end of human life that one can seek the means thereunto. The first general error in modern pedagogy is that it loses sight of this end. While Maritain is rather positive about the developments in pedagogical means found in twentieth-century educational theorists, the second error he finds is a flawed conception of man. Good technique wedded to various theories that undermine true human flourishing is what characterizes modern academia.

Maritain isolates four 'isms' that dominate in the schools: pragmatism, sociologism, intellectualism, and voluntarism. In light of the educational movements in American schools traced in the previous section, the two most important are pragmatism and sociologism. Both of these theories tend to reduce man to his individuality inasmuch as they treat him as a part of the social organism. Pragmatism does this by focusing on action, thus losing sight of contemplation and self-perfection as the end. The pragmatist fails to "trust in truth, ... [thus robbing action of] human effectiveness."[38] Sociologism utilizes the language of Benjamin Rush in "deriv[ing] the supreme rule and standard of education from social conditioning."[39] The individual is sacrificed to the needs of society and is viewed as a cog in the great machinery of the state. In both pragmatism and sociologism, man's transcendent end is completely neglected and, as John Henry Newman saw well before these movements had come into their maturity, such education turns out to be for the State rather than for the one educated.[40] The disillusionment found among American youth would not surprise Maritain, for it is to be expected that an educational system designed to transform the natural desire for Wisdom into a desire for useful social purposes would incite rebellion. Unless students' desires for transcendence are awakened through contemplative practices, they will settle for gross hedonism, rejecting thereby the good they never discovered they lacked.

36. See ibid., 14–15.
37. Ibid., 10.
38. Ibid., 13.
39. Ibid., 15.
40. See John Henry Newman, *The Idea of a University*, Discourse 7.

IV. Maritain on America

What do Americans love? There is no doubt that hedonism, materialism, consumerism, careerism, and similar unflattering terms would characterize the American soul, yet such a list is one-sided and overlooks the many other ways in which love appears on the American scene. Consider the popular images of farming, of nature, of the open road; all speak to a yearning for something more, a spark of the transcendent. While each is incomplete and tends to mask a failure to integrate the leisurely spirit of the contemplative into daily life, it would be remiss to overlook the American as a searcher, as one who longs for more than what quotidian affairs can provide. Americans may not love knowledge for its own sake; they may not grasp the monastic love of stillness and communion with God; yet this speaks not to a lack of love, but to an inability to articulate and interpret what everyone finds within his breast.

Whatever we may think of the accuracy of Benjamin's account of nineteenth-century American life, his concern is one that would have been shared by the American founders. While the pursuit of knowledge for its own sake may not have been on their minds, there was a strong commitment to the necessity of a citizenry dedicated, not just to living, but to living well. Even if monasticism and speculative philosophy were not seen as the *telos* of human life, political life was not seen as an end in itself.

George Washington's farewell as he resigned from the office of president in 1793 established a noble precedent in American political life: American presidents modeled the ideals of the regime by voluntarily limiting themselves to two terms, thus avoiding the possibility of tyrannical rule. As important as this lesson in good government was, Washington had to admit that his reasons for stepping down were personal. Quite simply, he felt that he had served his country and that he had finally earned the right to return to his beloved farm. In other words, Washington saw his political life as a necessary burden, the fruit of which would be the bucolic enjoyment of minding one's own business. As he said in closing,

> I anticipate with pleasing expectation that retreat in which I promise myself to realize, without alloy, the sweet enjoyment of partaking, in the midst of my fellow-citizens, the benign influence of good laws under a free government, the

ever-favorite object of my heart, and the happy reward, as I trust, of our mutual cares, labors, and dangers.[41]

For George Washington, first citizen, the political life is not an end in itself; politics is necessary because life in a well-constituted regime allows one to pursue a good life that otherwise could not be made secure. We have a duty to engage in politics so that we may be free to pursue more satisfying endeavors. While for Washington it was farming rather than contemplative study which fit this description, we find in his account of the joys of husbandry the inchoate contemplation of which Maritain spoke: as Washington wrote to Alexander Spotswood, "to see plants rise from the earth and flourish by the superior skill, and bounty of the laborer fills a contemplative mind with ideas which are more easy to be conceived than expressed."[42]

Such considerations are in the spirit of Maritain, who found in America "a certain hidden aspiration to contemplation."[43] In contrast to many European intellectuals, who found America to be the land of gross materialism and industrialized life, Maritain thought that Americans had, by "vanquish[ing] the inner logic of the industrial regime considered in its first historical phase, … almost without knowing it, inaugurated a really new phase in modern civilization."[44] Maritain was clearly in the "built better than they knew" camp, as he often found Americans' pre-reflective approach to life to shine through the public philosophy they espoused. Since Americans are practical by nature, they seek freedom now rather than in some messianic future. As such, they avoid the ideological extremes of Marxism or other forms of deliverance politics. And yet, despite their practical, even pragmatic, orientation, they are lovers of truth.

In a chapter entitled "The Old Tag of American Materialism," Maritain notes that the quest for truth is evident in the American emphasis on free discussion, that in the US "there is a perpetual process of self-examination and self-criticism … [and to making] wisdom the final battle."[45] Americans' thirst for knowledge and for spiritual life is evident in their attempts

41. George Washington, *Farewell Address*, 1796, *The Avalon Project* (Yale Law School, Lillian Golman Law Library).

42. Quoted in Bruce S. Thornton and Victor Davis Hanson, "'The Western Cincinnatus': Washington as Farmer and Soldier," in *Patriot Sage: George Washington and the American Political Tradition*, edited by Gary L. Gregg II and Matthew Spalding (Wilmington, Delaware: ISI Books, 1999), 44.

43. Maritain, *Scholasticism and Politics*, 192.

44. Maritain, *Reflections on America*, 23.

45. Ibid., 38–39.

to establish liberal arts institutions, and in the fact that monastic life flourishes more here than in Europe.

In closing, it is worth mentioning that the founder of the first Benedictine monastery in America, Boniface Wimmer, was told not to waste his time in this New World, for here there was no appreciation for the contemplative ways of monastics. Yet this determined *Projectenmacher,* who, incidentally, had a Jeffersonian view of the centrality of farming for stable political order, would not be deterred. His gamble paid off, and led either directly or indirectly to the founding of more than twenty abbeys and ten colleges in the US and abroad.

As Socrates says of democracy, Americans' characteristic love is freedom; while under such a constitution true liberty must coexist with license, the human longing for truth means that a community of learning or of worship will always be able to find a home on democratic soil. One can only wonder if Israel Benjamin would have found this to be the case had he not just been passing through. To put it differently, the freedom to move about the country is part of the American spirit; our land is a place where restless man can find a home if he is willing to keep traveling.

JAMES G. HANINK

Contemplation, Martyrdom, and the Principle of Gratuitousness

I. Introduction

Justice does not stand alone. Neither does peace nor the development of peoples that peace invites. Both, in part, are the work of justice.[1] But such a justice lives in the company of "the principle of gratuitousness."[2] For Benedict XVI, *this* principle reflects that "[t]he human being is made for gift," and it is this gift "which expresses and makes present his transcendent dimension."[3]

If we understand "principle" as a source rather than a formula or rule, we can say that we begin in and through a gift. It is a gift which we are to share. If now we speak theologically, we need not apologize. The non-believer hardly enjoys a default position in such matters. Josef Pieper more plausibly contends that "[t]heology is always prior to philosophy, and not in merely a temporal sense, but with respect to inner origin and their relationship in that origin."[4] Still, philosophy is a welcoming venue for the exploration of first things, and the deep structure of our existence has a pride of place among them. What, then, might a philosopher contribute to the language, the logic, and the reality of our lives understood as gift?

1. Pius XII chose *Opus jusitiae pax* as his motto. His source is Isaiah 32:17. Paul VI writes that "Development is the new name for peace." *Populorum progressio* (1967), no. 86.

2. Benedict XVI, *Caritas in veritate* (2009), no. 34.

3. Ibid.

4. Josef Pieper, *Leisure, The Basis of Culture*, translated by Alexander Dru (New York: Random House, 1963), 115.

II. A Philosophical Framework

A Thomist will begin with Aristotle, though the Philosopher himself took pains not to do so! Let's consider, then, the distinction between the transitive and intransitive dimensions of action; therein, we will already find a heuristic metaphysics. For Aristotle and St. Thomas, any action comes about along the metaphysical trajectory of potency and act.[5] This dynamic suggests a venerable corollary: *agere sequitur esse,* that is, "action follows on being."

But human action is distinctive. *Conscious* of our agency, we experience ourselves as present in our actions yet not "fused" with them.[6] Reflecting on the range of action, Aristotle says that "in general, motion is in the thing being moved," and offers as examples building a house or weaving a garment.[7] Both are transitive in character. But, of course, there are cases in which an act does not produce something external to the agent. They are intransitive in character. In such cases, he notes, "activity is present in these, as the act of seeing is in the one seeing, and the act of speculating in the one speculating, and life in the soul."[8] Note well: if we seek a happy life, we ought to look to the soul, since "happiness is in the soul [which] is a kind of life."[9]

Commenting on such activity, immanent rather than productive, Thomas writes that "the actuality then exists in the agent as its perfection," so that "the act of seeing is in the one seeing as his perfection" and, indeed, the activity of life is in the soul.[10] The distinction between transitive and intransitive is, for Thomas, of pivotal importance. In this same discussion, he appeals to the distinction to help explain the nature of happiness. "[J]ust as life is in one who lives, in a similar fashion happiness is in one who is happy," from which it follows that happiness is not a matter of external production;

5. For the general context of the trajectory of potency to act, see Aristotle, *Metaphysics,* 9. For a recent discussion of the significance of this trajectory, see Steven A. Long, *Analogia Entis: On the Analogy of Being, Metaphysics, and the Act of Faith* (Notre Dame, Indiana: University of Notre Dame, 2011), 13–51.

6. Robert Spaemann makes the point well; see Robert Spaemann, *Persons,* translated by Oliver O'Donovan (New York: Oxford University Press, 2006), 61.

7. Aristotle, *Metaphysics* 9.8, 1050a19–23. All quotations from the *Metaphysics* are taken from W. D. Ross's translation in *The Complete Works of Aristotle,* vol. 2, edited by Jonathan Barnes (Princeton: Princeton University Press, 1984).

8. Ibid.

9. Ibid.

10. Aquinas, *Commentary on Aristotle's "Metaphysics,"* translated by John P. Rowan (Notre Dame, Indiana: Dumb Ox Books, 1995), bk. 9, p. 617, no. 1885.

rather it "consists in understanding and willing."[11] Still elsewhere, he appeals to the distinction between transitive and intransitive in reference to predestination. Thus, while God's providence affects us all, the act of predestining remains within God.[12]

For his part, Maritain deftly profiles the two dimensions of action. The transitive brings movement to its object. Insofar as it transforms the material, this movement is visible; as such, it has temporal as well as spatial limits. Here we might think of a carpenter fashioning a door. The transitive also discloses the agent's need; because of this need, the transitive directs the agent toward some object or other. By contrast, the intransitive draws the world inward, within the agent, and thus perfects the agent. Here we might think of our coming to recognize a moral good. Maritain writes, "the soul, when it knows, becomes thereby something that it is not, and when it loves, it aspires toward what it is not, as to another self."[13] Like the soul, this immanent activity endures. It serves as the ground of both the moral life and the contemplative life.[14]

But what is it to live the contemplative life, which is embedded in the intransitive dimension of action? Aristotle tells us that it is to live the best of lives. And who is able to live such a life? Surely, he insists, neither the slave nor the artisan; surely neither the warring soldier nor the grasping politician. It is the activity of understanding that characterizes the best of lives and enjoys something of the divine. But slaves and artisans, politicians and soldiers? Either they cannot or they will not enjoy the leisure which invites understanding.[15] Even should there emerge a ruler superior in virtue, one who does not rule simply as a master, he too must direct his life to the contemplation that is virtue's crown.[16] Contemplation, then, is for the few. But now a further pair of questions arises: what is it that these few are to contemplate and how are they to do so? Skeptics might well suppose that even these few will find nothing more to contemplate than the very questions of what and how to contemplate. Is there anything more?

11. Ibid.

12. *Summa theologiae* (ST) I, q. 23, a. 2, ad 1.

13. Jacques Maritain, "Action and Contemplation," chapter seven in *Scholasticism and Politics*, translated and edited by Mortimer J. Adler (New York: The Macmillan Company, 1954), 171–72.

14. Ibid.

15. Aristotle, *Nicomachean Ethics* 10.7, 1177b.

16. *Politics* 7.3, 1325b.

III. A Theological Development

Christianity offers something more, something that no one could have anticipated. Maritain identifies four ways by which Christianity transforms what it is for us to contemplate.[17] First, it is in contemplation that love, *caritas*, takes us beyond knowledge and brings us into a closer union with God. This love deepens both our ontological and moral character. Second, in contemplation love becomes a light that lets us see beyond ourselves to the beloved. *Quia ubi amor, ibi oculus* ("because where there is love there is insight"). Third, this contemplative love directs our actions, even insofar as they are transitive, beyond the management of others as objects to the lasting service of others. Fourth, this love—God's free gift—brings *all* who accept it into the contemplative life. In both its mode and object, Maritain says, *caritas* "goes beyond anything that the energies of human nature, left to themselves, can achieve."[18]

Note how much is at stake. In large part, we find ourselves conditioned to a "rationed" recreation chiefly designed to prepare us for a fresh round of labor. By contrast, the philosopher's reflections and the poet's artistry set the stage for contemplation. It seems, though, that they do so only for the few. Yet beyond this natural achievement, there is a contemplation ordered to a share in the divine life, the life of grace. From this grace comes the transcendent action of the giving of one's self. Here Maritain finds in contemplation a *universal* call to holiness. In doing so, he anticipates Vatican Council II's *Lumen Gentium*, 39–42.

Contemplation itself, though, remains in the one who contemplates; it is an intransitive or immanent activity. But if one who contemplates shares in God's life, contemplation overflows in the free gift of self. Thus, indeed, it shows that it is of God. Recognizing this, Maritain expresses the mystery of grace in the language of metaphysics. "We have arrived," he says, "at a fundamental truth":

> Christian philosophy is a philosophy of being; more than that, a philosophy of the superabundance of being; and in this it stands incomparably higher than other great philosophies of being, such as Hindu metaphysics, where being does not give being and can but absorb in itself—*maya* and soul itself. Christian philoso-

17. Maritain, "Action and Contemplation," in *Scholasticism and Politics*, 173–78.
18. Ibid., 178.

phy, better than the Greek, has seen that it is natural that immanent activity should superabound, since it is superexisting.[19]

Thus, in our contemplation—an immanent activity—it is natural that we reach beyond ourselves to others. When, moreover, we consider God's gratuitous superabundance, we see how even God's glory, of which all creation speaks, is in a sense for us.[20] After all, God needs nothing from us. Thus, Thomas writes, it is "evident that God seeks glory, not for His own sake, but for ours."[21] Elsewhere he observes that "grace is nothing else than a beginning of glory in us."[22]

This superabundance of being helps us, as well, in approaching the mystery of the Trinity. Here, as Robert Spaemann observes, we can turn to both the Greek Fathers and the Latin Tertullian. The Greeks introduce the term *hypostasis* to signify a self-standing existent; they understand the God of revelation as mediated within by three *hypostases,* numerically but not qualitatively different. On this view, Spaemann comments, God's life is "a process of self-mediation" as well as "an eternal occurrence."[23] Later Tertullian borrows the term "person" from the grammarians to replace the Greek *hypostasis*. For the grammarians, of course, "person" figures into the analysis of speech-acts. As Spaemann notes, "The same individual can be spoken of now in the first, now in the second or third person, and persons are distinguished only by their relative position is a given speech-situation."[24] We come then to understand God as one in being and three in persons.

But this orthodox language calls for a further critical specification. Spaemann continues:

> [Being] was meant in the sense of a "first *ousia*," a particular, individual kind of being, which exists in the manner that the persons who realize it transmit it to one another in a definite order, having their reality in self-giving and self-receiving.[25]

Along with this specification of Being, there is an identification of the dynamic of gift, a gift we extend insofar as we share in God's life. But the receiving and giving of self as gift returns us to the grace that makes it possible.

What risk, one might wonder, comes with the glory of this grace? The

19. Ibid., 183.

20. Ibid.

21. St. Thomas Aquinas, *Summa Theologica,* translated by the Fathers of the English Dominican Province (New York: Benzinger Brothers, 1947), II-II, q. 132, a. 1, ad 1. All English quotations of the *Summa* are from this translation.

22. ST II-II, q. 24, a. 3, ad 2.

23. Spaemann, *Persons,* 25.

24. Ibid., 26.

25. Ibid., 26–27.

perfection to which this grace introduces us, Maritain says, leads to the "sacrificial privilege" of the contemplative life.[26] Admittedly, for most of us our contemplation is, as it were, "masked" in the particulars of the active life in which we find our vocation. But because the contemplative life to which God can lead us is superhuman, in some cases "the supernatural sweeps everything away" and does so "at the risk of breaking everything," a prospect which surely gives one pause.[27] What are we to make of this? And have not Christians, in any case, come a long and worrisome way from Aristotelian flourishing?

IV. An Objection and Reply

The skeptic's perspective on, and consequent wariness of, such a development is ready at hand. It comes in the context of the cumulative argument at issue. Thus far it is an argument that is philosophical in its account of the acting person, theological in its account of contemplation, and both in its thesis of the superabundance of being. In this context the skeptic will mince no words. He or she will admonish us to put ourselves on guard—straight way—against the religious fanaticism such a line of argument might encourage.

Having issued this immediate warning, the skeptic then turns to a weighty complaint. In a world replete with both physical and moral evil, we ought to challenge any theology of a gratuitously giving God. Indeed, the world is so replete with evil that there is a force about this objection that one must acknowledge. In some cases, moreover, one ought to thank the skeptic for calling by name the evils that others obscure. And yet a point of logic comes into play. How can we recognize what is evil if not as a distortion of what is good? Does not this disclose the primacy of the good? What, too, if hope wins out and we find that good overcomes evil?

But just where is it that we might see good overcoming evil? For Thomas, we should look for this triumph in the witness of the saints and martyrs. In the faith of the early martyrs, he writes, "there are truths preached that surpass every human intellect," and "for the minds of mortal men to assent to these things is the greatest of miracles, just as it is a manifest work of divine inspiration that, spurning visible things, men should see what is in-

26. Ibid., 185.
27. Ibid., 187.

visible."[28] Among the saints and martyrs, reaching even to today, we surely find the witness of contemplatives.

V. A Cloud of Witnesses

St. Paul writes famously of a cloud of witnesses who have helped shape God's work.[29] Contemplatives were, and are, in their number. Paul, of course, wrote of his own mystical experiences.[30] In Luke we read, too, that Jesus counsels the active Martha that Mary, her more contemplative sister, "has chosen the better part, which will not be taken away from her."[31] With an eye for detail, Thomas notes that Mary is described as sitting at Jesus's feet, thus showing the continuity of contemplative life.[32] With an artist's license, Jan Vermeer, in his early *Christ in the House of Martha and Mary*, adds a telling detail to the Gospel story: Mary's garment is red, the color of sacrifice.[33]

Let me offer, in this light, a short contemplative martyrology; it is only a brief listing of those who have shed their blood in the giving of self. The initial entries remind us, pointedly, of the bloodlust of false sovereignty. Consider, first, the Carthusians of the London Charterhouse; among Henry VIII's earliest victims, they were beheaded and quartered in 1535. These contemplative monks gave courage to the imprisoned Thomas More as he awaited his own death. Of them More said to his daughter, "Dost thou not see, Meg, that these blessed fathers be now as cheerfully going to their deaths as bridegrooms to their marriage?"[34] Perhaps Josef Pieper recalled this report when he wrote of some martyrs "that not even torture could tear them from the happiness of contemplation."[35] Consider, next, the Carmelite nuns of Compiègne whose courage George Bernanos celebrated in dramatic form.[36] Their death by guillotine came just ten days before

28. St. Thomas Aquinas, *Summa Contra Gentiles*, translated by Anton C. Pegis (Garden City, New York: Image Books, 1955), I, chap. 6, no. 1. Michael Torre explores what he sees as the strongest argument for the God of Christianity in his "Aquinas and the Credibility of God," *Logos* 3, no. 2 (2000): 7–17.

29. St. Paul, Hebrews 12.1.

30. Galatians 1:12 and Corinthians 12.2.

31. Luke 10.42.

32. ST II-II, q. 82, a. 1.

33. See Jem Sullivan's discussion, "To Choose the Better Part," *Magnificat*, July 2010, i-vi.

34. Thomas More, *Conscience Decides: Letters and Prayers from Prison written by Sir Thomas More*, edited by Dame Bede Foord (London: Geoffrey Chapman, 1971), 82.

35. Josef Pieper, *Happiness and Contemplation*, translated by Richard and Clara Winston (New York: Pantheon Books, 1958), 103.

36. In part George Bernanos based his *Dialogues of the Carmelites* on Gertrude von Le Fort's short novel *The Song at the Scaffold*.

Robespierre's own execution by the decree of a revolution that by then had become demonic. These sixteen contemplatives walked to their execution while chanting the *Miserere* and the *Salve Regina,* the *Te Deum* and the *Veni Creator Spiritus.*

The demonic, to be sure, led the past century to its own staggering horrors. In 1941 Edith Stein, as Sister Teresa Benedicta of the Cross, became one of the martyrs of Auschwitz.[37] As a philosopher she had known a natural contemplation; as a Carmelite she lived in a graced contemplation. Three years later, the Carthusians of the Charterhouse of Farneta, Italy, opened their cloister to give sanctuary to more than 100 refugees who were hiding from German SS troops. The sanctuary was violated, and twelve of the monks joined the hunted Jews in being numbered among the Nazis' victims.[38]

We ought not to close this martyrology without recalling a final and more recent pair of contemplative sacrifices. In 1996 the Algerian Armed Islamic Group murdered seven Trappist monks. The monks had been abducted three years earlier, but they had returned to Our Lady of Atlas Monastery in Tibherine, Algeria, as witnesses to peace.[39] In Yemen, in 1998, three Missionary Sisters of Charity also suffered martyrdom. Their assailant shot and killed them, because, he said, they were "preaching Christianity."[40] At the time of their deaths, they were doing so by working at a psychiatric hospital. The Missionary Sisters of Charity see themselves as contemplatives in the world. On Maritain's view, so should all who are baptized, if perhaps in a less evident way. For in their fashion, like the virtues, the Gifts of the Holy Spirit—which Baptism brings—form a unity; and it is in contemplation that we *develop* the Spirit's Gift of Wisdom.[41]

And what do such contemplatives tell us of their sacrificial privilege? Is it, as the skeptic charges, a grotesque fanaticism? A first point comes immediately to mind. None of these contemplatives engaged in violence. Unlike many who might now call themselves martyrs, for example, the Al-Aqsa

37. Paul Hamans, *Edith Stein and Companions: On the Way to Auschwitz* (San Francisco: Ignatius Press, 2010), especially 60–87.

38. *The 'Silent' Summer of 1944*, Charterhouse of the Transfiguration, 2006 (Carthusian Booklets Series, N. 10), 1–4.

39. George Dardess, "Remembering the Martyrs," *Commonweal* (January 31, 1997): 22–23.

40. See www.dailycatholic.com/issue/July/ 147news1.htm and www.indianexpress.com/ie/daily/ 19980729/210504p.html.

41. Jacques Maritain, *Scholasticism and Politics*, 186–87.

Martyrs' Brigades, these contemplatives are not practitioners of religious and political violence; often, rather, they are its victims.[42] Nor do these contemplatives seek martyrdom. Dom Christian de Cherge, the prior of the slain Trappists in Algeria, held that such a desire would amount to desiring that a terrorist sin.[43]

Of special interest, in light of the skeptic's charge, is the testimony of the guillotined Carmelites of the French Revolution. The Public Prosecutor of the Revolutionary Tribunal dismissed their steadfastness as "fanatic." One of the nuns, Sr. Marie Henriette, challenged him to define the term. He explained that their "attachment to religion" made them enemies of freedom.[44] In fact, Mother Teresa of Saint Augustine, the Sister Superior, had been at pains not to court martyrdom. It was for the Holy Spirit to decide whether to accept such a sacrifice. William Bush, a perceptive commentator on the witness of the Carmelites of Compiègne, identifies what is at stake. "[O]ne sometimes forgets that martyrdom is essentially a *theophany*, a manifestation of *God* rather than of man."[45] Bush tells us, too, that the Greek Orthodox liturgies speak of martyrs as "the bearers of God" and the "first fruits" of a redeemed universe.[46] Is it rash, one wonders, to see the work of Providence in that the worst bloodlust of the French Revolution ended with the execution of Robespierre ten days after the sacrificial death of the Carmelites?

VI. Envoi

Benedict XVI writes that the intellect reaches the truth about charity, both natural and supernatural, when it "grasps its meaning as gift," and this is the context for understanding the principle of gratuitousness.[47] James Matthew Wilson ably situates the foundational dynamic thus in play.

> Existence is chiefly informed *not* by necessity or natural fixed laws demonstrable to the natural reason any more than it is *founded* on the laws of justice. Rather, everything comes to us—we come to *ourselves*—in the mystery of the gratuitous

42. Holly Fletcher, "Al-Aqsa Martyrs Brigade," www.washingtonpost.com/wpdyn/ content /article/2008/04/02.

43. George Dardess, "Remembering the Martyrs," pp. 22–23.

44. William Bush, *To Quell the Terror* (Washington, D.C.: ICS Publications, 1999), 63.

45. Ibid., 229.

46. Ibid.

47. Benedict XVI, *Caritas in veritate*, no. 9.

[which] resituates those foundations—or *the* foundation of Being—as pure gift upon which we can make no prior claim of necessity.[48]

This pure gift is God's doing. It is, as Maritain would say, the bestowal of the superabundance of Being.

The graced contemplative extends this superabundance; he or she does so most strikingly with the gift of self in martyrdom. But the whole of creation speaks of the glory of the Creator. Poets celebrate this glory, as Gerard Manley Hopkins showed us in his "inscaping" of the beauties of nature. G. K. Chesterton did so, as well, in celebrating the sheer existence of the everyday. His penchant for paradox served, above all, to startle us into his own contemplative intuition of being. Hugh Kenner, the literary critic, comments that paradox "is rooted in the world-stuff which a contemplative sees, and Chesterton was first of all a contemplative."[49]

Kenner argues that the supreme paradox, for Chesterton, is the Incarnation. He offers in evidence the start of a poem Chesterton wrote in his early twenties. Therein he signals a modernity of just the sort that Henry Adams's education always lagged behind.[50] Even a blusterous modernity, as still it was, is caught up in the paradox of sacrificial gift.

> I live in an age of varied powers and knowledge,
> Of steam, science, democracy, journalism, art;
> But when my loves rises like a sea,
> I have to go back to an obscure tribe and a slain man
> To formulate a blessing.[51]

It is a blessing of what is old and of what is new and of all that is gift. It invites the martyrs to sing the music of silence. It lets justice rain down.[52, 53]

48. James Matthew Wilson, "Gratuitous Foundations: Benedict XVI's Humanism of the Gift, Part II," www.frontporchrepublic.com/2010/04; emphasis in original.

49. Hugh Kenner, *Paradox in Chesterton* (London: Sheed and Ward, 1948), 7.

50. Henry Adams, *The Education of Henry Adams* edited by Ira Nidel (New York: Oxford Paperback, 1998).

51. Cited in Maisie Ward, *Gilbert Keith Chesterton* (New York: Sheed and Ward, 1943), 66; Kenner calls attention to this early reflection; see his *Paradox in Chesterton*, 8.

52. See Amos 5.24.

53. Thanks to James Kintz and especially Errol Hughes and for their help in preparing this essay, a shorter of version of which was published as "Action, Contemplation, Martyrdom: The Cloud of Witnesses Speaks," in *New Oxford Review* 78, no. 2 (2011): 24–28.

ANNE FRANCES AI LE, O.P.

Contemplata aliis tradere

The Universal Call to Contemplation and Its Implications

Contemplata aliis tradere: "To hand on to others contemplated things" or, as more commonly expressed, "To give to others the fruits of one's contemplation." Though St. Thomas penned these words in the context of the excellence of religious orders, such as (or rather, especially) the Dominicans, whose preaching and teaching flow from the abundance of their union with God,[1] the expression also aptly illustrates Maritain's understanding of the relationship between contemplation and action presented in chapter seven of *Scholasticism and Politics*.[2] In his discussion of their relationship, Maritain does not engage in the debate per se concerning whether action or contemplation is greater; he instead operates under the explicit Aristotelian-Thomistic teaching of the intrinsic superiority of contemplation over action. To this end, Maritain calls for a rediscovery of the role and importance of contemplation for the West, which, contrary to any simplistic characterization of being solely devoted to action, once also had a rich tradition of contemplation. In his call to contemplation, Maritain emphasizes the significant influence of Christianity over the notion of contemplation that in effect paradoxically renders contemplation accessible to

1. St. Thomas Aquinas, *Summa Theologica* (ST), translated by the English Dominican Fathers (Westminster, Maryland: Christian Classics, 1981), II-II, q. 188, a. 6. All English quotations of the *Summa* are from this translation.

2. Jacques Maritain, "Action and Contemplation," in *Scholasticism and Politics*, translated and edited by Mortimer J. Adler (Garden City, New York: Doubleday Image, 1960), 163–83.

all rather than to Christians alone and at the same time rescues it from the elitist view of the ancient Greeks. Maritain's emphasis on contemplation in his lecture, however, in no way diminishes his understanding of the importance of action.

Maritain divides his lecture into five sections: (1) Greek Philosophy, (2) Christianity, (3) Superabounding Contemplation, (4) The Call to Contemplation, and (5) Orient and Occident. The purpose of the following reflection is not to analyze the entire lecture according to these points in the order presented; rather it is limited to demonstrating the consequences resulting from what Maritain sees as the fourfold innovation of Christianity. These consequences are (1) the universalism or universality of the call to contemplation, and (2) the complementarity of action and contemplation along with the implications of their mutual influence for the benefit of society.[3]

I. What Is Contemplation?

What exactly, then, is contemplation and what does it involve? A look at several definitions will suffice for our present purposes. In both the *Nicomachean Ethics* and the *Eudemian Ethics*, Aristotle gives three related meanings of contemplation: (1) a beholding, (2) an observation, examination, or study, and finally (3) the exercise or use of knowledge already possessed.[4] For Thomas Aquinas, contemplation is "simplex intuitus vertitatis," "the simple act of gazing on the truth."[5] Dietrich von Hildebrand defines contemplation as "a reposeful attention to an object fully present."[6] A more recent work similarly defines contemplation as "a long loving look at the real."[7] That Maritain

3. An analysis of Maritain's lecture in its entirety has already been provided by James Schall in his essay, "On the Prospect of a Paradise on Earth," in *Truth Matters: Essays in Honor of Jacques Maritain*, edited by John Trapani Jr. (Washington, D.C.: American Maritain Association, 2004), 11–25. Here I am only interested in exploring Maritain's theme of the universal call to contemplation while using other points and themes in the lecture to illuminate and direct my efforts.

4. It is not my purpose here to analyze these meanings as such. For a further discussion, see John Dudley's "La Contemplation humaine selon Aristote," *Revue Philosophique de Louvain* 80 (August 1982): 387–413, in which the first meaning is designated as the original, the second the most accepted, the third the restricted.

5. See ST II-II, q. 180, a. 3, ad 1 where St. Thomas distinguishes between contemplation, meditation, and cogitation in response to the objection that there are various acts pertaining to the contemplative life.

6. Dietrich von Hildebrand, *Transformation in Christ: On the Christian Attitude of Mind* (New York: Longmans, Green, and Company, 1948), 97.

7. Walter Burghardt, "Contemplation: A Long Loving Look at the Real," *Church* (Winter,

is of one mind with these authors can easily be established; his optimism regarding what he saw to be "great reserves and possibilities for contemplation" in America, even amidst its avowed activism, is illuminating. He states,

> The activism which is manifested here assumes in many cases the aspect of a remedy against despair. I think that this activism itself masks a certain hidden aspiration to contemplation. To my mind, if in American civilization certain elements are causing complaints or criticisms, those elements proceed definitely from a repression of the desire, natural in mankind, for *the active repose of the soul breathing what is eternal.*[8]

All the given definitions of contemplation contain certain common elements: a beholding, regard or attention, a repose, and an "other" that is the object of contemplation. Described as such, contemplation encompasses both philosophical and mystical contemplation. Maritain, however, clearly distinguishes between the two. In his lecture, Maritain criticizes the erring conclusion drawn from philosophic contemplation that limits its accessibility to only a small number of the human race, creating what can be called an "elitist" view of contemplation. Maritain acknowledges the merit of Greek philosophy in discovering the great truth of the superiority of contemplation over action. This superiority is due to contemplation being an immanent act that is self-perfective and as such does not require any external recipient for the perfection of its act. Maritain, however, laments that this great truth is practically transformed into a great error because it leads to an undesirable hierarchy, favoring the few intellectuals over the entire human race. Contemplation then becomes the business only of specialists—the philosophers—who live a super-human life while those incapable of contemplation live an ordinary life or a sub-human life.[9] To avoid this detrimental hierarchy, Maritain insists on the changes that Christianity introduced that resulted in what can be termed a "universalist" view in which Maritain argues that Christian contemplation or mystical contemplation is accessible and available to all souls, resulting in the universalization of contemplation, and thus, the universal call to contemplation.

1989). Douglas Steere's "Contemplation and Leisure," *Humanitas: Journal of the Institute of Formative Spirituality* 8 (November 1972): 287–306, also presents similar views.

8. Maritain, *Scholasticism and Politics*, 182; emphasis added. It is worth noting that Schall misquotes Maritain, substituting "response" for "repose," which fails to capture the essential characteristic of contemplation.

9. Ibid., 165.

II. The Universal Call to Contemplation

The universalization of contemplation culminates the fourfold innovation through which Maritain maintains Christianity to have "transfigured" the Greek understanding of contemplation. Preceding it are innovations that (1) involve reversing the order of will and intellect such that love is better than intelligence; (2) endowing contemplation with a new meaning, i.e., as an entrance into the very states of the Word Incarnate; and (3) giving a new meaning to action that goes beyond the mere transitive activity of the world of bodies, thereby redeeming the notion of work. All of these find their completion in the expansion of the call to contemplation to all souls.[10]

How, then, does Maritain understand and explain the call to contemplation to be universal? To begin with, he does not expressly use the phrase "universal call," but his emphatic words merit such a designation. In discussing the culminating innovation of Christianity, indeed an "astounding revolution in the spiritual order," Maritain affirms this universality, stating

> Greeks and Jews, masters and slaves, men and women, poor and rich (but the poor, first), souls who have known evil and souls (if there be such) who have not, whatever their condition, race and wounds,—all are called to the feast of divine Love and divine wisdom. That wisdom calls them all, it clamours in the public places and in the roadways.... [I]n a manner either close or distant, all are called to the contemplation of the saints, not the contemplation of the philosophers. All without exception. The universality of such an appeal is one of the essential features of Christianity's *catholicity*.[11]

It is also interesting to note that, from the start, Maritain specifically maintains the universality of the call to the contemplation of the saints, rather than of the philosophers. Maritain explains, citing St. Albert the Great, that the contemplation of the philosophers is "concerned with the perfection of the contemplator, and hence does not go farther than the intellect, so that their end is intellectual knowledge. But the contemplation of the saints is concerned with the love of the one contemplated—of God.... It attains to the heart through love."[12] Maritain, moreover, observes that theologians teach that the contemplation of the saints, or *contemplatio sanctorum*, is supernatural, that is, "it is achieved by the gifts which Sanctifying Grace ...

10. Ibid., 165–168.
11. Ibid., 168; emphasis in original.
12. Ibid., 166.

brings to the soul, ... and goes beyond anything that the energies of human nature, left to themselves, can achieve."[13] The contemplation which Maritain understands to be universal and designates as "an entrance into the very states of God, of God Incarnate,"[14] is therefore strictly theological in nature.

In arguing for the universality of the call to contemplation, Maritain recalls the various debates concerning contemplative graces: whether they are "exceptional not only *de facto* but also *de jure*, whether it is temerarious to desire or hope for them, or whether they are the normal flower within us of the living grace of virtues and gifts."[15] In order to resolve these difficulties, Maritain begins by establishing a clear understanding of the mystical life as "a coming of the soul under the regimen in which the gifts ... of the Holy Spirit predominate."[16] With the mystical life thus defined and understood, Maritain affirms that every soul is called at least remotely to this life, basing his conclusion on the call to the perfection of love addressed to all, a perfection that can only be attained with "radical purifications and substantial remouldings which are the mystical life's sacrificial privilege."[17]

Maritain designates various names for the different levels or degrees of contemplation attainable by individuals. Concerning the call to contemplation itself, Maritain, following Garrigou-Lagrange, refers to either a proximate or remote call. Simply stated, according to Garrigou-Lagrange, the proximate and individual call is addressed to those well-advanced in the spiritual life, while the general and remote call is for all souls who are in the state of grace.[18] Also noteworthy is the fact that all souls are indeed *called* to some degree of contemplation, meaning they are invited and given the necessary wherewithal, but they neither necessarily nor continuously fulfill or answer this calling. With regard to the degrees of contemplation, Maritain distinguishes them as typical or atypical and apparent or masked. Using such distinctions, Maritain's understanding of the universal call to

13. Ibid., 170.

14. Ibid., 167.

15. Ibid., 175.

16. Ibid., 176.

17. Ibid.

18. For a detailed explanation and more, see Reginald Garrigou-Lagrange, *Christian Perfection and Contemplation according to St. Thomas Aquinas and St. John of the Cross*, translated by M. Timothea Doyle (New York: B. Herder Book Company, 1937), 338–77. Garrigou-Lagrange names three signs of a proximate call mentioned by Johannes Tauler and St. John of the Cross: (1) meditation becomes impracticable; (2) the soul has no desire to fix its imagination on any particular interior or exterior object; and (3) the soul takes delight in being alone with God and fixing its loving attention upon Him; see 338–339 and 372–377.

contemplation can be stated as follows: all souls are at least remotely called to contemplation whether typical and apparent or atypical and masked. Maritain explains this diversification of contemplation as corresponding to the gifts of the Holy Spirit given to souls that enable each to behave according to its calling, noting that the gifts of Counsel, Fortitude, and Fear mainly concern action, while those of Intelligence and Wisdom are primarily related to contemplation. As a result,

> Some will be favoured in a pre-eminent manner with the highest gift, those of Wisdom and Intelligence; these souls will represent mystical life in its normal plenitude, and will have the grace of contemplation in its typical forms, be they arid or comforting.[19]

Mary of Bethany, Thomas Aquinas, John of the Cross, and Thérèse of Lisieux readily come to mind as representatives par excellence of such favored souls who experience the proximate call to contemplation and who faithfully respond to it. Maritain continues,

> In the case of other souls it will be primarily the other gifts of inspired freedom; their life will be indeed a mystical and dispropriated life but it will be such pre-eminently in relation to their *activities and works,* and they will not have the typical and normal forms of contemplation.[20]

Representatives of such souls, perhaps, do not come to mind as easily though their number is assuredly far greater than the former, as Maritain affirms that the forms of contemplation to which souls faithful to grace will actually attain most often will not be the typical one, but rather the atypical and masked forms.[21] These are souls that are called and experience only a remote call to contemplation. Elsewhere, Maritain states more emphatically that contemplation is "frequently the treasure of persons hidden in the world, known only to some few.... Sometimes, in a certain manner this treasure is hidden from the souls themselves who possess it—souls who live by it in all simplicity, without visions, without miracles, but with such a flame of love for God and neighbor that good happens all around them without noise and without agitation."[22]

19. Maritain, *Scholasticism and Politics,* 177. 20. Ibid.; emphasis added.

21. Ibid. It is noteworthy that in so saying Maritain suggests that there is a "price" to pay for the typical form of contemplation that most souls are not prepared or not willing to pay, "where the supernatural sweeps away everything, at the risk of breaking everything."

22. Jacques and Raïssa Maritain, *Liturgy and Contemplation,* translated by Joseph W. Evans (New York: P. J. Kenedy and Sons, 1960), 74.

Maritain bases the possibility of diversification of souls according to their differing calling, whether proximate or remote, on the basis of St. Thomas' teaching of the unity of the gifts such that they cannot be present in the soul without wisdom. In the latter case, that is, of "active" souls, wisdom is "exercised in a less apparent way, and in an atypical, attenuated, or discontinuous mode," resulting in forms of "*masked* and inapparent" contemplation that, as Maritain observes, render these souls "capable of only saying rosaries, and mental prayer will bring them only headache or sleep"; their way of praying will not consist in mysterious contemplation but instead in works and activities such as "the grace of their behavior, their sweet-minded hands, perhaps, or their way of walking perhaps, or their way of looking at the poor man or at suffering."[23] Maritain thus concludes, citing the growing agreement among theologians, that "all souls are called, if not in a proximate manner, at least in a remote one, to mystical contemplation as being the normal blossoming of grace's virtues and gifts."[24] Normal and universal though it may be, contemplation cannot be achieved on one's own, but only in and through God's grace in the gifts of the Holy Spirit.

III. Some Observations

Maritain's exposition of the universality of the call to contemplation anticipates both the teachings of the Second Vatican Council on the universal call to holiness and his own idea of "an adequately considered moral philosophy" presented in later works. First of all, Maritain's insistence on every soul's call to contemplation corresponds to and serves to elucidate the Second Vatican Council's teaching on the universal call to holiness,[25] wherein everyone is called to be holy in and according to his or her state of life. Both Maritain and the Council Fathers based their teachings on the universality of Christ's command to perfection ("Be ye perfect as thy heavenly Father is perfect") and the role of the gifts of the Holy Spirit as the cause of such perfection which is then displayed in the various forms of holiness or contemplation. The Second Vatican Council's *Dogmatic Constitution on the Church*, better known as *Lumen Gentium*, devotes a whole

23. Maritain, *Scholasticism and Politics*, 177.

24. Ibid., 178.

25. Second Vatican Council, *Dogmatic Constitution on the Church: Lumen Gentium*, edited by Austin Flannery (Northport, New York: Costello Publishing Company, 1975), chap. 5.

chapter, albeit the shortest but by no means the least significant, to the universal call to holiness. The document states:

> All in the Church, whether they belong to the hierarchy or are cared for by it, are called to holiness (#39). The Lord Jesus, divine teacher and model of all perfection, preached holiness of life (of which he is author and maker) to each and every one of his disciples without distinction: "You, therefore, must be perfect, as your heavenly Father is perfect" (Mt 5.48). For he sent the Holy Spirit to all to move them interiorly to love God with their whole heart, with their whole soul, with their whole understanding, and with their whole strength (cf. Mt 12.30), and to love one another as Christ loved them (cf. Jn 13:34; 15, 12).... It is quite clear that all Christians in any state or walk of life are called to the fullness of Christian life and to the perfection of love, and by this holiness a more human manner of life is fostered also in earthly society (#40).

Moreover, both Maritain's and the Council's classification of different forms and degrees of contemplation and holiness call to mind the beauty and order of God's providence and governance in the created world such that different creatures in their limited goodness and beauty reflect in diverse ways the infinite beauty and goodness of God.[26]

Furthermore, Maritain's understanding of the universal call to contemplation is indicative of his idea of "moral philosophy adequately considered," which he later presented in *An Essay on Christian Philosophy* and again in *Neuf leçons sur les notions premières de la philosophie morale*.[27] For Maritain, moral philosophy is adequately considered when it "takes into account existential data provided by sources of information of another order."[28] In the fifth *leçon*, entitled "Moral Experience and the Ultimate End," Maritain explains that this other order is theology which "will instruct [one] about this positive datum, that, in fact, nature is subject in us to the interior action of a gift of God—grace—which incites and elevates it, and which, if not infused, makes men and women participate in divine life."[29] In the case of contemplation, it is the "innovations" of Christianity that extends the notion to all souls, affirming that all souls can participate in some

26. Cf. ST I, q. 47, a. 1. St. Thomas argues that the multitude and distinction in things come from God who wishes to communicate his goodness to creatures and be represented by them. But because no one creature can adequately represent God's goodness, God created many and diverse creatures that together they may represent His goodness more perfectly.

27. Published in English under the title *An Introduction to the Basic Problems of Moral Philosophy*, translated by Cornelia N. Borgerhoff (Albany, New York: Magi Books, 1990).

28. Ibid., 98.

29. Ibid., 113.

measure in divine life through the act of contemplation enabled through the grace of the Incarnation and the gifts of the Holy Spirit.

IV. Mutual Influence and Complementarity of Action and Contemplation

The complementarity and mutual influence of action and contemplation is intimated in the Dominican motto, *contemplata aliis tradere*, mentioned at the beginning of this essay. These words of St. Thomas encompass elements both of action and contemplation with *tradere*, "to hand on," suggesting action while *contemplata*, "contemplated things," suggests contemplation.[30] In order to hand on something of intellectual value, one must have already possessed it, and delighted in it, and to such an extent so as to desire to share the delight of the possessed object with others. What is the delighting in an intellectual object if not the act of contemplation? Therefore, contemplation precedes action, indeed overflows into action because of the joy and delight that one finds in the contemplated things. This does not suggest that contemplation is ordered to action, that one contemplates in order to act, but that action is a natural overflow or a super-abounding of contemplation, as Maritain puts it.

After discussing the innovation introduced by Christianity that all souls are called to contemplation, Maritain soberly adds that at the same time and symmetrically, all are bound by the law of work: "Work is for everyone, as well as the sin of which everyone must be cured."[31] Maritain stresses, however, the analogical character of work against misinterpretations of modern societies which regard work to be only of one kind, one of economic value. Work as an analogical notion is substantiated in various "fraternal activities" directed to the good of others, activities which Christianity would call the spiritual and corporal works of mercy and from which no one can be dispensed, "be it to clothe or feed their bodies, to teach them or guide them, to feed them with the words of God, or, like those dedicated

30. I am not sure, then, whether *contemplata aliis tradere* requires any further "spelling out" to clarify its meaning, as Schall suggests the Jesuit motto *in actione, contemplativus* does. I would agree that *in actione, contemplativus* expresses what *contemplata aliis tradere* does and corresponds to it, but not that it "spells out something implicit in *contemplata aliis tradere*," which is sufficient in itself to contain elements of both action and contemplation. See Schall, "On the Prospect of a Paradise on Earth," 13.

31. Maritain, *Scholasticism and Politics*, 168.

to contemplative life, to wear oneself out in praying for them."[32] Although Maritain includes contemplation in the analogical notion of work, he is quick to clarify that contemplation is in fact not work, not a thing of utility, but rather a fruit, "a leisure coinciding with the highest *activity* of the human substance."[33] Thus, Maritain concludes that the analogical notion of work includes in varying degrees "all activities from manual labor to the gratuitously added utility of contemplative leisure" at the "extreme limit of refinement."[34] That the universal call to contemplation is counter-balanced by the universal subjection to the law of work should not be surprising, considering the varied forms of contemplation which Maritain expounds as "the multiform exercise of the gift of Wisdom, free and unseizable, and transcending all our categories, and capable of all disguises, all surprises."[35] Since most souls do not attain to the typical form of contemplation, they do, however, experience atypical forms in their activities and works.

Paradoxically, therefore, the complementarity of action and contemplation hinges on the nature of contemplation as an immanent act that is superabounding and superexisting. Indeed, Maritain states, "[I]n virtue of that generosity which is inherent in immanent activity at its highest degrees, loving contemplation overflows as a protection and a benediction to society."[36] Using fundamental distinctions between transitive and immanent actions,[37] Maritain explains that the superabundance of contemplation as an immanent act points to its self-sufficiency, so to speak, which does not require another upon whom to act, as do transitive acts, in order to obtain perfection. Schall similarly explains, "It is precisely because of this superabounding contemplation that our relation to others is not merely transitive, why it is not simply in need of objects to prove its own worth."[38] As a result, Christian contemplation overflows into action, not out of necessity but of its generosity, i.e., its superabundance, communicating its own good to others; "striving to be achieved in love, it strives to achieve the good of other men, disinterestedly, gratuitously, as a gift."[39]

32. Ibid., 168.

33. Ibid., 169.

34. Ibid.

35. Ibid., 178.

36. Ibid., 169.

37. Maritain, *Scholasticism and Politics*, 163–64. Maritain's use of contrasting sets of vivid, memorable adjectives and phrases to distinguish the two actions is worth repeating. Transitive activity is said to be "of the world of bodies," to "pass away in Time and with Time," to be "dependent on the patient to obtain perfection," "mendicant", and "egoistic." On the other hand, immanent activity is "above time," "of life and spirit," "self-perfecting," and "generous."

38. Schall, "On the Prospect of a Paradise on Earth," 16.

39. Maritain, *Scholasticism and Politics*, 174.

Maritain, therefore, proudly proclaims the superiority of Christian philosophy over Greek philosophy in seeing that "it is natural that immanent activity should superabound, since it is superexisting."[40] Christian philosophy, for Maritain, is not only a philosophy of being, but of the "superabundance of being" from which proceed actions directed to the good of others. Maritain, moreover, maintains that this superabounding of contemplation into action mirrors the creative act of God who is Love and Creator, i.e., God's ceaseless gift of Himself to the created world. Maritain states,

> God, whose essence is His own beatitude and His own eternal contemplation, God who creates, gives, has never ceased to give, He gives Himself through Incarnation, He gives Himself through the Holy Ghost's mission.... [In fact] when contemplation superabounds in efficacious love and in action, it corresponds within us to that divine superabundance communicative of its own good.[41]

For Maritain, then, since Christian contemplation is not confined to the intellect (contrary to the Greek notion of contemplation) but attains to the heart, "being the fruit of love in act through which faith becomes as it were a thing of experience, [it] also enters the sphere of action, in virtue of the generosity and abundance of love, which consists in giving oneself. Action then springs from the superabundance of contemplation, *ex superabundantia contemplationis*."[42] Maritain explains that action can proceed from the superabundance of contemplation in two ways. The first way is by the *nature* of the work produced to which Maritain parenthetically adds, calling to mind St. Thomas' teaching encapsulated in the Dominican motto, "thus preaching things divine must overflow from a heart united to God or be vain." Secondly, action proceeds from the superabundance of contemplation by reason of the *mode* of the production, which Maritain explains, "makes a work, whatever it is, an instrument employed by sovereign Love to touch and vivify the heart."[43] Maritain indicates the distinction between these two ways by the employment of italics: *nature* and *mode*, which require a little elaboration. "Nature" suggests the kind, or more precisely, the essence, of the action or work that is produced from the superabundance of contemplation, such as "the preaching of divine things." "Mode," however, suggests the manner in which action or work is produced or employed, such as to be used as an instrument for God "to touch and vivify the heart."

Such is Maritain's explanation of action proceeding from contempla-

40. Ibid., 174.
41. Ibid., 174–75.
42. Ibid., 173.
43. Ibid.

tion. What of the converse, namely, contemplation proceeding from action, or action leading to contemplation? Maritain, likewise, discusses the manner in which action, as preparatory measures, can lead to contemplation: "[T]here are in the spirit many activities, discursive activity and activity of desire, which are neither repose nor contemplation.... [T]his labour of the intelligence and of the heart tends toward contemplation and prepares for it, and in this measure participates in the end to which it is directed."[44] Maritain, thus, employs the notion of leisure[45] to speak of the "natural aspiration to contemplation" that supernatural contemplation "achieves and fulfils," without asserting, rather absurdly, the contemplation of the saints as the proper and direct end of the political life.

Maritain maintains that the law of work to which all humans are bound requires as the term of work, rest, not just any rest and relaxation that merely prepares one for renewed labor,—as sleep prepares for the toils of the day, Maritain notes—but an "active and self-sufficient rest, a terminal activity of an immanent and spiritual order, already participating in some measure in contemplation's supertemporality and generosity."[46] Lest one should ask what such rest is like, Maritain continues, "Let us say it is the active rest of the culture of the mind and the heart, the joy of knowing, the spiritual delectations which art and beauty offer us, the generous enthusiasm supplied by disinterested love, compassion and communion, zeal for justice, devotion to the commonwealth and to mankind."[47] Clearly, therefore, this "active rest" or leisure of which Maritain speaks is no ordinary leisure. Maritain includes within this "active rest," the contemplation of the philosophers from which flows delight or joy in knowing for the sake of knowing, i.e. intellectual delight. As for spiritual delectations from art or beauty, one can think of the delight which an individual might take in viewing Michelangelo's *Pietà* or Fra Angelico's *The Annunciation*. In sum, none of the above acts of leisure constitute contemplation properly speaking, i.e. supernatural contemplation, but Maritain confidently affirms that "if in this kind of leisure, instead of shutting up human concerns in themselves, man remains open to what is higher than himself, and is borne by the natural movement which draws the human soul to the infinite, all this

44. Ibid., 171.

45. Cf. Josef Pieper, *Leisure, The Basis of Culture*, translated by Alexander Dru (New York: Random House, 1963).

46. Ibid., 172.

47. Ibid.

would be contemplation in an inchoate state or in preparation."[48] As a result, whatever work one engages in, whether manual work, study, or natural contemplation, can only dispose one to receive supernatural contemplation, but never directly cause it.

Moreover, it can be said that the interplay between action and contemplation generates a social dynamism that can be continuous. Consider again Michelangelo's *Pietà*. Undoubtedly someone who views it for the first or twentieth time engages in a natural act of contemplation that Maritain calls an "active rest." In this rest one takes some delight, which can lead one to ponder the mystery of Christ's passion and death and so draw one into supernatural contemplation leading to some pious action that is in turn admired and pondered by another. So the cycle of action and contemplation is repeated. But what if we take a step back and look at Michelangelo? Surely, some measure of natural contemplation preceded the carving of his great artwork? It is said that when he was asked how he was able to create such beautiful sculptures, he replied that he simply chiseled away the extraneous material from the block of marble to unveil a *David*, a *Moses*, and so with all his other sculptures. In other words, his response illustrates the act of contemplation leading to action, i.e., Michelangelo envisioned his object in an act of contemplation to some degree and proceeded to the act of carving it and producing a masterpiece that continues to inspire to this day. The interaction between contemplation and action is, thus, not only intrapersonal but also interpersonal.

V. Conclusion

What does Maritain's understanding of the universality of the call to contemplation and the complementarity of action and contemplation accomplish? In other words, in what manner do the innovations of Christianity impact the Greek notion of contemplation? First of all, let Maritain speak for himself:

> The doctrine I have stated summarily means that Christian contemplation springs forth from that Spirit which bloweth where it listeth, and one hears His voice and no one knows whence He comes or whither He goes. It means that Christian contemplation is not the affair of specialists or technicians. The active ways through which the soul disposes itself to it are not techniques, but only fallible preparations to receive a free gift, fallible preparations which this gift always transcends.[49]

48. Ibid.

49. Ibid., 178.

Maritain recognizes that in Greek philosophy the "high truth of the superiority of contemplative life was bound up with the contempt for work and the plague of slavery,"[50] creating a degrading categorization of lives in which "mankind lives for the sake of a few intellectuals," which Maritain describes as follows:

> There is a category of specialists,—the philosophers,—who lead a superhuman life; then in a lower category, destined to serve them, come those who lead the ordinary human life, the civil or political one; they in turn are served by those who lead a sub-human life, the life of work,—that is, the slaves.[51]

Through the innovations introduced by Christianity, with its teachings on the gifts of the Holy Spirit, the notion of contemplation is expanded to include all souls and thus establishes a better society that acknowledges the worthiness of seemingly ordinary lives in which people are capable and most likely do experience supernatural contemplation to some degree, that is, in its atypical and inapparent forms. By universalizing contemplation, Christianity eliminates the hierarchy set up by the erroneous conclusion drawn from the Greek notion of contemplation. Maritain, therefore, succeeds through the teachings of Christianity in upholding the "great truth" discovered by the Greeks concerning the primacy of contemplation, as an immanent act, over action and also in avoiding the erroneous conclusion often drawn from that truth. In other words, Maritain succeeds in establishing a "universalist" over an "elitist" view of contemplation.

Maritain furthermore succeeds in uniting action and contemplation and thereby avoiding the extremes of both East and West with regard to the problem of action and contemplation. If the characterization of the East as contemplative and the West as active were absolutely true, each would be self-destructive when either action or contemplation is carried to the extreme and thus to the exclusion of the other. Thus Maritain's message to the West as a whole was as follows:

> We hold that the West will not surmount these crises [purely activistic, industrial, and warlike] in which it is engaged, unless it reconquers that vital truth [of the Incarnation], and understands that external activity must overflow from a superabundance of internal activity, by which man is united to truth and to the source of being.[52]

50. Ibid., 165.

51. Ibid.

52. Ibid., 181.

And, more positively, Maritain addressed the United States in particular:

> When in America some few come to realize better the value of contemplative activity, its superiority and fecundity, ... then this country will give some of its generosity, good will, confidence in the future and courage, to things contemplative, to contemplation overflowing in action.[53]

What, then, becomes of philosophic contemplation? How does Maritain view the contemplation of the philosophers in relation to the universalism of the contemplation of the saints, or supernatural, Christian contemplation? The contemplation of the philosophers still holds a unique place and plays a unique role. Schall points out that for Maritain the role of professional philosophers is to keep alive the reality of the transcendent realm, to contemplate being, *what is*, in order to maintain the order of reality.[54] Knowing the order of reality, however, does not necessarily make one a member of a privileged class, although the act of contemplating can still be maintained as the highest act consubstantial to the human person. The distinction between the act and the agent, therefore, must be maintained. The contemplation of the philosophers, moreover, can dispose one to supernatural contemplation that overflows into action. On the model of supernatural contemplation, one cannot help but hand on the knowledge of what one contemplates. Without this model, one might be trapped in one's own happiness and not care to hand on or share with others the fruits of one's contemplation, which is the great error to which Maritain sees the Greek understanding of contemplation as susceptible.

53. Ibid., 183.
54. Schall, "On the Prospect of a Paradise on Earth," 24.

About The Authors

PETER PAGAN AGUIAR is Associate Professor of Philosophy at Aquinas College, Nashville, Tennessee. He earned his doctorate at Fordham University and has taught previously at Wheeling Jesuit University (West Virginia) and Fordham University (New York). His interests include philosophical theology, natural law theory, Catholic social teaching, the thought of St. Thomas Aquinas, and the interface between science and theology. He has published articles and reviews in *The Thomist, National Catholic Bioethics Quarterly, ITEST Bulletin, National Catholic Register,* and previous volumes published by the American Maritain Association.

STEPHEN CHAMBERLAIN is Assistant Professor of Philosophy at Rockhurst University in Kansas City, Missouri. His areas of specialty are epistemology and metaphysics, particularly as these areas relate to the thought of Aquinas and movements in contemporary Thomism. More recently his research has been directed toward aesthetics in terms of the cognitive and ethical values of art. He has published articles and reviews in these areas, which have appeared in *International Philosophical Quarterly, Semiotics, New Catholic Encyclopedia,* and *Thomas Aquinas and Thomism Today* (Budapest).

JOHN J. CONLEY, S.J. holds the Henry J. Knott Chair of Philosophy and Theology at Loyola University Maryland. He specializes in ethics, aesthetics, and early modern philosophy. Major books include *Adoration and Annihilation: The Convent Philosophy of Port-Royal* (University of Notre Dame Press, 2009), *Madame de Maintenon: Dialogues and Addresses* (University of Chicago Press, 2004), *Jacqueline Pascal: A Rule for Children* (University of Chicago Press, 2003), and *The Suspicion of Virtue: Women Philosophers in Neoclassical France* (Cornell University Press, 2002).

HEATHER M. ERB is Assistant Professor of Philosophy at Lock Haven University in Pennsylvania. Her essays on the nexus between metaphysics and mysticism in the thought of Aquinas, on Boethius, and on issues in philosophy of religion and Christianity and culture have appeared in *Logos: A Journal of Catholic Thought and Culture, Verbum* (Hungary), the *New Oxford Review,* and in the Catholic University of America Press, Pontifical Academy of Saint Thomas Aquinas, and in publications of the American Maritain Association.

RAYMOND HAIN is Assistant Professor of Philosophy at Providence College in Providence, Rhode Island. His primary areas of research include ethics with an emphasis on theories of practical rationality and applied ethics, especially biomedical ethics and the ethics of architecture.

TERRY HALL is Director of the Honors Program and Associate Professor of Philosophy at the University of St. Thomas (Houston), where he has also served as Associate Dean of Arts and Sciences. During the administration of President Ronald Reagan, Dr. Hall was a member of the US Civil Rights Commission.

JAMES G. HANINK is Professor of Philosophy at Loyola Marymount University in Los Angeles, California. His interests center on metaphysics, epistemology, ethics, and political philosophy. He has contributed regularly to publications of the American Maritain Association, most recently "In Defense of the Intuition of Being," in *Distinctions of Being: Philosophical Approaches to Reality*. Other recent publications include "The Metaphysics of Moral Evil: Context, Truth and Character," *Études Maritainiennes / Maritain Studies* 26, and "Pro-Life Communitarianism and a Metaphysics of Relation," *Life and Learning* 19, the Proceedings of the University Faculty for Life, of which he is an active member. He and his wife, Elizabeth, long active in pro-life work, have five children and four grandchildren.

PETER KARL KORITANSKY is Associate Professor of History, Philosophy, and Religious Studies at The University of Prince Edward Island in Charlottetown, Canada. He is the author of *Thomas Aquinas and the Philosophy of Punishment* (CUA Press, 2012) and editor of *The Philosophy of Punishment and the History of Political Thought* (The University of Missouri Press, 2011).

MICHAEL P. KROM is Associate Professor and Chair of Philosophy at Saint Vincent College (Latrobe, Pennsylvania). He is the author of *The Limits of Reason in Hobbes's Commonwealth* (Continuum, 2011) and has published articles in such journals as *Journal of Religious Ethics, Hobbes Studies,* and *The Catholic Social Science Review.*

ANNE FRANCES AI LE, O.P. is a Ph.D. candidate in the Center for Thomistic Studies at the University of St. Thomas in Houston, Texas. Her dissertation is entitled, "*Nudus Sequens?*: Saint Thomas Aquinas on Evangelical Poverty and Christian Perfection."

ERIC MANCHESTER is Professor of Philosophy at Caldwell College in New Jersey, where he has taught for nine years, having taught full time previously at Viterbo University in Wisconsin. He has a Ph.D. in philosophy from Marquette University. Publications include essays in prior collections with the American Maritain Association, an article on pro-life philosophy in a Philosophy and Ethics supplement of the *New Catholic Encyclopedia, Proceedings for University Faculty for Life,* and *Conversations in Theology and Religion (*Blackwell). In addition, he has published in the *Wesleyan Theological Journal,* and contributed essays on philosophy of religion and political theology in volumes published by *Cambridge Scholars Publishing* in cooperation with the Wesleyan Philosophical Society. He and his wife Paula are members of Corpus Christi Catholic parish in Lansdale, Pennsylvania.

BERNADETTE E. O'CONNOR is Professor of Philosophy at the University of the Incarnate Word in San Antonio, Texas. She has several essays in the American Maritain Association book series.

JONATHAN J. SANFORD is Professor of Philosophy and the Associate Vice President of Academic Affairs at Franciscan University of Steubenville. He is the editor, with Michael Gorman, of *Categories: Historical and Systematic Essays* (CUA Press, 2004), and a book in Wiley-Blackwell's Philosophy and Popular Culture series, *Spider-Man and Philosophy: The Web of Inquiry* (2012). Many of his articles and book chapters address metaphysical and ethical questions from an Aristotelian-Thomistic perspective, and his latest book is forthcoming from CUA Press and is on virtue ethics.

DENIS A. SCRANDIS is Adjunct Assistant Professor of Philosophy at Saint John's University in New York City where he teaches health care ethics to pharmacy students as well as metaphysics and other core philosophy courses to university undergraduates. His recent published research includes "A Demonstration of the Personhood of the Human Embryo," *The National Catholic Bioethics Quarterly* 9, no. 4 (Winter 2009) and "Christian Morality: A Morality of the Divine Good Supremely Loved According to Jacques Maritain and John Paul II," *The Renewal of Civilization: Essays in Honor of Jacques Maritain* (2010), edited by Gavin T. Colvert, for the American Maritain Association Press.

FEDERICO TEDESCO received his Ph.D. in 2013 from the University of Verona. His thesis focused on theoretical models of logic (*ars speculativa, rationalis scientia, pars semeiotica*) in dialogue with Aquinas, Poinsot, and John Deely. He has published several reviews and articles in *Notes et Documents* and *Divus Thomas*. He is a member of the Istituto Internazionale Jacques Maritain.

MICHAEL D. TORRE is the recently elected President of the American Maritain Association (October, 2012). He had previously served as a Vice President of the *Institut International Jacques Maritain*. He is a professor of philosophy at the University of San Francisco. His book *Do Not Resist the Spirit's Call: Francisco Marín-Sola on Sufficient Grace* has just been published (July 2013) by The Catholic University of America Press. He previously edited the American Maritain Association volume *Freedom in the Modern World: Jacques Maritain, Yves R. Simon, Mortimer J. Adler* (1989, second printing: 1990), and has contributed numerous articles to its series, of which he was the General Editor from 2009–2013, bringing its last eight volumes to print. 2009 also saw the publication of his *God's Permission of Sin: Negative or Conditioned Decree?* by Fribourg University Press.

CORNELIA A. TSAKIRIDOU is Associate Professor in the Department of Philosophy at La Salle University and Director of the Diplomat-In-Residence Program. She is the author of *Icons in Time, Persons in Eternity: Orthodox Theology and the Aesthetics of the Christian Image* (Ashgate Publishing, 2013) and the editor of *Reviewing Orpheus: Essays on the Cinema and Art of Jean Cocteau* (Bucknell University Press, 1997). She is currently working on a book for the University of New Mexico Press, titled *An Art of Their Own: Holiness, Aesthetics and Culture in the New Mexican Santo and the Greek Folk Icon*.

ANNE M. WILES is Professor of Philosophy at James Madison University in Harrisonburg, Virginia. She is the author of several articles, in journals and collections, on the epistemology and metaphysics of Plato and Aristotle, and on the philosophy of Wittgenstein, Dante, and Rabindranath Tagore, among others. Her dissertation, directed by A. D. Woozley, was on Plato's Theory of Forms.

Index

Index

PUBLICATIONS OF THE
AMERICAN MARITAIN
ASSOCIATION

GENERAL EDITORS
Anthony O. Simon (1990–2004)
Michael D. Torre (2009–2013)
Giuseppe Butera (2013–)

Jacques Maritain: The Man and His Metaphysics
Edited by John F. X. Knasas, 1988
ISBN 978-0-268-01205-2, (out of print)
Distributed by the University of Notre Dame Press

Freedom in the Modern World: Jacques Maritain, Yves R. Simon, Mortimer J. Adler
Edited by Michael D. Torre, 1989, Second Printing, 1990
ISBN 978-0-268-00978-6
Distributed by the University of Notre Dame Press

From Twilight to Dawn: The Cultural Vision of Jacques Maritain
Edited by Peter A. Redpath, 1990
ISBN 978-0-268-00979-3
Distributed by the University of Notre Dame Press

The Future of Thomism
Edited by Deal W. Hudson and Dennis Wm. Moran, 1992
ISBN 978-0-268-00986-1
Distributed by the University of Notre Dame Press

Jacques Maritain and the Jews
Edited by Robert Royal, 1994
ISBN 978-0-268-01193-2
Distributed by the University of Notre Dame Press

Freedom, Virtue, and the Common Good
Edited by Curtis L. Hancock and Anthony O. Simon, 1995
ISBN 978-0-268-00991-0
Distributed by the University of Notre Dame Press

Postmodernism and Christian Philosophy
Edited by Roman T. Ciapolo, 1997
ISBN 978-0-8132-0881-7
Distributed by the Catholic University of America Press

The Common Things: Essays on Thomism and Education
Edited by Daniel McInerny, 1999
ISBN 978-0-9669226-0-8
Distributed by the Catholic University of America Press

The Failure of Modernism:
The Cartesian Legacy and Contemporary Pluralism
Edited by Brendan Sweetman, 1999
ISBN 978-0-9669226-1-5
Distributed by the Catholic University of America Press

Beauty, Art, and the Polis
Edited by Alice Ramos, 2000
ISBN 978-0-9669226-2-2
Distributed by the Catholic University of America Press

Reassessing the Liberal State:
Reading Maritain's Man and the State
Edited by Timothy Fuller and John P. Hittinger, 2001
ISBN 978-0-9669226-3-9
Distributed by the Catholic University of America Press

Faith, Scholarship, and Culture in the 21st Century
Edited by Alice Ramos, and Marie I. George, 2002
ISBN 978-0-9669226-5-3
Distributed by the Catholic University of America Press

Jacques Maritain and the Many Ways of Knowing
Edited by Douglas A. Ollivant, 2002
ISBN 978-0-9669226-4-6
Distributed by the Catholic University of America Press

Truth Matters: Essays in Honor of Jacques Maritain
Edited by John G. Trapani, Jr., 2004
ISBN 978-0-9669226-6-0
Distributed by the Catholic University of America Press

The Human Person and a Culture of Freedom
Edited by Peter A. Pagan Aguiar and Terese Auer, O.P., 2009
ISBN 978-0-9669226-7-7
Distributed by the Catholic University of America Press

Maritain and America
Edited by Christopher M. Cullen, S.J. and
Joseph Allan Clair, 2009
ISBN 978-0-9669226-8-4
Distributed by the Catholic University of America Press

The Renewal of Civilization:
Essays in Honor of Jacques Maritain
Edited by Gavin T. Colvert, 2010
ISBN 978-0-9669226-9-1
Distributed by the Catholic University of America Press

The Vocation of the Catholic Philosopher:
From Maritain to John Paul II
Edited by John P. Hittinger, 2010
ISBN 978-0-9827119-0-3
Distributed by the Catholic University of America Press

Reading the Cosmos: Nature, Science, and Wisdom
Edited by Giuseppe Butera, 2011
ISBN 978-0-9827119-1-0
Distributed by the Catholic University of America Press

Distinctions of Being: Philosophical Approaches to Reality

Edited by Nikolaj Zunic, 2013

ISBN 978-0-9827119-2-7

Distributed by the Catholic University of America Press

Love and Friendship: Maritain and the Tradition

Edited by Montague Brown, 2013

ISBN 978-0-9827119-3-4

Distributed by the Catholic University of America Press

Aquinas and Maritain on Evil: Mystery and Metaphysics

Edited by James G. Hanink, 2013

ISBN 978-0-9827119-4-1

Distributed by the Catholic University of America Press

CPSIA information can be obtained
at www.ICGtesting.com
Printed in the USA
FFOW03n0650140214
3601FF

9 780982 711958